Web Publishing For Tea...

Cheat Sheet

Claris Home Page 2.0 Shortcuts

Want an easy way to do routine tasks? Use this handy chart that gives you all the COMMAND and CONTROL you need!

File Menu	Command Mac	Shortcuts Windows 95
New Page	⌘+N	Ctrl+N
Open	⌘+O	Ctrl+O
Close	⌘+W	Ctrl+W
Save	⌘+S	Ctrl+S
Print	⌘+P	Ctrl+P
Preview in Browser	⌘+R	Ctrl+R
Quit	⌘+Q	—

Edit Menu	Command Mac	Shortcuts Windows 95
Undo	⌘+Z	Ctrl+Z
Cut	⌘+X	Ctrl+X
Copy	⌘+C	Ctrl+C
Paste	⌘+V	Ctrl+V
Clear	Delete	Delete
Select All	⌘+A	Ctrl+A
Document Options	⌘+J	Ctrl+K
Document Statistics	⌘+K	No shortcut
Find/Change	⌘+F	Ctrl+F
Find Next	⌘+G	F3
Check Spelling	⌘+=	ALT+=

Insert Menu	Command Mac	Shortcuts Windows 95
Insert From Library	⌘+Y	No shortcut
Insert List	⌘+Return	F8

Windowing Style Menu	Command Mac	Shortcuts Windows 95
Show Object Editor	⌘+E	No shortcut
Show Link Editor	⌘+L	No shortcut
Edit Page View	Shift+⌘+E	Shift+Ctrl+E
Preview Page View	Shift+⌘+P	Shift+Ctrl+P
Edit HTML Source	Shift+⌘+H	Shift+Ctrl+L

Format Menu	Command Mac	Shortcuts Windows 95
Normal Text	⌘+U	Ctrl+U
Heading 1 (Largest head-line size)	⌘+1	Alt+1
Heading 2	⌘+2	Alt+2
Heading 3	⌘+3	Alt+3
Heading 4	⌘+4	Alt+4
Heading 5	⌘+5	Alt+5
Heading 6	⌘+6	Alt+6
Blockquote	⌘+]	Alt+]
Remove Blockquote	⌘+[	Alt+[

Text Style Menu	Command Mac	Shortcuts Windows 95
Reset	⌘+T	Ctrl+T
Bold	⌘+B	Ctrl+B
Italics	⌘+I	Ctrl+I

Other Goodies	Shortcuts Mac	Windows 95
Move window without bringing it to the front	Command-click on title bar and drag it	No shortcut
Open Link Editor	Enter	Enter (on numeric keypad)
Select next line	Shift+Down Arrow key or Shift+Up Arrow key	Shift+Down Arrow key or Shift+Up Arrow key
Insert non-breaking space (word break without a hyphen)	Option+space	No shortcut
New List Item (indented)	⌘+Option+Return	F9
New List Item (outdented — all but first line indented)	⌘+Shift+Return	F7

...For Dummies: #1 Computer Book Series for Beginners

...For Dummies®

COMPUTER
BOOK SERIES
FROM IDG

Web Publishing For Teachers™

Cheat Sheet

Online Safety Rules for Students

- ✔ I will not give out personal information such as my address, telephone number, my parents' work numbers or addresses, or the name or location of my school without my parents' permission.

- ✔ I will tell my parents right away if I come across any information that makes me feel uncomfortable.

- ✔ I will never agree to get together with someone I "meet" online without first checking with my parents. If my parents agree to the meeting, I will be sure that it is in a public place and I will bring my mother or father along.

- ✔ I will never send a person my picture or anything else that belongs to me without first checking with my parents.

- ✔ I will not respond to any messages that are mean-spirited or in any way make me feel uncomfortable. I realize that it is not my fault if I get a message like that. And, if I do, I will tell my parents right away so that they can contact the online service.

- ✔ I will talk with my parents so that we can set up rules for going online. We will decide upon the time of day and the length of time I can be online, and the appropriate areas for me to visit. I will not break the rules or access other areas without my parents' permission.

Adapted from information available from the National Center for Missing and Exploited Children (1-800-THE-LOST)

Basic Steps to Create a Web Page

1. Plan your content.

2. Type your content into a word processor or Claris Home Page.

3. Add formatting, HTML tags, links, and graphics (or other multimedia).

4. Quality-check your page off-line first with your browser before posting it to the Web.

5. Use FTP (File Transfer Protocol) or your local area network to transmit your Web page files to your Internet service provider's computer.

6. Test your Web page by logging onto the Net, launching your Web browser, and entering your home page's URL.

7. Visit your Web site frequently to refresh the page content and update your links.

My Favorite World Wide Web Sites

Site	URL
_____	_____
_____	_____
_____	_____
_____	_____
_____	_____
_____	_____
_____	_____
_____	_____

IDG BOOKS WORLDWIDE™

...For Dummies: #1 Computer Book Series for Beginners

WEB PUBLISHING FOR TEACHERS™

by Bard Williams, Ed.D.

Foreword by Guy Kawasaki

IDG Books Worldwide, Inc.
An International Data Group Company

Foster City, CA ♦ Chicago, IL ♦ Indianapolis, IN ♦ Southlake, TX

Web Publishing For Teachers ™

Published by
IDG Books Worldwide, Inc.
An International Data Group Company
919 E. Hillsdale Blvd.
Suite 400
Foster City, CA 94404
www.idgbooks.com (IDG Books Worldwide Web site)
www.dummies.com (Dummies Press Web site)

Library of Congress Catalog Card No.: 97-71810

ISBN: 0-7645-0111-9

Printed in the United States of America

10 9 8 7 6 5 4 3 2 1

IDD/ST/QW/ZX/IN

Distributed in the United States by IDG Books Worldwide, Inc.

Distributed by Macmillan Canada for Canada; by Transworld Publishers Limited in the United Kingdom and Europe; by WoodsLane Pty. Ltd. for Australia; by WoodsLane Enterprises Ltd. for New Zealand; by Longman Singapore Publishers Ltd. for Singapore, Malaysia, Thailand, and Indonesia; by Simron Pty. Ltd. for South Africa; by Toppan Company Ltd. for Japan; by Distribuidora Cuspide for Argentina; by Livraria Cultura for Brazil; by Ediciencia S.A. for Ecuador; by Addison-Wesley Publishing Company for Korea; by Ediciones ZETA S.C.R. Ltda. for Peru; by WS Computer Publishing Company, Inc., for the Philippines; by Unalis Corporation for Taiwan; by Contemporanea de Ediciones for Venezuela. Authorized Sales Agent: Anthony Rudkin Associates for the Middle East and North Africa.

For general information on IDG Books Worldwide's books in the U.S., please call our Consumer Customer Service department at 800-762-2974. For reseller information, including discounts and premium sales, please call our Reseller Customer Service department at 800-434-3422.

For information on where to purchase IDG Books Worldwide's books outside the U.S., please contact our International Sales department at 415-655-3000 or fax 415-655-3295.

For information on foreign language translations, please contact our Foreign & Subsidiary Rights department at 415-655-3021 or fax 415-655-3281.

For sales inquiries and special prices for bulk quantities, please contact our Sales department at 415-655-3200 or write to the address above.

For information on using IDG Books Worldwide's books in the classroom or for ordering examination copies, please contact our Educational Sales department at 800-434-2086 or fax 817-251-8174.

For press review copies, author interviews, or other publicity information, please contact our Public Relations department at 415-655-3000 or fax 415-655-3299.

For authorization to photocopy items for corporate, personal, or educational use, please contact Copyright Clearance Center, 222 Rosewood Drive, Danvers, MA 01923, or fax 508-750-4470.

 is a trademark under exclusive license to IDG Books Worldwide, Inc., from International Data Group, Inc.

About the Author

Bard Williams, Ed.D., is an educator, writer, and an educational technology consultant. He's the author of *The Internet For Teachers, The World Wide Web For Teachers,* and *America Online For Teachers* (all from IDG Books Worldwide, Inc.). He likes to give presentations (you'll find him jumping between keynotes at educational conferences), to write (he is the author of more than 150 articles), to plan (helping school districts with technology planning is a obsession for him), to travel with friends, munch on M&Ms, and ride his bike around Boston.

Dr. Williams left the classroom after 12 years as a middle school science and computer teacher and district technology coordinator to join Apple Computer, Inc., as an Education Technology Consultant. Bard now spends his time helping teachers, administrators, school board members, and politicians understand and harness the power of the world's leading educational computer.

Finding Bard these days takes lots of technology. His family wishes he were wearing a global positioning satellite transmitter, and the folks at his office run around chasing "Bard Was Here" bumperstickers. Somehow, though, with the help of telephones, e-mail, and frequent-flier points he keeps in touch with his friends and jumps around the country evangelizing the use of educational technology. Somewhere in between he's been able to write several successful titles in the *...For Teachers* series of books. In his spare time, he mines the Internet for new resources, helps college students with their homework, and answers truckloads of e-mail (you can e-mail Bard at EDUBard@aol.com).

ABOUT IDG BOOKS WORLDWIDE

Welcome to the world of IDG Books Worldwide.

IDG Books Worldwide, Inc., is a subsidiary of International Data Group, the world's largest publisher of computer-related information and the leading global provider of information services on information technology. IDG was founded more than 25 years ago and now employs more than 8,500 people worldwide. IDG publishes more than 275 computer publications in over 75 countries (see listing below). More than 60 million people read one or more IDG publications each month.

Launched in 1990, IDG Books Worldwide is today the #1 publisher of best-selling computer books in the United States. We are proud to have received eight awards from the Computer Press Association in recognition of editorial excellence and three from *Computer Currents'* First Annual Readers' Choice Awards. Our best-selling *...For Dummies®* series has more than 30 million copies in print with translations in 30 languages. IDG Books Worldwide, through a joint venture with IDG's Hi-Tech Beijing, became the first U.S. publisher to publish a computer book in the People's Republic of China. In record time, IDG Books Worldwide has become the first choice for millions of readers around the world who want to learn how to better manage their businesses.

Our mission is simple: Every one of our books is designed to bring extra value and skill-building instructions to the reader. Our books are written by experts who understand and care about our readers. The knowledge base of our editorial staff comes from years of experience in publishing, education, and journalism — experience we use to produce books for the '90s. In short, we care about books, so we attract the best people. We devote special attention to details such as audience, interior design, use of icons, and illustrations. And because we use an efficient process of authoring, editing, and desktop publishing our books electronically, we can spend more time ensuring superior content and spend less time on the technicalities of making books.

You can count on our commitment to deliver high-quality books at competitive prices on topics you want to read about. At IDG Books Worldwide, we continue in the IDG tradition of delivering quality for more than 25 years. You'll find no better book on a subject than one from IDG Books Worldwide.

John Kilcullen
CEO
IDG Books Worldwide, Inc.

Steven Berkowitz
President and Publisher
IDG Books Worldwide, Inc.

Eighth Annual Computer Press Awards ≥ 1992

Ninth Annual Computer Press Awards ≥ 1993

Tenth Annual Computer Press Awards ≥ 1994

Eleventh Annual Computer Press Awards ≥ 1995

IDG Books Worldwide, Inc., is a subsidiary of International Data Group, the world's largest publisher of computer-related information and the leading global provider of information services on information technology. International Data Group publishes over 275 computer publications in over 75 countries. Sixty million people read one or more International Data Group publications each month. International Data Group's publications include: **ARGENTINA:** Buyer's Guide, Computerworld Argentina, PC World Argentina; **AUSTRALIA:** Australian Macworld, Australian PC World, Australian Reseller News, Computerworld, IT Casebook, Network World, Publish, Webmaster; **AUSTRIA:** Computerwelt Osterreich, Networks Austria, PC Tip Austria; **BANGLADESH:** PC World Bangladesh; **BELARUS:** PC World Belarus; **BELGIUM:** Data News; **BRAZIL:** Annuário de Informática, Computerworld, Connections, Macworld, PC Player, PC World, Publish, Reseller News, Supergamepower; **BULGARIA:** Computerworld Bulgaria, Network World Bulgaria, PC & MacWorld Bulgaria; **CANADA:** CIO Canada, Client/Server World, ComputerWorld Canada, InfoWorld Canada, NetworkWorld Canada, WebWorld; **CHILE:** Computerworld Chile, PC World Chile; **COLOMBIA:** Computerworld Colombia, PC World Colombia; **COSTA RICA:** PC World Centro America; **THE CZECH AND SLOVAK REPUBLICS:** Computerworld Czechoslovakia, Macworld Czech Republic, PC World Czechoslovakia; **DENMARK:** Communications World Danmark, Computerworld Danmark, Macworld Danmark, PC World Danmark, Techworld Danmark; **DOMINICAN REPUBLIC:** PC World Republica Dominicana; **ECUADOR:** PC World Ecuador; **EGYPT:** Computerworld Middle East, PC World Middle East; **EL SALVADOR:** PC World Centro America; **FINLAND:** MikroPC, Tietoverkko, Tietoviikko; **FRANCE:** Distributique, Hebdo, Info PC, Le Monde Informatique, Macworld, Reseaux & Telecoms, WebMaster France; **GERMANY:** Computer Partner, Computerwoche, Computerwoche Extra, Computerwoche FOCUS, Global Online, Macwelt, PC Welt; **GREECE:** Amiga Computing, GamePro Greece, Multimedia World; **GUATEMALA:** PC World Centro America; **HONDURAS:** PC World Centro America; **HONG KONG:** Computerworld Hong Kong, PC World Hong Kong, Publish in Asia; **HUNGARY:** ABCD CD-ROM, Computerworld Szamitastechnika, Internetto online Magazine, PC World Hungary, PC-X Magazin Hungary; **ICELAND:** Tolvuheimur PC World Island; **INDIA:** Information Communications World, Information Systems Computerworld, PC World India, Publish in Asia; **INDONESIA:** InfoKomputer PC World, Komputek Computerworld, Publish in Asia; **IRELAND:** ComputerScope, PC Live!; **ISRAEL:** Macworld Israel, People & Computers/Computerworld; **ITALY:** Computerworld Italia, Macworld Italia, Networking Italia, PC World Italia; **JAPAN:** DTP World, Macworld Japan, Nikkei Personal Computing, OS/2 World Japan, SunWorld Japan, Windows NT World, Windows World Japan; **KENYA:** PC World East African; **KOREA:** Hi-Tech Information, Macworld Korea, PC World Korea; **MACEDONIA:** PC World Macedonia; **MALAYSIA:** Computerworld Malaysia, PC World Malaysia, Publish in Asia; **MALTA:** PC World Malta; **MEXICO:** Computerworld Mexico, PC World Mexico; **MYANMAR:** PC World Myanmar; **NETHERLANDS:** Computer! Totaal, LAN Internetworking Magazine, LAN World Buyers Guide, Macworld Netherlands, Net, WebWereld; **NEW ZEALAND:** Absolute Beginners Guide and Plain & Simple Series, Computer Buyer, Computer Industry Directory, Computerworld New Zealand, MTB, Network World, PC World New Zealand; **NICARAGUA:** PC World Centro America; **NORWAY:** Computerworld Norge, CW Rapport, Datamagasinet, Financial Rapport, Kursguide Norge, Macworld Norge, Multimediaworld Norge, PC World Ekspress Norge, PC World Nettverk, PC World Norge, PC World ProduktGuide Norge; **PAKISTAN:** Computerworld Pakistan; **PANAMA:** PC World Panama; **PEOPLE'S REPUBLIC OF CHINA:** China Computer Users, China Computerworld, China InfoWorld, China Telecom World Weekly, Computer & Communication, Electronic Design China, Electronics Today, Electronics Weekly, Game Software, PC World China, Popular Computer Week, Software Weekly, Software World, Telecom World; **PERU:** Computerworld Peru, PC World Profesional Peru, PC World SoHo Peru; **PHILIPPINES:** Click!, Computerworld Philippines, PC World Philippines, Publish in Asia; **POLAND:** Computerworld Poland, Computerworld Special Report Poland, Cyber, Macworld Poland, Networld Poland, PC World Komputer; **PORTUGAL:** Cerebro/PC World, Computerworld/Correio Informático, Dealer World Portugal, Mac*In/PC*In Portugal, Multimedia World; **PUERTO RICO:** PC World Puerto Rico; **ROMANIA:** Computerworld Romania, PC World Romania, Telecom Romania; **RUSSIA:** Computerworld Russia, Mir PK, Publish, Seti; **SINGAPORE:** Computerworld Singapore, PC World Singapore, Publish in Asia; **SLOVENIA:** Monitor; **SOUTH AFRICA:** Computing SA, Network World SA, Software World SA; **SPAIN:** Communicaciones World España, Computerworld España, Dealer World España, Macworld España, PC World España; **SRI LANKA:** Infolink PC World; **SWEDEN:** CAP&Design, Computer Sweden, Corporate Computing Sweden, Internetworld Sweden, it.branschen, Macworld Sweden, MaxiData Sweden, MikroDatorn, Nätverk & Kommunikation, PC World Sweden, PCaktiv, Windows World Sweden; **SWITZERLAND:** Computerworld Schweiz, Macworld Schweiz, PCtip; **TAIWAN:** Computerworld Taiwan, Macworld Taiwan, NEW ViSiON/Publish, PC World Taiwan, Windows World Taiwan; **THAILAND:** Publish in Asia, Thai Computerworld; **TURKEY:** Computerworld Turkiye, Macworld Turkiye, Network World Turkiye, PC World Turkiye; **UKRAINE:** Computerworld Kiev, Multimedia World Ukraine, PC World Ukraine; **UNITED KINGDOM:** Acorn User UK, Amiga Action UK, Amiga Computing UK, Apple Talk UK, Computing, Macworld, Parents and Computers UK, PC Advisor, PC Home, PSX Pro, The WEB; **UNITED STATES:** Cable in the Classroom, CIO Magazine, Computerworld, DOS World, Federal Computer Week, GamePro Magazine, InfoWorld, I-Way, Macworld, Network World, PC Games, PC World, Publish, Video Event, THE WEB Magazine, and WebMaster; online webzines: JavaWorld, NetscapeWorld, and SunWorld Online; **URUGUAY:** InfoWorld Uruguay; **VENEZUELA:** Computerworld Venezuela, PC World Venezuela; and **VIETNAM:** PC World Vietnam.
3/24/97

Dedication

This book is dedicated to those who believe that it's easier to invent the future than to predict it and to my incredibly supportive friends and family.

Author's Acknowledgments

Projects like this just don't happen without the help of many friends and colleagues. I'm fortunate to have had the wisdom of many for this project. I apologize, in advance, for any I may have missed.

Tommy Hann, a Senior Systems Engineer for Apple Computer, did the technical editing of this book. You'll find nobody with more troubleshooting and Net skills (and a bigger grin on his face) than Tommy.

One thing you'll learn if you ever write a book — it's the editorial and production team that makes the work something special. Turning out great content is one thing, but shaping that content into readable, syntactically correct material takes an artist. I'm lucky to have worked on this project with Nancy DelFavero, my project editor, who let my voice remain in the work and laughed at most of my jokes. Thanks to Mary Bednarek and my contract-dude Mike Kelly for championing the project.

One of the things that makes this book special is the CD. I want to especially thank IDG's own Joyce Pepple and Kevin Spencer for their hard work getting the disc together. And, thanks also to IDG's production team, who worked hard to make this book look so good.

The good people at Claris Corporation pitched in and helped with this book, too. Jeff Orloff and Robert Perrier assisted in getting the software on board and gave me some super tips to share, and Nancy Freeman and Ed Staton helped with that great Claris educator discount coupon (see the back of the book).

I probably wouldn't have finished this book on time if it weren't for the friendship and support of Nita Seng, my Buffett-lovin', manatee-saving buddy. Even though there are miles between us, her reach exceeds her grasp. (I smile just thinking of her.)

My family is very special to me and they've also been incredibly supportive through four books and several second editions. Mom, Dad, Tom, Laura, Susan, and the rest of the Cook and Wilson crews — I love you all!

And last, but not least, thanks to my friend Michelle Robinette, who persuaded me to jump on the author roller coaster and assured me that what I had to say was worth saying.

Publisher's Acknowledgments

We're proud of this book; please send us your comments about it by using the IDG Books Worldwide Registration Card at the back of the book or by e-mailing us at feedback/dummies@idgbooks.com. Some of the people who helped bring this book to market include the following:

Acquisitions, Development, and Editorial

Project Editor: Nancy DelFavero

Acquisitions Editor: Michael Kelly, Quality Control Manager

Product Development Director: Mary Bednarek

Media Development Manager: Joyce Pepple

Associate Permissions Editor: Heather H. Dismore

Technical Editor: Tommy Hann

Editorial Manager: Mary C. Corder

Editorial Assistants: Chris H. Collins, Steven H. Hayes, Darren Meiss

Production

Project Coordinator: Sherry Gomoll

Layout and Graphics: Angela F. Hunckler, Todd Klemme, Jane E. Martin, Anna Rohrer, Brent Savage

Proofreaders: Nancy Price, Robert Springer, Ethel M. Winslow, Phil Worthington, Karen York

Indexer: Sherry Massey

Special Help: Kevin Spencer, Associate Technical Editor, and Access Technology, Inc., Diana R. Conover, Associate Editor, Stephanie Koutek, Proof Editor, Joell Smith, Media Development Assistant

---

General and Administrative

IDG Books Worldwide, Inc.: John Kilcullen, CEO; Steven Berkowitz, President and Publisher

IDG Books Technology Publishing: Brenda McLaughlin, Senior Vice President and Group Publisher

Dummies Technology Press and Dummies Editorial: Diane Graves Steele, Vice President and Associate Publisher; Judith A. Taylor, Product Marketing Manager; Kristin A. Cocks, Editorial Director

Dummies Trade Press: Kathleen A. Welton, Vice President and Publisher; Stacy S. Collins, Product Marketing Manager

IDG Books Production for Dummies Press: Beth Jenkins, Production Director; Cindy L. Phipps, Supervisor of Project Coordination, Production Proofreading, and Indexing; Kathie S. Schutte, Supervisor of Page Layout; Shelley Lea, Supervisor of Graphics and Design; Debbie J. Gates, Production Systems Specialist; Tony Augsburger, Supervisor of Reprints and Bluelines; Leslie Popplewell, Media Archive Coordinator

Dummies Packaging and Book Design: Patti Sandez, Packaging Specialist; Lance Kayser, Packaging Assistant; Kavish + Kavish, Cover Design

♦

The publisher would like to give special thanks to Patrick J. McGovern, without whom this book would not have been possible.

♦

Contents at a Glance

Cartoons at a Glance

By Rich Tennant

page 301

page 85

page 9

page 261

page 51

page 179

page 233

Fax: 508-546-7747 • E-mail: the5wave@tiac.net

Table of Contents

Foreword

● ●

*1*f you're reading this book, you're probably an evangelist: You believe that technology has great promise for the classroom and that moving students from consuming information to providing information is a good thing. You're moving up the digital food chain!

Being an evangelist is important — especially when you're talking about technology in education. Whether you're pitching your school board to buy the right computers (Macs, of course) or brainstorming ways for your school to use a Web page to connect to the community, it's all about communication and empowerment.

As I e-mailed Bard this Foreword to his book, I realized that educational technology evangelists are no different than other evangelists. They both believe in a cause (for teachers, it's educated and motivated students), they both believe that you motivate folks through constant positive contact, and both often have to fight hard to be heard.

Why should you read this book? Because you want to make the world a better place. Think of this book as a way to get a jump on this process. Bard's cool tips, techniques, and projects can inspire the most reticent student (or teacher) and light a fire under the most skeptical parent.

While yet-another-Internet book would get lost in the morass of junk, this one's different. *Web Publishing For Teachers* is a great book for anyone — budding educational technology evangelist or not — to learn about the Web and its power in the classroom.

Not to put any pressure on you, but it's only the future of society that you control.

Guy Kawasaki

Chief Evangelist, Apple Computer, Inc.

Author of *Rules for Revolutionaries*

Introduction

● ●

*W*elcome to *Web Publishing For Teachers*. This book is written for educators who are ready to move from *consuming* information on the Internet to *producing* new information and adding to the wealth of resources available in this exciting medium.

You've come to the right place to learn about Web publishing. From the very beginnings of the Internet, educators like you and me took the lead in developing strategies for applying the amazing technology of telecommunications to the real world.

You'll be happy to know that you have three important qualities that many noneducators lack. The following will very quickly move you way out ahead of the other folks on the infobahn:

- ✔ You are enthusiastic about lifelong learning and your enthusiasm is contagious.
- ✔ You know enough about learning and teaching to teach yourself.
- ✔ You work with hyperactive, growing brains every day.

The first two factors probably got you to buy this book in the first place. (I thank you and the publisher thanks you!) The third factor will keep you hopping, and in no time you'll leapfrog beyond all those snails on the information superhighway. Relax and enjoy the ride.

If you're like many educators, your mind keeps racing well after the lights go out and you're supposed to be snug in your bed. You lie awake thinking about grading periods, dissertations in progress, convincing the world that Johnny can really read and won't admit it, and (of course) all the other zillion things going on in your life. If you have any problems at all going to sleep, do *not* read this book just before you've scheduled a date with the sandman. Why? Because it may give you some great new ideas — you know, those special ideas that start as little twitches inside your head and then blossom so quickly it's scary. You may find yourself up all night long (or at least until Tom Snyder and Conan O'Brien sign off) because you're so excited at the prospect of trying out the ideas the next day with your students. (Yes, it's a tough job and we're proud to do it!)

There are literally hundreds of books about the Internet and Web publishing available today, but precious few of those books view the Net from the unique perspective of an educator. Whether you're an assistant professor at a large college or university or a struggling preschool teacher who just got access to your first computer, this book helps you understand and apply some of the most powerful Web publishing tools, such as Claris Home Page 2.0 (a demo is included on your CD!), and also gives you the intellectual tools you need if you want to "go native" and write your own HTML code.

Inside *Web Publishing For Teachers,* you'll find information on how to design, create, and publish pages on the Internet's World Wide Web. I've also included hundreds of Internet Web addresses (URLs) that provide models for Web page creation and some teacher-tested ideas for building classroom activities around Web publishing. Other URLs you'll find in the book can guide you in obtaining the tools you need to get the job done.

So, here it is in plain English. All the technobabble has been stripped away and here are *just the facts* that tell you how to get started using the Web, how to do some cool things after you get online, and how you can harness the power of the Internet in your classroom.

About This Book

Web Publishing For Teachers can be used by anyone who is interested in designing, producing, and publishing Web pages on the Internet. If you're like most educators, you are anxious to explore this brave new world of the Internet, so I've taken care to bring the information to you in a clear, easy-to-read format that allows you to jump right into any chapter, get what you need, and then jump back to the real world.

In this book, you'll discover handy information that answers the following questions (and many others):

- ✔ What is the World Wide Web?
- ✔ Why should I use the Internet in my classroom?
- ✔ What tools do I need to become a Web publisher?
- ✔ What are some of the barriers to Internet use and how do I get around them?
- ✔ How do I use a Web browser?
- ✔ How do I use a "Web page processor," such as Claris Home Page 2.0 (included on the CD), to create a Web page?

    By the way, there are loads of great Web publishing tools for you to choose from, but I picked Claris Home Page 2.0 because it's easy to use and readily available to schools who use other Claris products.

- ✔ What is HTML and do I really need to learn it to publish on the Web?

 ✔ How can I publish my Web page on the Internet?

 ✔ What can I do to help other educators learn about the Internet and Web publishing?

 ✔ How can I find other schools that have published pages on the Web?

How to Read This Book

Grab this book when you need a quick reference. Glance at the Table of Contents, peruse the Index, and zip right to the page that has the answer you need.

Web Publishing For Teachers has been written so that each chapter pretty much stands alone. This book is great for those five-minute (or two-minute?) reading breaks between classes.

Conventions

I've done some things to make your life easier. Watch for them.

Internet addresses (sometimes called *URLs*) and the commands for writing your own Web pages look like this:

```
http://www.mindspring.com/~bardw/bard.html
```

Type the address in, just as it appears, capitalization and all, and then press the Return or Enter key on your keyboard. When you make a boo-boo, just type the address again. Sometimes the keyboard gremlin is active (kind of like the gremlin that steals your grade book and car keys now and then). Just be patient. It'll work.

When you use your World Wide Web browser or Claris Home Page, you need to use commands from the menu bar. I used the Macintosh version of Netscape Navigator and Claris Home Page when writing this book (and my screen shots are from this version), but the version for Windows is just about the same. To avoid having to give separate commands for Mac and Windows users, I've often combined them such as with this example:

File⇨Open Location (⌘+O or Ctrl+O)

This means that from the menu bar you simply choose Open Location from the File menu. The underlined letters are *hot keys* for Windows users, who can just press Alt+F and then O, instead of using the mouse. You can see the underlined letters on the Windows version of the browser. The *command key* symbol in parentheses is for Mac users, who can use this sequence instead of using the mouse, and the Ctrl abbreviation in the parentheses stands for the Control key, which is used for the equivalent shortcut in Windows.

Who am I talking to? (also known as, to whom am I speaking?)

In preparing this book for you, I've assumed the following:

- ✔ You have (or would like to have) access to the Internet.

- ✔ You intend to work with students (or just fly solo) as you design, create, and publish a home page on the Internet.

- ✔ You are an educator who is wondering how you can learn about the Internet and the World Wide Web and how you can use them in what you do every day.

- ✔ You are responsible for managing instruction in a situation where students meet the Internet head-on.

- ✔ You are itching to build a Web site that everyone will want to visit.

- ✔ You have heard everyone on the planet talking about the Internet, you've seen Internet URLs all over television and in the newspapers, and the Internet is driving you crazy. You want to learn more about it.

Whether you're a Macintosh user or a Windows guru, I've got you covered. The *Web Publishing For Teachers* CD-ROM that comes with this book is equipped with a trial version of Claris Home Page 2.0 software (for Mac or Windows users) and a few other tools, such as Adobe PageMill 2.0 for the Macintosh and a Windows program called Home Site, that allow you to create Web pages in the blink of an eye. I've also stuffed lots of interesting Web tools on the disk — perfect for editing graphics, sound, or movie files as your site goes multimedia.

By the way, if you want to know more about the Internet as a whole and things such as FTP, IRC, Gopherspace, and telnetting for fun and profit, grab a copy of *The Internet For Teachers,* 2nd Edition (IDG Books Worldwide, Inc.). The author's a great friend of mine. ;-)

(That thing at the end of the last paragraph is called a *smiley* or *emoticon*. You're likely to see many of those as you telecommunicate. In case you missed it, turn your head sideways to the left, and I'm winking at you.)

How this book is organized

This book has seven parts. The parts are designed to be read either in sequence or on their own. You can jump in anywhere you like, but I recommend that you peek at Part I so that you'll know a bit about the World Wide Web before you take the plunge.

Here are the parts of the book and what they contain:

Part I: The Web, It's Elementary

In this part, you can take a quick journey into the history of the Web, find out how the Web is becoming more important to everyone from shopkeepers to politicians, and take on the tough issues like copyright, student safety, and security when using the Net in your classroom. We'll also take a quick ride on a Web browser — no helmet needed — just to make sure you're up to speed on being a consumer of information before you take the jump to becoming a producer of information.

Part II: Webbing 101

In this part, you can get your feet wet learning how the best designers on the Web handle the design and creation process surrounding a home page. I've even thrown in lots of information about other tools that are available, besides Claris Home Page, that you can use in the Web-creation process. Plus, I talk about the dangers of using copyrighted designs in your Web page. Use the basic tenets of Web design presented in this part to storyboard your Web page and you're ready to take the next step.

Part III: Weaving Together a Web Page

Enough of this getting started stuff! Time to rev your computer's engine and get going. In this part, you'll explore the basics of opening, editing, and manipulating Web pages that Claris Home Page helps you create. Just so you know what you're missing, I've also taken steps to be sure you know what's happening under the hood. I've included lots of raw HTML code as examples of what Claris Home Page can help you write on your own.

Part IV: Jazzing Up Your Web Page

Time for the jump to light speed! Your page is ready for energizing with frames, forms, sound, QuickTime movies, and some healthy Java fuel. While you're cruising along in your Web page development process, take time out to look to the future of Web site design in Chapter 18, where you'll find the latest Net goodies to sample.

Part V: Sharing and Using Your Web Page

Now that you've created your page, what do you do? This chapter guides you through your options for publishing your Web page to the Internet. I also give you some tips and techniques for managing your Web site.

Part VI: The Part of Tens: Tens of Ideas, Tens of Sites

Get ready to take a cyber-ride through the sprawling Internet. This part contains ideas for great Web projects, tips for teaching other teachers about using the Net, and loads of URLs to visit to see how other schools have captured and applied the power of the Internet in their classrooms.

Part VII: Appendixes

Here you can find a glossary that's been exorcised of all technobabble, a summary of *HTML* (Web-scripting language) commands, and some teacher-tested tips for creating acceptable use policies should your school want to use a safety net when it begins flying on the Web trapeze. An About the CD appendix also answers your questions about what's on the CD and how to access those programs and files.

Icons Used in This Book

Here are the pretty pictures that signal something interesting you should know:

Learning Link

Learning Link icons indicate opportunities for you and your students to participate in Internet-related educational activities.

On the CD

This icon points out programs that are on the *Web Publishing For Teachers* CD-ROM, which is included with this book.

Teacher Approved

This icon highlights an item or an activity that I think is a "must use" in your classroom.

Techno Terms

The Techno Terms icon points out vocabulary items that the teacher (you!) should know in order to be a *true* Net surfer.

Tip

The Tip icon points out handy things that you should watch for or things that can make your life easier. These tips are time-savers and frustration savers.

Warning!

A danger sign. Hold the mouse!

Cool Web Site

My favorite icon! This icon alerts you to useful and/or fun Web addresses that you can use in your classroom.

Just Do It!

Repeat after me:

- ✔ "I can do this."
- ✔ "It's easier than the entrance exam for graduate school."
- ✔ "This is more meaningful than the last memo I received from the district office."
- ✔ "It's worth my time to learn this stuff because I want to have all the advantages that I can get when I walk through the door and face the raging hormones in fifth-period science class."

Whatever your reason, you've gone so far as to buy this book and read this introduction. As you delve further into this book, you'll find that your journey into World Wide Web publishing will be *a piece of cake*. Have a great meal!

Feedback!

I really, really want to know what you think about *Web Publishing For Teachers*.

Send feedback to:

IDG Books Worldwide, Inc.
7260 Shadeland Station, Suite 100
Indianapolis, IN 46256

Or (even better) show us that you've learned something by sending an
e-mail message containing the URL for your new Web page to IDG Books at

```
feedback/dummies@idgbooks.com
```

Part I
The Web,
It's Elementary

"I don't mean to hinder your quest for knowledge, however it's not generally a good idea to try and download every file on the Web."

In this part . . .

As educators, we experience many "mysterious" things. You know, those things that happen during a school day that seem inexplicable. For example: Why is there never any chalk in the chalk tray when you just put out a whole box yesterday? Or why do class periods seem to get longer as the school year nears its end? Hmm . . . maybe chalk pieces are like socks that get lost in the wash. I know! Someday you'll walk into a mini-mall and see a whole store selling nothing but little stubby pieces of chalk and unmated socks, all at an unbelievably low price!

The World Wide Web (also known as the Web) might seem like a mysterious thing, but it really isn't. This part of the book will help demystify the Web (and a few other parts of the Internet), while suggesting some great reasons why your Internet access in classrooms should be as vital as access to pen and paper. You also get a heads-up on what you'll need before you and your students jump onto your Web surfboards and take off.

Chapter 1
What Is the Web?

*R*emember your first day in the classroom? Years of preparation and student teaching couldn't possibly have prepared you for what you were to face on Day One.

Teaching, as you're well aware, is one of those wonderful professions that is vastly more difficult than it appears. It's not enough that you have to master a convoluted curriculum. You've also got to know what to do when Sally falls over backward in her chair ("I told you so" is no longer an appropriate response), or when Johnny doesn't show up to school for three weeks (truant officers are hard to come by these days), or when you get a jargon-filled memorandum from the superintendent proclaiming the introduction of a new "outcome-based, interactive, collaborative, learner-centered, whole-language" science curriculum.

You successfully jumped that first hurdle; and even though you were excited and nervous on that first day (on about three hours sleep?), you knew that you could sift through the complexities of classroom life and get on with the art of teaching. For me, my first introduction to telecommunications (and later to the Internet) gave me the same feeling.

The Net seemed really complex (at first, so did operating a purple ditto machine), and the Net had its own jargon standing in the way of my complete understanding. It took far less time than I had imagined, however, to get through the basics and realize that the Internet could be a valuable personal and teaching resource that, with a little practice, could help me transform my classroom into an information-rich learning environment.

I think you'll find that learning to create your own Web pages is worth the effort and tons easier than your first day in the classroom. Web page creation is just the next step in your evolution toward the classroom of the future and the world of tomorrow. (No pressure, huh?)

The Bus Stops Here

The wait is over. The bus has pulled up to your stop, and it's time to head out for your journey on the information superhighway. Remember to keep your arms and head inside the window at all times and keep your hand on the mouse. For our first stop, I offer a brief primer on the structure of the Internet and help you see how Web publishing fits in. Don't worry. Reading this guidebook to the "infobahn" is much easier than grading 50 essays or writing "works well with others" on 125 report cards. Step carefully, please.

It's a bird. It's a plane! It's a network?

The *Internet* is no more than a collection of computer networks linked together so that its users can share vast data resources. To get onto the Internet, all you have to do is make arrangements to link your computer to an online service (such as America Online), a local area network with Internet gnnections, or a commercial Internet service provider (such as AT&T) that offers Internet access.

Of course, you can't *touch* the Internet — the Internet isn't a place at all. *Internet* is just a name for the union (get out your math books and turn to page 27) of many data sources. The Internet is the pathway that allows us to access information anytime, any place for just about any purpose. The "intangibility" of the Net confuses many beginning users. The Internet is about *how* resources are linked and *what* resources are available (and there are many, many of them).

How many resources? Millions of computers provide data on the Net, and that number is growing hourly. Colleges and universities, research organizations, government entities, and businesses are all rushing to find ways to connect to (and exploit) Internet resources. Schools are no exception. As of mid-1996, more than 85 percent of schools had access to the Internet, and many schools around the world were not only *consuming* information, but *producing* it. Figure 1-1 shows a Web page created by students and teachers at Wachusett Regional High School in Massachusetts. The really neat thing about this page is that the kids at the school created the whole thing and they included things that are useful *beyond* the walls of the school. Way to go, Wachusett!

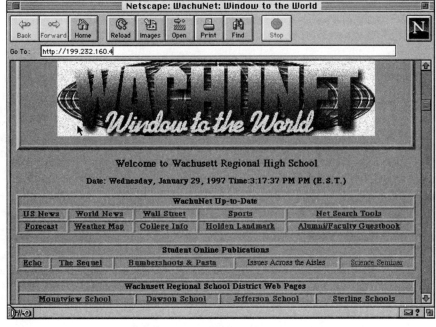

Figure 1-1:
Thousands of schools, such as Wachusett Regional High School in Massachusetts, have their own presence on the Net.

Big computers and bunches of wire

The Internet began with nothing more than a bunch of wire, a telephone network, a few blinking behemoth computers, and an idea that people needed better ways to communicate. In 1969, the Department of Defense (DoD) funded a project to link DoD engineers with civilian research contractors, including a large number of universities that were doing military-funded research. The resulting interconnection of computers (in the beginning, there were only three) — a network known as ARPAnet (Advanced Research Projects Agency Network) — formed the basis for future work in information exchange and data storage.

Educators, it turns out, were a major force in helping the Internet idea spread like wildfire. In the Net's early days, universities began to shift from centralized computing to a distributed workstation architecture. In plain English, that meant that *mainframe computers* (called "big iron" in some circles) became overwhelmed with byte-chomping insignificant traffic (such as electronic mail, or e-mail). So, the gurus of Silicon Valley figured out that computing power could be spread over many computers to free up the mainframes for more important tasks, like calculating pi to the 10,000th significant digit. (That's a lot of pi!)

In fact, the Internet spread throughout institutions of higher learning because of electronic mail. Colleges, universities, and research institutions (such as the CDC and NASA) began to exchange online information, and soon the Net was established — as valuable a tool as chalk or a pencil.

Not too much later (in the late 1980s), the Internet (as it existed then) became overwhelmed with traffic. Enter the commercial Internet providers who saw profit potential. With their larger, faster, less-expensive computers and faster telephone transmission lines, these service providers quickly expanded Internet resources to free up the information logjam. Nowadays, virtually every college and university offers free Internet access (or at least e-mail access) to all their students and employees.

Today, there are thousands of Internet on-ramps (*nodes*) and millions of users. So many new users jump on the Internet each day that service providers can't keep up with the demand and the Internet is headed for another traffic jam. As you may expect, K–12 is one of the fastest-growing populations of new users and we're contributing our share to slowing down the Internet to a dribble of information. It's up to us educators to assess the value of online communications and determine the best use of Internet resources for our kids. Teachers and students must realize that folks shouldn't use the Internet because they *can*, but because *it makes sense*. It's a matter of using the right tool for the right job.

A Web is born

The *World Wide Web* (an interactive, graphical presentation of information on the Internet) is a relative newcomer on the Internet timeline. The Father of the Web is generally thought to be Tim Berners-Lee of the European Particle Physics Laboratory. Lee developed the Web concept in 1989 as a means for building communication bridges between scientists throughout an organization of physicists called CERN. (Trivia: CERN stands for Conseil Européen pour la Recherche Nucleaire. Now you know why they use an acronym.)

Web browsers (software tools like Netscape Navigator, Cyberdog, and Internet Explorer used to access the Web) didn't appear until late 1990. Developers latched onto what was certainly a great idea and began to develop and expand the capabilities of the early Web software. As the developers worked, they developed a set of rules that assures that software and computer systems work together peacefully. These rules are referred to in techno-speak as *protocols*.

The Web got its name from its ability to create a virtually infinite number of interconnections, called *links,* between different types of data at different locations. Whether the resource is a scientific report from Rome, Italy, or a book report from a third-grader in Rome, Georgia, the data can be interconnected using clickable text (called *hypertext*).

What Is Web Publishing?

If you're familiar with HyperStudio or HyperCard, you have a great reference point for learning about the World Wide Web (also known as the Web). The aforementioned "hyper-programs" present users with cards that are linked together with clickable *buttons*. The buttons on the cards can do different things in the hyper-world: They can launch programs, play sounds, show digital movies, or display simple animation. Put a bunch of cards together in HyperStudio or HyperCard, and we call them a *stack*.

In the world of the Web, cards become *pages,* buttons become *hypertext links*, and stacks become *Web sites*. Got it? *Web pages* are online documents that feature clickable hypertext links that transport you to documents, graphics, or other Web pages; or they connect you to other kinds of Internet resources such as *file transfer protocol (FTP)* or *newsgroups* (electronic bulletin boards). Get all that? If so, you've got a pretty good operational definition of the Web. (See Figure 1-2.)

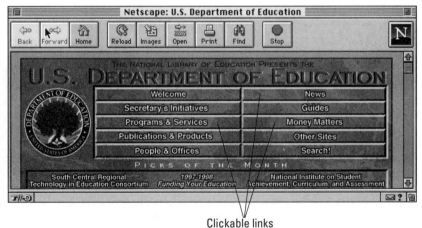

Figure 1-2: The Web features pages connected by clickable text called *hyperlinks.*

Clickable links

Take a breath and go back and re-read that third sentence in the preceding paragraph. The keywords are "other kinds of Internet resources." People especially like the programs used to view Web pages, called *Web browsers,* because these programs are kind of the Swiss Army knife of Internet tools. In the beginning of Internet access, folks used a separate program to access file transfer (using a program such as Fetch), another to view newsgroups (using a program called a *newsreader*), and another to search or access computer databases (with a program called *telnet*). Most Web browsers available today allow you to do almost all those things, and more, from within one program.

Before you get too excited about this Mother of All Internet Tools, I'll give you one caution. The tools that I mentioned previously (newsreaders, Fetch, and such) do only one thing, but they do it very well — and with lots of bells and whistles. Web browsers typically do many things, but they're primarily designed to display Web pages, so you'll still find the need to access the other programs if you want to do something quickly or access the Internet without going through the Web.

One final note about the Web: The Web has grown exponentially over the last few years. Schools (and everyone else on the planet who knows a mouse from a rat) are using the Web for entertainment, to get information, to purchase products, to communicate, and more. It's not going away — it's only going to get bigger, better, and more versatile. (Of course, that's why you so wisely purchased this book — *you* want to drive the info-highway bus, not just be a passenger. Good for you!)

Your School Supplies

Time for your yearly trip to the store to get all the goodies you'll need for school. This year, whip out your American Express card and get ready to spend — but gaining Internet access will likely cost you far less than you think. Using the Web requires only a computer, a modem, an Internet connection, and a software program called a *Web browser.*

If you're already a graduate of the Web Browser's Institute and are ready to build your own Web pages, you'll need a tool to create the language (HTML — Hypertext Markup Language) that's read by Web browsers. Luckily, you can use any word processor to write HTML code, or you can grab one of the "what-you-see is-what-you-get" Web page processing tools I've included on your CD.

In Parts III and IV of this book, I've chosen to highlight Claris Home Page 2.0 because it's one of the easiest Web authoring tools to learn and one that's readily available to most teachers. In case you want to sample some others, I've also included demo versions of Adobe PageMill 2.0 and a few more tools on your *Web Publishing For Teachers* CD.

Are you hyper yet?

The Web offers users an adventure in hypermedia, fueled by hypertext and hyperlinks. It's a truly hyper place that's perfect for hyper students (and teachers).

Hypermedia is a term used to describe the union of hypertext and multimedia. The term *hypertext*, coined by techno-culture guru Ted Nelson, describes text that, when selected with the click of a mouse, zips the user to another source of related information. For example, clicking on the hyperlinked word "projects" in the sentence "There are many online projects that NASA offers to students" might whisk you away to another site (residing on another computer halfway across the globe) that offers a list of specific projects and information about how to participate.

Multimedia refers to the union of different data types, such as text, graphics, sound, and sometimes movies. Hypermedia connects these data types together. With hypermedia, highlighted and linked text, called *hyperlinks* (or just *links*), allows a user to move between data in a non-linear manner. You're just as likely to hear a sound when clicking on a hyperlinked word when browsing a hypermedia file, for example, as you are to view a picture.

The language that Web programs use to create hyperlinks is called *Hypertext Markup Language (HTML)*. The HTML language follows a set of rules (called a *protocol*) known as HTTP (Hypertext Transfer Protocol). This set of rules allows any users to create their own Web pages and post them to the Internet and ensures that the files will be readable by Web browsers. When you enter a WWW (World Wide Web) address, you enter the following text before the Web address:

`http://`

The prefix tips off the Internet that the *URL* (*Uniform Resource Locator* — an Internet resource address) that you're looking for is a WWW address rather than a Gopher or FTP site. So, in the address `http://www.idg.com/`, the `http://` tells you, and the Net, that the site you seek is on the Web.

To help you remember to add the prefix, we've appended the `http://` prefix to WWW addresses in this book. Most browsers these days are smart enough to tell what kind of Internet resource the URL you enter refers to, so, even though we meticulously added the `http://` prefix to each address, you don't necessarily have to. Try it both ways and see what works for you.

I'm sure lots of teachers out there are visual learners like me, so a diagram may be handy to illustrate exactly what you need to make an Internet connection and to design your own Web pages. The diagram in Figure 1-3 shows the "big five" items that you need: hardware, software, a modem, a phone line, and an Internet account.

You'll find an extended explanation about exactly what color of notebooks and what kind of lead for your pencils you'll need, as well as specifics on the aforementioned hardware and software accouterments, in Chapter 6. Happy shopping!

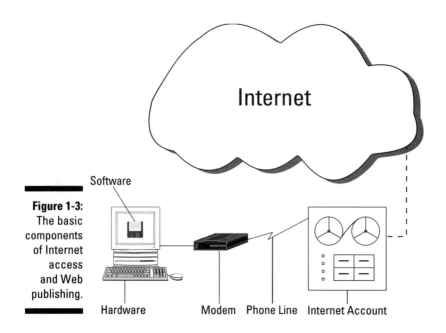

Figure 1-3:
The basic components of Internet access and Web publishing.

How Will We Pay for This?

I know what you're thinking. This Web thing is great, but how in the world will I ever pry enough money out of the school coffers to fund access or a place to produce our school's Web page? It once took me an entire school year to convince a principal that the school should supply each teacher with his or her own personal $5^1/_4$-inch floppy disk — floppies that cost a whopping 50 cents each. (This event occurred back in the Dark Ages when we had 50 Apple IIs and no supply budget. Now we have a bunch of Macintoshes, a few PCs, and a mammoth $50 per year for supplies.)

How much you need to budget for Web access (including Web page storage and other telecommunications) depends largely on the deal you strike with your Internet service provider, or if you decide to establish your own Web server. If you're connecting to the Internet through an online service, such as America Online or CompuServe, you get space for your Web site for free, plus an easy all-in-one interface. However, the space isn't unlimited (usually around 10MB per person), and you lose the ability to collect information using forms or to do some of the fancier formatting tricks on your Web page.

If you purchase time and hard-drive space (a place for the content of your Web site) through an Internet service provider, or ISP, you can negotiate for Web services and for the ability to do forms and fancy things on your site. If your school is in a rural area, however, you may also have to contend with long-distance charges from the school to the nearest Internet service provider.

Is it safe to publish student work online?

Hear that sound? It's the collective head-scratching of thousands of educators and parents trying to come to terms with the notion that if a school's Web site highlights and celebrates student work, and that work is tagged with a student's *name*, unscrupulous folks will turn the budding authors into unsuspecting prey.

In my consulting work, I hear this concern almost every day. I'm going to go out on a limb and take a stand on this issue. The reality of the electronic age is this:

✔ If someone wants to prey on children (or prey on anybody, for that matter), that person can do so in a number of ways, either by using the Net, or by walking through the local phone book.

✔ If you spot someone's name on the Internet, it's like reading it in a newspaper. It's not necessarily any easier to find out personal information, such as an address or phone number, on the Net than in the news.

That said, you can stop the head-scratching by hammering out a (hopefully *simple*) school policy about privacy and your Web site. Consider the following guidelines:

✔ Don't publish any personal information about students (*or teachers*) online. Use only the school address and main phone number for contact information. A list of names is okay, but eliminate any phone numbers or personal information from that list.

✔ Require parents to sign a letter of permission before any student work is published on the Web. (Some schools handle this by setting a guideline, publishing it in the Student Handbook, and requiring it to be signed at the beginning of each school year.)

✔ Think of the Web as your online local newspaper. Follow the same rules you would follow in submitting student work to a paper. Would you (or your child) sign his or her name in a letter to a newspaper editor? Is that really any different than publishing a name online?

✔ Don't, under any circumstances, publish student e-mail addresses. Even with a letter of permission from parents, this invites problems. If you want to solicit feedback, somewhere on the Web page post a general "school e-mail" address that's screened by responsible adults.

One last question I'm asked a lot: What about photos of students and teachers online? I really don't see much of a problem with this, as long as you first get permission from a parent or guardian. Plenty of yearbooks are widely circulated, some even in video or CD format, that unscrupulous individuals can get their hands on. Why add unnecessary worry about photos published to the Web? Go ahead and use those mug shots online, if it makes sense with your goals and objectives for the page. But, again, keep any personal information about faculty and students under wraps and off-line.

The best way to estimate the cost of your school's Web presence is to think about how you'll use the Web site and if the site will actually be a part of your school's local area network (sometimes referred to as an *intranet*). If you set up your own Web site as part of a bigger local network plan, you need a Web *server* (a computer with lots of memory and storage space), some software tools (such as Web management software), and you *still* need high-speed access to the Internet through some kind of intermediary (college, university, statewide education network, or ISP). Don't be afraid to approach local providers or your school's business partner and make a case for a free account for school use. This kind of deal is good for their business.

Ultimately, a direct high-speed connection to the Internet is the best of all worlds. While these high-speed lines can be expensive, there is a growing pot of money out there filled by Federal and State government telecommunications initiatives that your school may be able to tap into. In addition, local initiatives such as a "Netdays" event, can help raise enough awareness in your community to get things rolling. There's a great chapter in *The Internet For Teachers* (IDG Books Worldwide, Inc.) that explains how to raise big bucks for telecommunications support; but if you don't want to shell out the money for that wonderful resource, just post a message on an online service in the education forum and watch the ideas grow.

Internal Internet?

What's hot these days in networking? It's not the Internet — it's the *intranet*. Schools are finding out that the Web metaphor of browsers, links, and cross-platform communication works just as well as an internal method of spreading information as it does for sharing information with the world.

Basically, the concept is that you take information (student handbooks, teacher's manuals, and so on) and place them on Web pages that reside on a Web server in your school's network but aren't connected to the Internet or accessible by outside sources. Using the Web internally jumps over such pesky questions as

✔ What if I don't have the same kind of computer? (The Web is blind to platform differences and works well with virtually any kind of hardware.)

✔ How do I keep information within our school safe from naughty hackers? (An internal network not connected to the outside world is inherently safer than connecting to all 23 million or so users on the Net.)

✔ How can we post calendars, timelines, schedules, and other information to every person in our school regardless of how they're connected to the Net? (Intranet's the way!)

So . . . yet another use of the Net's technology. It's inexpensive, it's easy for people to develop their own content, and it's a great first step to publishing information to the world on the Web.

Speaking of Money

Throughout this book, I share lots of great places to visit on the Web. Because we're talking about money, a list of sites follow that'll help you learn about grants available to fund Internet access and the establishment of your own Internet server. Don't worry if you don't understand what to do with the Internet address yet; just stick a mental bookmark here and remember it for later.

Here's a short list of just a few of the places on the Internet packed with useful information about how to get other folks to give you lots of money for your Internet habit:

```
http://www.ed.gov/Technology/Challenge/challenge.htm
http://www.carnegie.org/
http://www.yahoo.com/Education/Financial_Aid/Grants/
http://www.ed.gov/money.html
http://www.nsf.gov/home/grants.htm
```

or use the keyword **Grants** on America Online.

Chapter 2

Why Use the Web in Education?

. . . .

In This Chapter

▶ Webbing in the classroom for a world of information

▶ Eight reasons to take the Net plunge

▶ Getting the most out of the Internet

. . . .

During my fifth year as a middle school teacher, I was matched with a wonderful new teaching partner. We worked well together. I was the one who broke up the fights; she was the one who taught me how to braid a lanyard for use with our compasses in our orienteering activity. I was the one who showed her how to use a computer grade book; she taught me a nifty new way to handle classroom discipline. We were a great team.

We were decidedly different in one major way, however: I was a *drawer* person, and she was a *pile* person.

Drawers and Piles

A casual observer would think that my science classroom was immaculate: each piece of lab equipment in its place — lots of clean lab tables and seemingly organized shelves. Those who knew me, however, knew that I was an expert at hiding my messes. Opening my file cabinet took a crowbar, and the cabinets in the science workroom were filled with boxes marked "Bard's junk." I knew, of course, which drawer held each paper or piece of equipment, and I often amazed students as I extracted their Fall Quarter science projects from a drawer to give to them as they left for the summer. My teammate used to giggle that she'd probably come into class one day and find me asleep in a drawer.

Peek into my teammate's classroom and you'd immediately realize that she was different — she was a *pile* person. Now, before you snicker too much, think about your own classroom (or your home). You are a pile person if you look around and see virtually every flat surface festooned with a pile of books, papers, folders, or boxes. As a pile person, she knew exactly which pile contained the exact paper/project/assignment sheet at all times. A glimpse into her file cabinets (not that I glimpsed there) revealed very neat and organized trays and material organizers, but those cabinets weren't packed full like mine were. Everything in her piles was in plain sight and easy for her to locate.

The fact is that no matter what our organizational methods were, we always knew where to find things. Using the Internet is no different. With zillions of bytes of information floating around on the information highway, knowing where to find things is perhaps the most important skill (next to knowing what to do with the things that we find). Whether you're a pile person or a drawer person, you'll find a tool or strategy that can help you explore Internet resources in a way that makes you and your students comfortable.

The World Wide Web (the Web) offers order to the chaos of the Internet. Creating Web pages with your students will help them (pile or drawer people just like you) understand more about the information that's out there and develop a better feel for how much of our own knowledge we might share with others.

The Web: Good for Education?

What can the Web and Web publishing offer your classroom? That depends, for the most part, on your teaching style and how you think. A famous puzzle challenges you to connect a matrix of nine dots with four single, straight, unbroken lines. If you haven't seen the puzzle, here's your chance:

> •   •   •
>
> •   •   •
>
> •   •   •

The answer to the puzzle, like the answer as to whether the Internet will be effective in your classroom, lies in your willingness to think "out of the box." As educators, we're conditioned to be locked into a standard set of materials that supports a curriculum: traditional things such as textbooks, workbooks, calculators, and computers. It's taken us quite a bit of time to become comfortable with computers in the classroom (we still have a long way to go on this one), and becoming comfortable with the Internet tool is no different.

Harnessing the power of Web publishing is a great way to think "out of the box" with your students. Be a risk-taker. Be curious. Explore with your students. Learn together. If you are willing to experiment with new ways to do new things, you'll no doubt be successful.

Want the solution to the matrix puzzle? The answer lies in the first sentence of the preceding paragraph. The puzzle can be solved. Try it!

Welcome, Webmasters!

The Web offers access to more information resources than you can imagine. Web pages created by *Webmasters* offer a way to organize the Web's content and make access to that content easier and more efficient. The Web can also be your access point for many different types of Internet resources. For example, as Web surfers, you and your students will have the opportunity to:

✔ Exchange information via global communication links

✔ Retrieve information "just in time" for use in the classroom (or anywhere else)

✔ Send and receive files, including programs, graphics, sounds, and movies

✔ Log in and search remote databases

✔ Add to the body of human knowledge (Whoa! Think about the potential of being able to *publish instantly* to millions of people. Kind of gives you chills, doesn't it?)

✔ Have a lot of fun browsing the ideas, thoughts, and creations of others

Building a *Distributed Learning Environment*

One of the biggest challenges now facing educators is the lack of *access* to technology in today's classrooms. In most schools, we still trot students down a hallway to a computer lab or media center for Internet access. This means that instruction halts while students gather up their belongings and move.

Worse yet, because the technology is not physically connected to the classroom, the activities completed in labs are disassociated from what's being studied in the classroom. Students end up using the Net "because it's Thursday" and not because it's appropriate for that time or for that unit or project. That makes a huge difference in whether you're using the Internet constructively. But, help is on the way: Enter the concept of a *Distributed Learning Environment* (DLE).

In a true Distributed Learning Environment, the technology is so ubiquitous that it becomes available *anywhere, anytime,* to *anyone* who needs assistance them with teaching and learning. What a nice thought! DLE ultimately is the goal of most school, district, and state technology plans.

Building a DLE means not only more access to traditional desktop technology, but also access to learning tools that are more portable and less expensive and can be taken out of the school when necessary. It seems that the gurus in the technology industry are finally waking up to the fact that giving every student a laptop PC (or, worse, making students lug around a 60-pound computer) just isn't the answer. New technologies, such as Apple Computer's eMate, bridge the gap between cost and benefits while helping to answer concerns about accessibility. Technologies like these bring us closer to a true DLE and make the Internet available to everyone. For more information on eMate, visit the Apple Education Web page at www.education.apple.com.

In case you need specific education-related reasons to jump onto the information highway and begin to create your own Web pages, the following section should help convince you.

Eight Great Reasons to Use the Internet and Publish on the Web

It takes a bit of imagination, but picture that you've just opened a box containing the first piece of Velcro you've ever seen. At first glance, Velcro seems useful, but you're not sure of its purpose. Show your piece of Velcro to a few friends, and soon you'll stumble onto hundreds of uses. The day will come when that odd connection of tiny hooks and loops becomes invaluable.

The Internet is like Velcro. The more you think about the resources that are out there on the Internet, the more ideas you generate for its use. The time we spend with our students is precious, so the "because it is there" rationale doesn't really cut it when we're talking about using the Net in a classroom. The fact is, some pretty compelling reasons exist to access the Internet, including a few reasons that may strongly appeal to you.

In *The Internet For Teachers*, 2nd Edition (IDG Books Worldwide, Inc.), I wrote about "Six Great Reasons to Get Your Class on the Information Superhighway." With the help of lots of other teachers who have attended several staff development activities that I've taught, I've redirected the focus to Web publishing — and added a couple more reasons.

The following eight reasons for using the Net and publishng to the Web come from lots of conversations, both electronic and real time (a.k.a. face to face) with people like you who are pondering the possibilities.

Web publishing offers opportunities to explore integrated knowledge

The Internet provides a bunch of electronic information that's organized in different ways and represents many different topics. You'll rarely see a Web page that features information on only one specific subject for one specific purpose. If students access the Web site at the Centers for Disease Control and Prevention in Atlanta (`http://www.cdc.gov`), for example, they may expect to see information limited only to the science of virology or biology. Instead, they see that the CDC maintains geographic information about

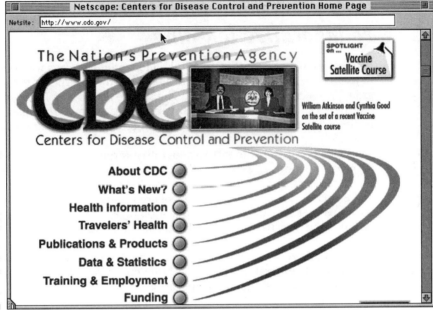

Figure 2-1: The CDC site is a great example of an inter- disciplinary collection of information.

landforms and climate as well as medical databases (see Figure 2-1). For the scientists and researchers who use the site on a daily basis, this integration of science, geography, and mathematical information makes their work more efficient.

At NASA's Web site, students see much more than just information about rockets and the sciences: They find libraries packed with technical writing, graphics, and newsletters describing the design and specifications of the latest shuttle payloads. NASA's Web site contains an elegant combination of writing, science, and mathematics. The site also has links to many Internet sites that support or extend the work of NASA's wondermakers. As with the CDC, the crafters of the NASA Web pages decide what knowledge to present and how to link that knowledge together. The result is truly interdisciplinary (NASA's URL is `http://www.nasa.gov`).

As you navigate through this book, you and your students will learn to create your own Web pages and explore new opportunities to link interdisciplinary resources together in new and useful ways. The Web is a place where, by using electronic tools, we can form the link between learning and life.

Web publishing facilitates collaborative learning

You will soon discover that one of the most efficient ways for your students to use and explore the resources available on the Internet is through small-group, project-centered activities. The simple fact is that because the Internet is so big and offers so many resources, teamwork makes a huge positive difference in the quality of the outcome of any Internet search.

Send four groups of students to separate Internet connections to search for information about any subject; they'll all come back with different information, from different sources, written with different biases, for different audiences, and with differing levels of credibility. Bring those four groups back together and ask them one question to get the collaboration going: "What is the best (or most useful) information and why?"

Of course, there's that "excited learners are contagious" thing that we educators all understand. You'll find that creating really terrific and effective Web pages requires lots of collaboration among students (inside and outside of your classroom). Put one student on a Web production project and watch how quickly many others flock around. Imagine the possibilities!

Web publishing offers opportunities for telementoring

Everyone out there has looked to a friend or colleague for information at one time or another. The Internet offers incredible opportunities to meet and learn from people around the globe on just about any topic you can imagine. Telementoring, literally helping or receiving help via telecommunications links, is the way most of us learned to use the Internet — back in the days before the ...For Teachers books hit the shelves, of course. Electronic mail, newsgroups, and Internet chat all provide ways to interact with your peers, learning all the while. You'll also find that other educators are a great source of information on tips and techniques for making your Web site extra-special and extra-useful. You will find that the Internet is useful both for teaching and for learning (and even for some curbside psychiatry when the going gets rough).

Web publishing is all about communicating

Editing a Supreme Court decision and posting it to the Internet takes about eight hours. Finding it takes about eight seconds. The Internet represents a communication opportunity that will probably have a profound impact on everything from politics to potato farming. Posting a message on the Internet and getting replies from Russia is cool. Logging on to the Internet and chatting live with anthropologists exploring Mayan ruins is an amazing experience. Building Web pages that share the culture of your school is enlightening and a rich source of powerful lessons. Students telecommunicating with their peers, no matter where in the world they live, is about as exciting a prospect as I can imagine.

Web publishing can cater to different learners in different ways

Like a good library, the Internet has print, sound, photograph, and video resources. The kind of information students choose to access and the way that they choose to access it is often as revealing about the students' capabilities as the quality of the information they collect. The Internet offers opportunities to browse or to target information with excruciating precision. You'll find that everyone, from the reluctant learner to the bookworm, can be an effective user and publisher on the Web. Helping them explore their interests and channel their efforts toward furthering their educational goals is up to us teachers, of course. With sufficient goals and direction, virtually every student can experience success.

The Internet is a culturally, racially, physically, and sexually blind medium

It is truly a strange feeling when you first meet someone with whom you've telecommunicated for a long period of time. In the early years of Macintosh technology, I had occasion to sign on to America Online (actually, its prede-cessor, called Q-Link) and ask for help. A clear and accurate response came almost immediately from someone who had seen my posting on the net-work. Over the next year, I came to rely on "Person X" to help me with problems that ranged from installing new network wiring to resurrecting hard drives that had crashed and burned.

At an educational conference two years later, while wandering the aisles looking for free demo disks and cheesy mousepads for my classroom, I stumbled upon a bright young lady playing a MIDI keyboard, connected to her Macintosh, in front of a crowd buzzing with excitement. After her stunning performance, I walked up to congratulate her. On her name tag was written her AOL screen name (the name by which everyone on the network knew her). I was floored. I had been corresponding with a young lady who was ten years my junior — what's more, she was an accomplished performance artist. I suddenly felt the need to give her a hug, or write her a check, or *something*. Now she's writing musical scores for movies, and I'm writing books — go figure!

Through this experience, and many others since, I realized that communication through the Internet was *blind*. Suddenly race, religion, appearance, speech — all the things we may use to form opinions about the people that we meet — become invisible. Communication through the Internet is pure communication.

The downside is that because much of communication is nonverbal you can lose something — for example, observing facial features, silly grins and all — in the translation. But that makes the challenge even sweeter.

The top ten ways to be a good Internet citizen

Want people to smile when they see your name on the information highway? Think about these ten tips before you surf!

1. Never knowingly post or forward information that's not true.

2. Have good manners.

3. Tell people when you like their work.

4. Be creative, not destructive.

5. Always obey copyright laws.

6. Think before you send.

7. Be yourself.

8. Don't use someone else's account or password.

9. Ask for help when you need it.

10. Think before you upload.

(Adapted from "Ten Commandments for Computer Ethics," Computer Ethics Institute, 1995)

Figure 2-2: The Web might be just the thing to rekindle a teacher's (and a student's) interest in learning.

Exploring the world of Web publishing can rekindle a teacher's interest in learning

As educators, we pride ourselves in valuing education. We spend our lives helping others learn *how* to learn. Unfortunately, there seems to be precious little time to learn things that will help *us* teach or live better. Unlike other new initiatives in education, I've seen exposure to the possibilities of telecommunications and technology motivate even the most reluctant teacher-learners to learn more and try different things in their classrooms. The excitement brought about by an infusion of so many resources is hard to resist. (See Figure 2-2.)

Other teachers are learning about the Internet because they don't want to drown. These teachers feel, perhaps with justification, that if they *don't* learn about the Internet and other technologies, the tidal wave of change will wash them out of a job. Of course, you've taken the time to buy this book, so you'll be smugly surfing on top of the Web publishing crest, doing the "queen's wave" to all the little people treading water below.

We have an obligation to society

Okay. It's soapbox time. (Just for a minute!) I'm scared not to tell folks about the Internet. We are all used to dealing with students from radically different backgrounds — some from families that have two cars and four computers, and some that are lucky to get three meals. I'm afraid that the ever-present socioeconomic gap will be further widened into two distinct groups: those who know about, can use, and have access to technology, and those who don't. It is already apparent that investors can use the information they gain over the Net to make more informed decisions that result in increased wealth. People with e-mail addresses seem to communicate with more people more often. What about all the people who don't have access to telecommunications technology? Will they be left behind?

It's like science fiction. Will we face a future society of the information-rich versus the information-poor? I may be overreacting, but I think that educators can help prevent that not-so-wonderful scenario from becoming a reality. We've got to help *all* students appreciate the value of knowledge and information. Knowledge gained from the Internet is certainly no exception. Moreover, we've got to fight to make sure that anyone and everyone can get access to the Internet if they have the desire. In the not-too-distant future, not having an e-mail address may be like not having a mailing address. I can go on forever about this topic, but I think that you get the point. Let's spread the word about the good, the bad, and the ugly of the Internet to all of our students — it will probably help them lead better lives in the future.

End of sermon.

That's the big eight! You can surely think of more as you think about the role the Internet may play in your classroom. In the next section, I'll tease your brain cells with a bit of prose about what you and your students can do with Internet access.

Beyond the Web: What Can I Do with the Internet?

The Internet is not the total answer to all the challenges facing an educator today. The Internet does not

- ✔ Watch your class while you hit the lounge for a well-deserved encounter with the "tastes almost like coffee" machine
- ✔ Make the school cafeteria stop serving mystery meat
- ✔ Cause your students' scores on standardized tests to jump dramatically

Some really cool Net statistics

Pick up most magazines and you'll find Internet statistics sprinkled throughout. Funny thing, though, is that none of the stats seem to match. One source says there are more than 100 million Net surfers; another reports fewer than 2 million. Who's right? After scouring the Net and my most reliable sources, I've put together this list of statistics for your reading pleasure. Use these when you present your How to Get the Net into My School plans to your administration or school board:

- From July 1994 to July 1996, the number of registered host computers (computers accessing or providing content on the Net) grew from 3.2 million to 12 million. By the year 2000, more than 120 million machines will be connected. (From Internet Society at http://www.isoc.org)

- The education domain (sites that end with the .edu extension) is second only to the growth of the commercial (.com) sites on the Internet. In July of 1994, there were 856,243 sites; by February 1997, the number had grown to an amazing 2.1 million sites. (From Internet Society)

- As of early 1997, there were more than 105 million people who had used the Internet and close to 2 million unique World Wide Web sites. (From http://www.netree.com/netbin/internetstats)

- An estimated 9 million adult Americans use the Web daily. (From http://www.openmarket.com/intindex/)

- The biggest issues facing Internet users today? In a survey by The Georgia Institute of Technology, 35.9 percent of respondents said censorship, privacy was next with 26.2 percent, followed by navigation at 14.1 percent. (From http://www.cc.gatech.edu/gvu/user_surveys/)

- The average Web user in the U.S. is 34.9 years old. About 45 percent are married. Thirty-nine percent are female. Average income of all users is $55,000. Most have college degrees. About 30 percent access the Web through an online service like CompuServe or America Online. (From Georgia Institute of Technology at http://www.cc.gatech.edu/gvu/user_surveys/)

- More than 10,000 schools have created and posted their own WWW sites on the Internet. (From Yahoo! at http://web66.coled.umn.edu/schools/Stats/USA.html)

For additional resources, check InterNIC (at http://www.internic.net) and Matrix Information and Directory Service (MIDS) (at http://www1.mids.org/), or do a Yahoo! search for "statistics" and "Internet."

I mention standardized tests because that seems to be the way that many professionals measure the success of a new tool in education. Carefully orchestrated use of the Net can help students develop both critical-thinking skills and skills in accessing and evaluating information, but it's unlikely that using the Net can help them answer Number Three on the ITBS (you know, that wonderful standardized test that consumes #2 pencils and too many brain cells). But then again . . . who knows?

Setting reasonable expectations and accessing the Net only when it's appropriate are keys to using the Net effectively with your students as a learning tool. How do you decide when it's appropriate to use the Internet instead of a workbook, for example? Knowing what the Internet can offer you and your students helps:

- ✔ **Global electronic mail:** Send a note to anyone else in the world with an Internet address at any time. Suddenly, you have the ability to build links between people everywhere without regard to those things that blind us from appreciating the knowledge of others — things such as race, color, creed, gender, and physical disabilities all disappear when you board the information highway.

  A teacher in my school district used electronic mail to correspond with a teacher in Alaska who gave a mush-by-mush description of the Iditarod dog sled race. Every day, the teacher in my district checked to see what condition the dogs were in, who the front-runner was, and what interesting anecdotes the windblown racers had about the challenges they faced. She then passed the information on to her students, who wrote articles for an "Iditarod Update," made maps of the trip, charted weather conditions, and even calculated windchill temperatures. Is this project interdisciplinary or what?

- ✔ **Knowledge navigation:** Zip around the world via the Internet to locate documents, pictures, sounds, and even digitized movies to keep your knowledge, skills, and curriculum up to date. Glance over at your bookshelf, tug on the textbook that says, "Someday, man will go to the moon," and think about how useful having instantaneous information for use in the classroom can be.

  Got a unit on weather coming up? Use Internet resources to pop over to NASA (`http://www.nasa.gov/`) to access ready-made classroom activities. Then surf over to the Library of Congress (`http://www.loc.gov/`) or your local library and build a bibliography, and then head for the Jet Propulsion Lab (`http://www.jpl.nasa.gov/`) for digitized satellite photos.

- ✔ **File exchange:** Send and retrieve files containing documents, pictures, movies, sounds, and programs. Need the latest version of virus protection software? Jump onto the Net, hop to the vendor's file server, and copy the program (`http://www.yahoo.com/Business_and_Economy/Companies/Computers/Software/Virus_Protection/`).

- ✔ **Discussion groups:** Engage in a discussion with other Internet users about any topic you can think of. A media specialist using a discussion group (also called a newsgroup) began a discussion about selecting software for a circulation system. Four weeks later, he went before the Board of Education with testimonials and facts from 23 school systems from around the country about the system he had selected. His board of education bought it — lock, stock, and bar code.

TECHNO TERMS

Surfing, mining, browsing — we need a new metaphor!

In one of those rare quiet moments driving to a meeting, I got a great chance to talk to a fellow Net user about the semantics of the Net. Words are important. The way you say things really does have an effect on how people react. So, what does the word surf really mean?

My friend suggested that surfing is a term that indicates pointing yourself in one direction and ending up somewhere you don't expect. It suggests a lack of control over where the user ends up. Perhaps. She prefers to use the term mining. She said that mining means that you know what you're looking for, you go find it, and along the way you find lots of other good and bad stuff. Not a bad metaphor, I think.

How about browsing? Is this an aimless activity? Maybe. Is doing an activity "aimlessly" all bad? Maybe not. One the ways I've found some of the best resources is by browsing from site to site. When I see a great site, I add it to my browser's address storage list (called a *bookmark list*) and move on. Later, when I need a specific resource (I guess I'm mining then), I call upon those things that I found while I was browsing.

Okay. I think I've figured it out. When you first sit down at your computer, you're likely wearing your surfer clothes. You point yourself toward a search page or a known point and use it as a jumping-off point for what comes next. You don't really know what's next, but you're pretty glad that you're there.

Next, you *browse* a bit, searching the items you found when you entered your search terms on the search page. You may stumble now and then and find places that you wish you hadn't or places that you want to remember for later. Soon you begin to focus on the task at hand — time for the miner's hat.

As you mine, you're looking for specific information and choosing links and jumps in a very organized and purposeful way. So . . . maybe the sequence is surf, browse, mine . . . or maybe not. <grin>

I think that we have a much richer word to describe what we're doing. When we access the Net we're not surfing, mining, or browsing. What we're doing is tapping. Not the shuffle-ball-change thing, not the beer thing, but the other kind of tapping. Tapping implies that we're making a connection or opening an outlet for information. The key words here — *connection* and *outlet for information* — make me think more about what we're really doing. The word doesn't have a value judgment — it doesn't suggest that what we're doing is a bad, good, or even fun thing. It's value-neutral, unlike surf. We're connecting with others and using our computers and lots of phone lines as an outlet for information that we use to make decisions, solve problems, or just file away for later use. Maybe it's a stretch, maybe not. Next time you jump on the Internet, *see* what resources you can tap.

✔ **Live conferencing:** Talk "live" to other Internet users. Get into a debate about outcome-based education, or Bloom's Taxonomy, or whether to have Coca-Cola or Pepsi in the faculty lounge machines.

And, there's much, much more. By its very nature, the Internet is a dynamic medium. It changes just about every nanosecond as people add or delete information. The body of knowledge on the Internet is growing exponentially. Between the time that I wrote this page and the time that you read it, there have been thousands of new resources added to the Internet.

Whether it's the rich resources or the chance to collaborate globally that attracts you and your students to the Internet, the potential benefits (both tangible and intangible) can be substantial. Once linked into the Net, the emphasis in your classroom will shift quickly toward fostering the quest for new knowledge and helping students interpret, navigate, evaluate, and apply the knowledge they gain. The Web is good for students, good for teachers, and, yes, good for education. Web and learn!

Chapter 3

Let's Go Web Surfing!

. . . .

In This Chapter

▶ Webbing with Netscape Navigator

▶ Getting your free copy of Navigator

▶ Meeting the Netscape Navigator interface

▶ Navigating the Web

▶ Untangling the tangled Web

. . . .

*I*n the prehistoric telecommunications era (1970 – 1980), going online was a major production. You had to know baud rate, stop bits, parity, checksum, log-on codes, modem strings (that looked like something from that college statistics class that you skipped at least once), and much more. Thank goodness that telecommunications in general (and the Net, specifically) is easier today than ever. You need know none of the above terms to get started on your Internet journey.

This section guides you on a quick journey through the Web using a browser called Netscape Navigator (http://www.home.netscape.com). I've chosen to highlight Netscape because more than half the people using the Web have and use this program on their computers. (Netscape has been free to educators for some time now; Internet Explorer is also free to download.) Most of the browser screen shots in *Web Publishing For Teachers* were created with Navigator, so your screen may look different than those shown in this book. (See the sidebar on Netscape Communicator later in this chapter for more information on future versions of Netscape.)

The general operation of most Web browsers other than Netscape, including its main competitor Microsoft Internet Explorer (http://www.microsoft.com/ie/), is very similar to that of Netscape. So if you're using a browser other than Navigator, your job of understanding this information (and my job of writing it) has been made a lot easier.

Internet 101: Netscape Navigator

A browser such as Netscape Navigator is a program that enables users to cruise the World Wide Web. The program is actually the offspring of another browser called Mosaic, a freeware program that paved the way for the enhanced capabilities of Netscape.

Netscape and other browsers provide users of Macintoshes and PCs running Windows with a fast, easy-to-use interface that makes zipping around the Web easy. Netscape Navigator is feature-rich; provides access to WWW, Gopher, and FTP resources; and — here's the best news — some versions are *free* for educators!

Get Your Free Copy!

First things first. It's time to grab your copy of Netscape Navigator. The good news is it's *free* and can be downloaded from Netscape's home page at `http://www.netscape.com`. (Note that other browsers are also downloadable from the Internet, too. For instance, Microsoft Internet Explorer is also free for the downloading. For a good one-stop shopping place for browsers, visit `http://www.download.com`.)

You can use the AOL browser to download Netscape Navigator, or use AOL's built-in browser, Internet Explorer. Note, however, that the AOL browser doesn't (yet) support all the bells and whistles that Navigator does. It's also possible to use Netscape Navigator while logged on to AOL if you have Netscape Navigator Version 3.0 or later. (Check your AOL software manuals, which you can find online by using the keyword Help, for how to do this.)

To use Netscape Navigator, you need Internet access (via an Internet service provider or an online service such as AOL) and a Macintosh or PC running Windows. Here are the easy installation instructions:

1. **Obtain a copy of Netscape Navigator from your Internet service provider or download it like I just described.**

2. **Double-click on the Netscape Navigator installer icon to start the installation program.**

   You need about 3MB of free space on your hard drive for the program.

3. **After you've installed the program, connect to your Internet provider.**

   This step physically connects you to the Internet so that Navigator can do its work.

   (If you need more help with this, try *The Internet For Teachers,* 2nd Edition (from IDG Books Worldwide, Inc.).

4. Double-click on the Netscape Navigator icon to start the program.

That's it! Now a recent version of Netscape Navigator is safe and sound on your hard drive, and you're ready to begin to do some Web surfing! For updates of your software, you can visit the Netscape Web page at

```
http://www.netscape.com/
```

The Netscape Interface

When you launch the Netscape Navigator Web browser by clicking on the Netscape Navigator icon, you are presented with a screen containing ten major components:

- ✔ A menu bar
- ✔ A toolbar
- ✔ A title bar
- ✔ Directory buttons
- ✔ A status bar
- ✔ A viewing area
- ✔ Scroll bars
- ✔ A URL bar
- ✔ A mail icon
- ✔ A security icon

Figure 3-1 can help you match the components with their locations on your computer screen. By the way, Figure 3-1 shows the Weather Underground page from the University of Michigan (`http://groundhog.sprl.umich.edu`). (Your screen may look a little different, depending on what version of Netscape you are using.)

Here's a brief summary of each of the components that make up the Netscape Navigator main window and the functions of each component. If you'd like to get started right away (those of you who still rip the wrapping off holiday gifts faster than someone can say "Wait!"), skip to the next section and come back and read this section later.

The *title bar* shows you the name of the current Web page that you're viewing.

Directory buttons   URL bar   Menu bar   Toolbar   Title bar

Figure 3-1:
The
Netscape
Navigator
main
screen,
shown here
in the
University
of Michigan
Weather
Underground
home page.

Security icon   Status bar   Viewing area   Scroll bars   Mail icon

The *menu bar* has lots of pull-down menus. Many of the commands in these menus are replicated on the Netscape Navigator toolbar.

The *Netscape Navigator toolbar* contains many useful buttons. Figure 3-2 gives you an up-close look at the toolbar. Basically, the toolbar gives you easy access to commonly used features. To use the tools, simply click on the buttons.

Figure 3-2:
An up-close
look at the
Netscape
Navigator
toolbar.

TECHNO TERMS

Meet URL

URL (pronounced "you-are-elle") stands for *Uniform Resource Locator.* A URL lists the exact location (address) of virtually any Internet resource, such as a file, hypertext page, or newsgroup.

URLs look like this:

Resource	Example
a WWW page	`http://www.info.apple.com/education/`
a picture file	`ftp://fabercollege.edu/graphics/otter.gif.sit`
a newsgroup	`news:alt.binaries.great.fraternity.pkt`
a Gopher site	`gopher://gopher.tc.umn.com`
a telnet session	`telnet://teachable.tech.com`

URLs are made up of a *resource type* (Web, newsgroup, FTP, and so on) followed by a colon and two forward slashes, the Net address of the resource, and (sometimes) the pathway that locates the files among all the sub-directories on the destination server.

What do you *do* with these URLs? Type them into the Open box in your Web browser (or other Internet tools), press Return (or Enter), and you're on your way!

Here's a rundown of the buttons on the toolbar:

Tool/Button	Function
Back	Returns you to the previous Web page or document.
Forward	Moves you forward to the Web page or document from which you've used the Back command. (If you're on the last item in your Recent list, the command will be grayed out.)
Home	Returns you to the first page that you see when you launch Netscape Navigator.
Reload	Reloads current Web page or document. (Use this when your screen looks strange or if images [pictures] don't load correctly the first time.)
Images	Loads pictures into your Web page if your Autoload Images preference is set to off (isn't checked).
Open	Enters a new URL (Internet pathway).
Print	Prints the current document.
Find	Finds text in the current document or current page.
Stop	Cancels incoming graphics or text information. (Useful if you're impatient and don't want to wait for long image transfers.)

An area called the *URL bar,* just below the toolbar, shows the full Web address of the site to which you've surfed.

The *directory buttons* whisk you away to Netscape Navigator resources, such as the popular "What's New" (new Web pages) and several Web search resources.

You find that all the text and images (graphics) reveal themselves in the largest area on your screen, the *Viewing Area.* This is where the good stuff comes in.

On the bottom of the screen is a *status bar.* The status bar shows you where you're headed and whether the document is *encrypted* (electronically coded before transmission). If you're at a site that's protected by encryption, an unbroken key shows up if the file you're reading is encrypted for security; most sites aren't protected. The status bar also gives you information about how large a Web page is and how long it will take for the images and text to download to your computer.

Scroll bars help you move up and down (or, in some cases, side to side) on Web pages that are larger than the viewing area of your screen.

You can hide the directory buttons and other items to give you more screen real estate by choosing Options⇨Show directory buttons.

Connecting to the Web via Your Browser

You've retrieved your copy of Netscape Navigator (or another browser) via FTP (using Fetch, the AOL FTP, or another program), and now you're ready to fire up the program and get surfing! Netscape has been a leader in browser interfaces for a very good reason — it's easy to use and very powerful. Using the program is as simple as starting the program and entering a URL (an Internet address). Here's how:

1. **Connect to your Internet provider (usually this means launching a Mac control panel like MacPPP or an online service such as AOL, or launching Netscape in Windows).**

   You can double-click on the Netscape Navigator icon, and your computer automatically accesses the proper resources and makes your Net connection as it launches Navigator. (Note that this feature can be turned on and off via the Preferences menu.) Figure 3-3 shows the Netscape home page.

The browser that spawned them all

NCSA Mosaic, the granddaddy of all brows-ers, is currently in Version 3.0 and is also free. (NCSA stands for the National Center for Supercomputing Applications at the University of Illinois.) This product has some pretty powerful features, but it also has some drawbacks. NCSA Mosaic doesn't support certain HTML extensions, so it isn't the greatest browser for looking at or working with certain Web pages. You can download Mosaic from http://www.ncsa.uiuc.edu/sdg/ software/WinMosaic/ HomePage.html.

As you move your mouse over some of the words and pictures on the home page (they're probably blue or purple if you have a color monitor), the mouse pointer turns into a pointing hand. Clicking on these words or pictures takes you to another Web page. Clicking on the words Netscape Destinations, for example, zips you to a Web page that lets you find people, visit cutting-edge sites, and download software.

Figure 3-3:
Netscape Navigator automatically takes you to the Netscape home page.

2. **To browse the World Wide Web, either click on one of the hypertext (blue) items on the screen or choose File⇨Open Location (⌘+O) at the top of the screen.**

3. **Enter a URL.**

Want a cool place to start? Try the home page of the Public Broadcasting System (PBS). The PBS page has links to your favorite PBS broadcast shows, as well as lots of general reference education information. Click on the Open button or press ⌘+O (or choose File⇨Open Location) and enter this URL (address):

```
http://www.pbs.org
```

When you click on OK, you are whisked away to the PBS site. Easy, huh?

Figure 3-4 shows one of the many sites you can access through the PBS main menu. This one, Newton's Apple, is one of my favorite! (Can you tell I was a science teacher?)

Use the button bar to activate commands such as Back (⌘+[ ) to return to the last Web site you visited, Home to return to the Navigator home page, and Stop (⌘+.) to cancel your request and try another Web site.

Figure 3-4:
Grab
Newton's
Apple
through the
PBS home
page.

Don't get excited if you encounter a 404 not found error message. This just means that the Web site is busy, has moved, or that your URL wasn't entered correctly.

Occasionally, your browser will fail to load pictures correctly and will display a "broken icon" graphic. Click on the Reload button (⌘+R) at the top of the screen, and Navigator refreshes the graphics on your screen.

Exiting Netscape and Saving Pages

When you finish surfing, exit Netscape Navigator by choosing File⇨Quit (⌘+Q).

Remember that you've only quit the browser and have not quit the Net itself. You must return to your PPP, SLIP, or WinSock tools to terminate your connection.

Use File⇨Save (⌘+S) to save the contents of a Web page on your disk for later viewing.

When you save a page, you can save the text but not all the graphics. The format is also somewhat scrambled, but you'll eventually view and print from a word processor and not a Web browser.

Navigating the Tangled Web

Finding things hidden in the Web can be as tough as finding a free moment to make a phone call during the school day. Hundreds of thousands of Web pages are out there, with more pages being added every day, so it's tough for any one place to have a full listing of what's on the Net.

How suite it is: Netscape Communicator

Netscape Navigator is soon to become integrated with a suite of programs from Netscape called Netscape Communicator. Navigator will become one of a number of programs in the Communicator Suite, which should be very affordably priced (in the neighborhood of 50 bucks). Navigator will become even snazzier and easier to use in its new home, and the entire Communicator Suite will include enhanced e-mail capabilities, sound and graphics updates, and an HTML editing tool called Netscape Composer, which you can use to create and upload Web pages. Check out http://www.home.netscape.com for the latest on Communicator updates, pricing, and availability.

What's more, URLs come and go and change structure regularly. This means that some links that you come across, or have collected yourself, may evaporate at a moment's notice.

The Web provides several pages that are either lists of other sites or that contain a searchable database of Web addresses. Try one or more of the jumping-off points given in the list below. Use the Open button (⌘+L) to reveal a window where you can enter any URL. Here are a few jumping-off points that you and your students may enjoy. From these, you can get virtually anywhere on the World Wide Web.

```
http://www.yahoo.com
http://www.exite.com
http://www.altavista.digital.com
```

The search is on!

After you've dialed in to the Net and launched your Web browser, you can visit specific sites, called *search engines,* that feature fill-in-the-blank forms that allow keyword searches of Web sites and content. One of the best Web search engines is called Excite. Like other search engines, Excite is merely a specially written Web page designed to take a user-entered query and find all the sites on the Net that match the query's criteria. The Excite URL is

```
http://www.excite.com/
```

Excite searches for documents whose title or content matches your key-word. As with any search engine, you get "hits" only on those sites whose URLs have been entered (either by crafty Web robots or a college student staying up all night — for a year) physically into a searchable list of URLs. That's why people use more than one search site when they're really looking for something.

Using Excite is easy; simply enter the search term and click on the Search button. (See Figure 3-5.)

Some Web search pages actually serve as a jumping-off point for *other* search pages. The Beaucoup! site lists more than 600 search engines, categorized by how they work. Get to Beaucoup! by traveling to

```
http://www.beaucoup.com/engines.html
```

FAQ and other TLAs

When you learn to surf the Internet, you and your students are learning a new language with lots of new jargon and, of course, lots of acronyms. Many of the acronyms dealing with technology tend to have three letters, so we affectionately call them *TLAs* (three-letter acronyms). One very useful TLA that you'll find all over the net is FAQ. *FAQ* stands for *frequently asked questions,* and a FAQ is a document containing answers to all the questions swirling around in your brain right now. Most sites have FAQs, especially those sites dealing with newsgroups or FTP (file transfer) sites.

One cardinal rule for students and teachers. If you spot a FAQ file, read it. You'll save everyone lots of grief. FAQs often contain information that can save you embarrassment, ridicule, time, and money. I know! All you folks out there who are now staring at all the software and hardware manuals on your shelf (those manuals that are still hermetically sealed in their original shrink-wrap) are going to chuckle. Just wait, though; eventually someone will throw the "Didn't you read the FAQ?" message at you. This message is similar to *RTSM* (read the stupid manual).

A great activity for students is to send them on a hunt for TLAs and have them make an Internet dictionary. Here are a few to get them started:

FAQ TCP LAN FTP BBS DNS
URL AOL GIF RFC IRC MUD

And for extra credit: NII.

Figure 3-5:
Excite offers a simple and very comprehensive search engine for the Web.

Once you're there, be sure to check out the *Multiple Search Engines* category. These multi-search Web pages provide you with the ability to enter one search term (called a *keyword*) and search more than one search engine at a time.

For you teachers-in-training, or for those of you who just can't give up an opportunity to go to graduate school, here's a particularly useful search engine that saves you lots of miles on the old Pinto wagon:

```
http://ericir.syr.edu/Eric/
```

It's the ERIC database online! Yippee! Use ERIC to search for education topics. The URL above searches ERIC Digest (a summary of topics), but links to full-text search at the U.S. Department of Education are also found on that page.

Trouble on the highway

When you have a room full of wide-eyed fifth-graders at 2:30 p.m. on a Friday afternoon, things will fail. (This situation is the educator's corollary of Murphy's Law.) The kinds of errors you see, and how you handle them, depend mostly on your Web browser software. Netscape Navigator and Internet Explorer give you lots of feedback when problems arise; other Web browsers may sometimes leave you hanging.

Following is a short list of the most common problems that you and your students might encounter and what you can do about them:

Problem/Message	Remedy
"The server may be down or unreachable"	It's busy (so wait) or it's off-line for maintenance (so wait some more).
"404 not found"	Check your URL; the cause is usually a typo or a link that's moved or evaporated.
"The server does not have a DNS entry"	Check your URL; another likely typo.
"Broken pictures" (a fragmented icon that represents where a picture should be)	Reload the image or Web page.

Sometimes your browser just freezes and doesn't seem to be doing anything at all. Most of the time, you can press ⌘+. (that is, press the ⌘ key and the period key on a Mac) or Ctrl+C (that is, the Ctrl key and the C key in Windows) to stop the execution of a browser command. With most browsers, you can check the bottom of the active window for a message that tells you what request the browser has made. The big chill sometimes happens when the messages reads as follows:

- ✔ Looking up a host (The farther away the host, the longer it's likely to take to find it.)

- ✔ Contacting host (Your browser is awaiting access; sometimes the requested server is too busy.)

- ✔ Host contacted. Waiting for reply. (The host computer knows you're there, but you're in a queue awaiting access.)

- ✔ Transferring data (Moving the text or images from the host to your computer; this stage can take a *long* time if the Web page features large graphics or lots of text.)

How to End Up with Fewer Gray Hairs

Here are some points to ponder that can save you loads of time (and a few gray hairs):

- ✔ If images are coming in too slowly, deselect Options⇨Auto Load Images. This action gives you a text-only interface. After you've reached a page that you'd like to examine more closely, click on the Reload button (⌘+R) to see the Web page's graphics.

- ✔ If at first you don't succeed . . . sometimes the third time's the charm. Web pages can be very busy.

- ✔ Remember that you can copy, print, or save the text and graphics that are displayed on any Web page.

- ✔ *Bookmark files* (files that allow you to keep a running list of your favorite WWW sites — read more about these in Chapter 8) can quickly fill up with lots of dead-end links. Determine a policy and/or organizational method for storing your Web bookmarks and share the policy with your students.

You've seen that surfing the Web is really not much more than pointing and clicking on words and pictures. It's easy — no kidding! I've had great success with surfers from my neighbor's first-grader to my friend's grandmother. My dad spent several hours pointing and clicking his way to an expanded stock portfolio. Once your students understand the metaphor of a point-and-click "hot-linked" environment, you can shift their focus to the more important tasks of evaluating the Net's wealth of information and developing strategies for capturing and using the information that they find.

Navigate with SurfBoard

SurfBoard (a program for Macs that I've included on the CD) provides a fast and easy way to navigate the Internet. SurfBoard is really a control panel that lets you use a menu to create bookmarks pointing to your favorite spots on the Internet.

The interface looks like that all-too-familiar TV remote control, but get ready — SurfBoard is a blast! All you need to do is click on a SurfBoard bookmark; the program then launches the appropriate application and takes you where you want to go. With SurfBoard, you can even set up categories for your bookmarks (by subject, grade level, whatever!) and organize your bookmarks accordingly. Some neat sound effects (which you can disable when the cacophony in the computer lab gets unbearable) help make this a really great bookmark manager program.

Part II
Webbing 101

The 5th Wave — By Rich Tennant

Principal

"I found these two in the computer lab morphing
faculty members into farm animals."

In this part . . .

*B*efore you can *hang 33.6* (that's 33,600 bits per
second, in modem language), you and your students
will need to put some radical thought into the purpose,
design, and style of your home page. You also need to
choose the right tools for your job of creating a Web page.
This part of the book guides you step by step as you learn
the elements of effective Web page design and Web page
style.

Chapter 4
The Grand Web Site Design

. . . .

In This Chapter

▶ Dissecting a Web site

▶ Getting hierarchical or going straight

▶ Thinking about content

▶ Going for the goal

. . . .

*W*alk around your school and look at the keyboards attached to the computers on people's desks. If the home-row keys are dark and look dirty, you've just found out a very important thing about the user: He or she reads a newspaper. Newspapers would be much better if their ink didn't magically jump from the paper onto your computer keyboards. When I get to school (before the rooster crows), I like to take a second to catch up on education and technology news from the local paper. Next, I move to answer the zillions of e-mail messages that spontaneously generate in my mailbox between 11 p.m. the previous evening and rooster time. Oops! More newsprint ink on the keyboard. Sigh. Wait. There *is* a point to this story, I promise!

If you glance at the front page of your daily newspaper, you see that it consists of the name of the paper (the masthead), various "hot" stories with headlines of different sizes, and lots of references to what's inside.

A Web site is just like its distant cousin, the newspaper. The first page (screens in Web space are called *pages*) that you see when you enter a Web site gives you information about the location of the server (school name, company name, and the like — a virtual masthead) and just enough information to tickle your fancy ("teasers"); it then points you to other pages (*links*). This chapter leads you though a brief look at the components that make up a Web site. Be sure to wash your hands before using your keyboard!

Dissecting a Web Site

A Web *site* is basically all the text, graphics, sounds, hypertext links, and other resources that make up your presence on the World Wide Web. A Web site is made up of three basic components:

- ✔ A home page (the top-most page in your site)
- ✔ Local and remotely stored pages linked to your home page
- ✔ Supporting content (documents, images, and sounds)

In the following sections, I'll hold a "faculty meeting" to brief you on how these components work together. Reading these pages can give you a great idea of how Web pages are structured, and these pages also give you several options for creating your own Web site.

While surfing around the Internet, experiment by using multiple browsers. Web pages tend to look different when viewed with different tools. For example, Netscape Navigator supports a command that allows for the display of various types of fonts; others browsers generally do not. Therefore, it's important to try accessing sites you admire by using more than one browser. Just because you're using the latest version of Navigator or Internet Explorer doesn't mean that everyone else will be or that your page will look the same to every reader.

Going home

A *home page* is the first page that users see when they enter your Web site. Because it sets the tone for the organization and content in your site, careful planning of your home page is important. First impressions, after all, are important.

Figure 4-1 shows an example of a home page created by yours truly. Visit the real-time version at `http://www.mindspring.com/~bardw/bard.html`.

Home pages usually contain a *header* (like a newspaper's masthead) that gives the name or affiliation of the creator. These electronic mastheads can be just simple text, or a combination of text and a graphic, such as in the home page of North Hollywood High School (`http://www.lausd.k12.ca.us/North_Hollywood_HS/`), shown in Figure 4-2.

Home pages can also be complex — containing graphics with "hot spots" where users can click and be whisked away to other pages. Figure 4-3 shows a home page from Queen Elizabeth Elementary School (`http://wqsb.qc.ca/queenvd/`) in Quebec, Canada — one of the better examples of school-level Web pages to pop up on the Web. The buttons on the left side of the screen are part of an image that features "live" areas — clicking on different parts of the image takes you to other pages or other Web sites.

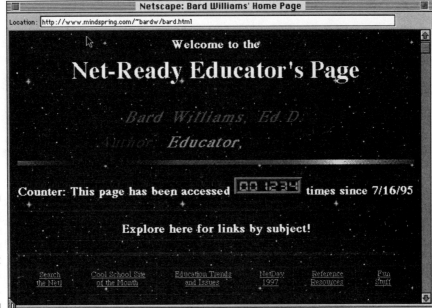

Figure 4-1:
A home
page is the
top-most
page in a
Web site.

Figure 4-2:
Many
school Web
sites
feature
simple
headers
and easy-
to-read text.

Clickable "hot spots"

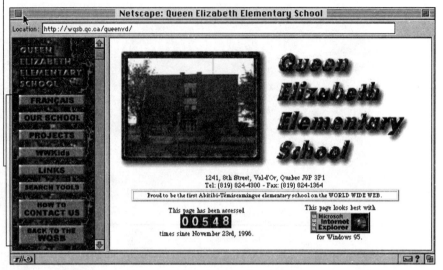

Figure 4-3:
Some Web
pages
contain
clickable
graphics
(like the
buttons
shown
here) that
sweep you
away to
new places
to explore.

Don't be too intimidated by fancy graphics and artwork, though. Your school or district can begin with a much simpler page and work its way up. Note that students are very often the perfect Webmasters at education sites. First, the students are much more comfortable with the technology (in general); and second, they'll never turn down a challenge (especially when you explain that your Web page can be seen by millions of people).

Links-R-Us

Most of the time, a home page contains text that, when clicked with a mouse, performs one of several magical tricks. In Netspeak, we refer to clickable text (sometimes graphics are clickable, too) as *links* or, more correctly, *hypertext links.* Clicking on a text or graphic link may do one of the following:

- ✔ Transport you to other Web pages at the same site
- ✔ Zip you along to other Web pages at different sites
- ✔ Jump your cursor to another place on the same page
- ✔ Cause a file to be downloaded (copied) from the Web site to your computer
- ✔ Link you to other Internet resources, such as mail, FTP, newsgroups, or Gopher sites

The ability to create your own links easily gives you and your students the power to create anything from a simple list of "favorite sites" to a complex mini-Web of interconnected pages.

Are You Linear, Hierarchical, or Web Crazy?

Sorry for the personal question. What I'm asking is if you'd like to design a Web site that is *linear*, one that is arranged in a more complex *hierarchy*, or one that has a highly complex *web* arrangement. The design style you choose is based largely upon what type of content you intend to deliver and your expertise in designing Web pages.

Going straight

The easiest Web page organization is to "go straight," that is, create a linear design. Linear designs are like books. You begin with the title page (your home page), and links take you from your home page to page 2, from page 2 to page 3, from page 3 to page 4, and so on (see Figure 4-4).

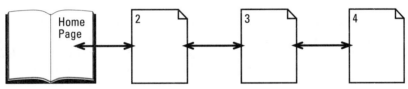

Figure 4-4:
Linear Web
sites are
designed
like books;
access is
sequential.

Linear design is perfect if you are presenting a series of steps or tracking a process from start to finish. Linear organization makes sense when you're presenting a series of documents. Its simple design keeps users from clicking into never-never land. Good linear organization offers clickable buttons that allow users to select "next page," "previous page," or "back to home page" options.

Getting hier

Hierarchical structures are the most common Web-site designs. This design type looks kinda like your family tree. In hierarchical design, the home page serves as a contents page that branches to other pages that, in turn, branch to still other pages. Unlike linear design, hierarchical design provides more than one path that a user may take (see Figure 4-5).

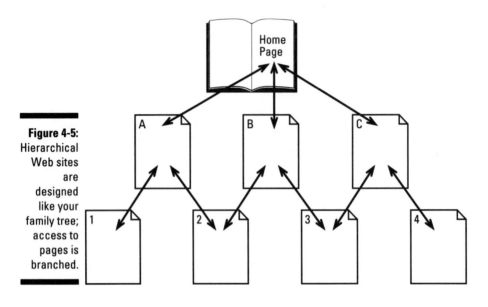

Figure 4-5:
Hierarchical
Web sites
are
designed
like your
family tree;
access to
pages is
branched.

The spider's choice

The most daring type of Web design allows users to jump (branch) from any point in a Web site to any other point in that site with the click of a mouse. With web structure, your home page can take people to lots of different places; but no matter where each link takes them, they find multiple links to other pages, including back to your home page (see Figure 4-6).

It's easy for educators to imagine the complexity of this design if we think of *that food web* that we drew in fifth grade; you know, the one where you start with the "bears," and students eventually connect virtually every living thing on the planet with their bear's food chain.

The Web itself, of course, is designed like the food web. If you choose to build very complex web structures, giving your viewers lots of visual cues as to where they are and what they're seeing is a great idea. Using standard pointers such as "forward," "back," and "return to home page" on every page helps keep folks from wandering endlessly in cyberspace.

Form Follows Function

No matter how snazzy your Web site's design, if nothing is important, interesting, or particularly useful on your Web page, you're just "computing in the wind." It's a good idea to begin your discussion with what content you intend to offer to fellow Internet surfers.

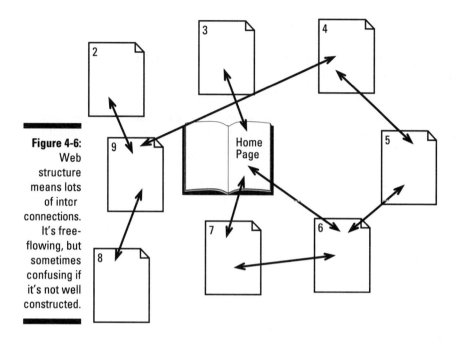

Figure 4-6:
Web structure means lots of inter connections. It's free-flowing, but sometimes confusing if it's not well constructed.

Content on your Web page can take one of many forms. Here are some things that you might consider placing on your Web page:

- ✔ Documents (about your school, community, education in general; student writing, public-domain reference resources, and the like)

- ✔ Images (pictures of your school, community, students, mascot, football team — whatever — a WWW yearbook!)

- ✔ Sounds ("Bueller? Anyone? Anyone?" — for the Ferris Bueller fans!)

- ✔ Downloadable movies (a visit with the principal?)

- ✔ Links to other interesting or useful sites (chosen by students and teachers)

In Part IV of this book ("Jazzing Up Your Web Page"), you learn how to incorporate all the aforementioned goodies into your Web page!

From Basic Design to Master Plan

The time has come to move up the Internet food chain from Web consumer to Web producer. Ready or not, read on for the first steps to take.

If you're like most educators, you want to create a Web page for one of the following reasons:

✔ You can't find what you really need on anyone else's Web page, so you want to make your own.

✔ You can't wait to see your school's name splashed across its own billboard on the information highway.

✔ Your administration said, "Make a Web page."

✔ You're steamed because at least 5,000 schools around the globe have already created their own Web pages, and you hate being left behind.

✔ You know that if you build it, they will come!

 Before you can go any further, pull together a committee of your peers and figure out why you want to create a Web page. Fact is, creating something useful takes a bit of time, and creating a Web home page requires that you find a place (an Internet provider) willing to host your new creation. All of this means an investment of time and a bit of money, resources that are mighty scarce around most schools. Planning is critical to ensure time well spent in building a product that meets your goals. So what do you do first? Set goals, of course!

Set your goals

Creating a Web presence is not unlike deciding on a slogan for a marketing campaign. Your Web page is your school's electronic greeting card and annual report, all rolled into one neat package. Obviously, you want your Web page to be the most friendly and most attractive home page that it can possibly be. Don't forget, though, that it's the content that makes your page something more than just another pretty electronic face.

Choose your content

Deciding on the type of content that you would like to share really depends on three factors:

✔ Your goals for the Web page

✔ Copyright-free resources that your school can collect and share

✔ What resources your school values

Your school's Web page can be designed to share information about your school and community; provide access to databases of text, graphics, movies, and/or sound; provide a handy jumping-off point to links that you and your students have collected; or any combination of the above!

If your school's goal in creating a Web page is to share new information, you should think about what kinds of new information you can access, or generate, that would be of interest to others. Be sure to think in terms of local and global information, because lots of people who aren't from your hometown will flock to see your new Web page. While local items such as school calendars, local sports scores, and important phone numbers are helpful resources for your immediate community, you might consider posting student writing, newsletters, custom-built documents containing new information, or other resources for the "virtual visitors" to your school.

Decide what's really important

Another important consideration as you plan your Web site is the type of information your school values. Think about the kind of information that's important to both your local community and audiences outside of your community — whether they consist of global visitors, school board members, local politicians, businesspeople, or students dialing in from home. *Remember:* Your Web page is your world calling card. First impressions are important. Making your Web pages content-rich and visually magnetic becomes an easier task if you plan well.

The next chapter reviews the final steps in the design process — developing a storyboard for your Web page and thinking about matters of style. Ah, style —the FUN part! Will your page be "hot" or "rad," "cool" or "conservative," or "totally bodacious"? However it turns out, between student input and your creativity, it definitely won't be boring!

The copyright monster

Beware of the copyright monster. You may be tempted to take advantage of the gigabytes of information that your school has on CD-ROM or on floppy disks, but beware. Copyright laws most certainly extend to protect information, even if you've paid for it, from being shared free of charge over the Internet. Be sure to first check with a vendor before you try to offer any commercial or shareware product through your site. Also, be careful to obtain any required permissions before using any art on your Web page.

Some starving artist likely worked hard to create those snazzy logos or nifty lines you admire so much. That artist deserves compensation (or at least a request for permission to use the artwork) before you release your page to the public.

To avoid copyright problems with use of graphics, check out the large libraries of public-domain artwork available at most Web development sites. One of the largest collections of copyright-free artwork can be found at http://www.netscape.com/, the home of Netscape Navigator. Turn to Chapter 3 to see how you can get a free copy of Netscape Navigator.

Chapter 5

Elements of (Web) Style

● ●

In This Chapter

▶ Webbing with style

▶ Touring the Web: the best of the best

▶ Setting the ground rules

▶ Creating a storyboard

● ●

As you and your students create customized Web pages, think *style.* Style is the element that keeps the reader interested. Adhering to a style helps you write clearly and concisely. When you and your students face the challenge of creating your own Web page, you've got a terrific opportunity to reinforce good writing habits. Go ahead and dig out your copy of Strunk and White's *The Elements of Style* or grab a fantastic book called *If You Want to Write* by Brenda Euland. These books will help you remind students how to write understandably and concisely for a wide audience — and the Internet is the widest audience you can imagine. Keep in mind that Web pages are not dissertations — go ahead and have fun with them!

Cut to the Chase

As you create your Web pages, think about how people use the Internet. Typically, they hop around from place to place while glancing to see what's interesting or useful. They *browse.* As a Web author, it's your responsibility to show users what's on your pages in as concise a manner as possible, so that when they zip to your site, they can quickly see what's in store for them. The top of your Web page should give the reader an idea of the content, a reference point (the name of your school or location, perhaps even a picture), and an overall view of the site, through graphic representations, menus, or clickable lists or tables.

Here are some tips you can use to make even the boldest browser smile:

- ✔ Use bullets for lists (student names, school activities, and the like) whenever you can. Bullets are terrific for browsers (the human kind) and are easy to create with browsers (the software kind).

- ✔ Put the important stuff first. People who design television commercials will tell you that they seek to capture your attention in the first five seconds. If they miss, you'll likely hit the channel button or dash off for a quick snack. Web pages should grab a reader's attention with important content (and a bit of flash on the side).

- ✔ Keep images small. (You can find tricks throughout this part, and in the next part of this book, to help you do that!)

- ✔ Consider placing text over a plain white or plain black background (especially for your home page). Pictures, colors, and patterns underneath your words can make them harder to read. Format the text so that it can be seen by people *without* their bifocals.

Proofread

Imagine for a moment that your school has decided to advertise by billboard. Think one step further: Imagine the implications of having a spelling error on the billboard. What would that say about your school (directly or indirectly)? What would the thousands who see it think?

Your Web page is the Mother of All Billboards. There is the potential for millions to view it. The caveat here: No matter how hurried you are to publish your Web page, always proofread your documents before you release them. In fact, have someone else (students, parents, or both) read the documents and check for errors.

If your computer has text-to-speech capability, have your computer read the document to you. You'll undoubtedly find that a useful way to catch errors, and (given that no computer has truly mastered speech) the experience should be entertaining as well. I have to admit that I tried having my Macintosh read back a couple of chapters from this book. I found myself talking like the "Fred" voice for two days.

All emphasis is no emphasis

Remember when you created your first Macintosh or PC document? Most beginning users have the philosophy that if you have 20 fonts in your computer, you should use each and every one of them. And how about those boldface and outline styles — they look so cool you should use them everywhere, right? Nope. Resist the urge to overuse any type of emphasis **(boldface,** *italics,* SPECIAL FORMATTING) or else you ultimately lose the effect.

KISS

As in most writing, the KISS rule applies. Keeping it simple means that, in addition to being careful about how you use emphasis in your text, you don't overuse graphic elements or images (pictures). Remember that some users view your Web pages using very slow connections, so no matter how great it would look to have a color photo of each and every student in your class on your home page, don't do it. Having too many images places the viewer into "download limbo," and most viewers won't wait — they'll surf on to another site. Also remember that some users can't view images at all, so you should make sure to use the ALT (alternative image) tag for those using Lynx or some other text browser so that those "graphically challenged" folks will see words that describe what they are missing.

What's the bottom line? Say what you want to say as concisely as possible. When it comes to words on your home page, less is more.

As a rule, use rules

As with anything you read, white space helps to keep a page from appearing too crowded. Rules (a.k.a. lines) come in handy for just the same purpose. HTML (the computer language that you use to create your Web pages) allows you to easily insert horizontal lines to separate graphics or text elements. Horizontal lines have lots of uses on Web pages, including:

✔ Spacing your text for readability

✔ Dividing categories or topics (useful when organizing hypertext links)

✔ Separating parts of your Web page (head, body, tail, and so forth)

Like other graphical elements, use rule lines with care. Too many lines distract the reader. If you want to get fancy, use an image of a rule (a colored or textured line graphic) instead of HTML's built-in rule line.

Ground yourself

Everyone likes compliments. Just as I try to write positive comments on their papers when students do exemplary work, I also make it a point to drop a note to the Webmaster whenever I encounter a really useful or graphically stunning Web page. Most good Web designers list their e-mail or snail mail (sorry, postal service!) address on the bottom of their home page. The hypertext language (HTML) also has a command called `mailto` (see Appendix B) that lets you dash off a note with the click of a mouse.

Although a return e-mail address is a good feature on your home page, letting the reader know where your school is geographically located is also important. The person accessing your Web page is just as likely to be from Australia as they are from Akron. An important piece of information for your school's home page should be text or a graphic that tells where your school is and a bit about it.

Your home page is like an advertisement of good will to other global cybersurfers — road signs help on the information superhighway!

Pages with pizzazz

Your classroom is no doubt personalized. From your favorite posters (thank goodness for book clubs and computer shows!) to that burlap on the bulletin board, your classroom reflects your style. A Web page is no different. A great Web page reflects the style and personality of its creator or the school, business, or other entity that it represents. As you surf the Net and visit other Web sites, think about the personality each page conveys.

A visit to Ben DeLong's home page (`http://www.unix.oit.umass.edu/~bdelong/index.html`) as shown in Figure 5-1, for example, shows an intelligent student with a playful personality. I like this page because it shows not only the business (serious) side of the student, but has connection to hopes, dreams, and aspirations. (Ben and his colleagues have now started a successful Web-authoring company!) A glance at the home page for a commercial enterprise like Microsoft (`http://www.microsoft.com/`) presents a businesslike approach. Think about what's most appropriate for your Web page, and then create it. No matter how wacky your ideas, try them out. Just be sure that the medium doesn't overwhelm the message (that is, that your content isn't overshadowed by the flash of your page).

Go modular

As you think about the content that you'll provide via the Web, think about how the average user will access your page. Try to keep the topic and content of each page focused, and make each page one complete thought or idea. Pages should stand alone, if at all possible. The key to modularity in Web page design is *storyboarding*. I talk about storyboarding at the end of this chapter, and you can check out Chapter 4 for more on the subject.

Visual overkill

Be aware that lots of folks will view your Web pages; most folks don't have much time to spare, and many have slow connections. How can you help? Use images only when necessary to support content. Your students' first

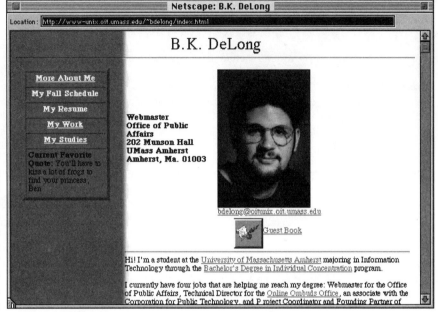

Location : http://www-unix.oit.umass.edu/~bdelong/index.html

B.K. DeLong

More About Me

My Fall Schedule

My Resume

My Work

My Studies

Current Favorite Quote: You'll have to kiss a lot of frogs to find your princess, Ben

Webmaster
Office of Public Affairs
202 Munson Hall
UMass Amherst
Amherst, Ma. 01003

bdelong@oitunix.oit.umass.edu

Guest Book

Hi! I'm a student at the University of Massachusetts Amherst majoring in Information Technology through the Bachelor's Degree in Individual Concentration program.

I currently have four jobs that are helping me reach my degree: Webmaster for the Office of Public Affairs, Technical Director for the Online Ombuds Office, an associate with the Corporation for Public Technology, and Project Coordinator and Founding Partner of

Figure 5-1: A personal home page such as this one reflects the character of the author.

impulse will be to scan everything in sight and splash those graphics across your Web page. While visually stunning, a person seeking access to your Web page will mostly notice is how stunningly long it takes for all those graphics to download. Testing your Web page with a "slow" connection (9600 bps or 14.4 Kbps) is a good idea (just to discover about how long Web surfers from average schools may have to wait to see your handiwork).

Link it

Most schools on the Web feature a list of their favorite Web sites. Instead of just listing the *URL* (Internet address), it's good practice to make the text representing those Web sites into hypertext links. *Hyperlinks* allow users to zip away to other Web pages and Net resources with the click of a mouse.

Basically, there are five types of links that you'll find on a Web page:

- ✔ Links to other Web pages
- ✔ Links to documents
- ✔ Links to Web pages on the local Web server
- ✔ Explanatory links (definitions, footnotes, and the like)
- ✔ E-mail links (allow you to send e-mail from within your Web browser program)

Strunk gets Webbed

You can't talk about style without mentioning the Father of All Style Manuals. That's right, William Strunk, Jr. of *Elements of Style* fame, is on the Web at `http://www.columbia.edu/acis/bartleby/strunk/index.html`. You and your students can access all the tips and techniques without having to search for the dog-eared copy of the Strunk and White style manual in your school media center. The Web page was created according to HTML 3.0 standards (that's cyberspeak for a new set of hypertext language commands readable by cutting-edge Web browsers such as recent versions of Netscape Navigator) and offers great examples of the enhanced formatting available with the newer HTML 3.0 command set (that's cyberspeak for "it looks way cool").

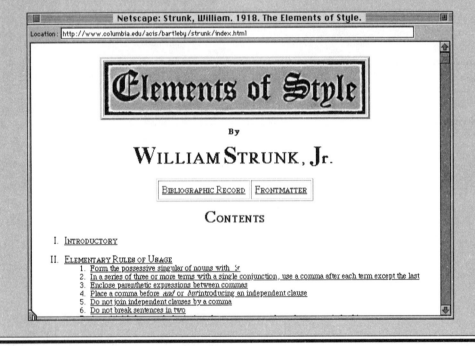

Netscape: Strunk, William. 1918. The Elements of Style.

Location: http://www.columbia.edu/acis/bartleby/strunk/index.html

Elements of Style

By

WILLIAM STRUNK, Jr.

BIBLIOGRAPHIC RECORD | FRONTMATTER

CONTENTS

I. INTRODUCTORY

II. ELEMENTARY RULES OF USAGE
1. Form the possessive singular of nouns with *'s*
2. In a series of three or more terms with a single conjunction, use a comma after each term except the last
3. Enclose parenthetic expressions between commas
4. Place a comma before *and* or *but* introducing an independent clause
5. Do not join independent clauses by a comma
6. Do not break sentences in two

If you choose to use lots of links on your Web pages, be sure to organize them by topic or category for easy reference. Changing your links on a monthly (or more frequent) basis ensures that users keep coming back for more. Some Webmasters talk about not putting too many outside links on their pages because surfers tend to leave their site without ever viewing much of it. Be sure to put the "important stuff" at the top of your Web site!

Style on the Net

Table 5-1 lists commercial and educational Web pages that are among those that get my award for "style" in publishing. The Thurgood Marshall High School's Web page (`http://nisus.sfusd. k12.ca.us/schwww/sch853/ tma_page.htm`) shown in Figure 5-2 is a good example. What distinguishes such pages are the use of common elements (such as toolbars); stunning graphics; open, readable designs; and, of course, lots of useful content.

Table 5-1	Award-winning styles
Site	*URL*
The Coca-Cola Company	`http://www.cocacola.com/`
Town School for Boys	`http://www.town.pvt.k12.ca.us/`
Netscape Communications	`http://www.netscape.com/`
Cupertino Union School District	`http://www.cupertino.k12.ca.us/`
Apple Computer, Inc.	`http://www.info.apple.com/ education`
Estonia (an international delight!)	`http://www.edu.ee/`

Surf first, before you create!

Allow plenty of time to browse other sites before you craft your own Web page. Other schools' sites can serve as useful guidelines for what works (and what doesn't) in Web page design. Some Web addresses that serve as jumping-off points to help you find your way to the thousands of schools (and other sites) on the World Wide Web include the following:

✔ `http://www.webcrawler.com/` Enter **school** or **K–12** as a search term

✔ `http://www.yahoo.com/educa-tion/` The Mother of Search Engines

✔ `http://web66.coled.umn.edu/` More school Web sites than you can imagine

✔ `http://k12.cnidr.org:80/ janice_k12/k12menu.html` Extremely well-connected Web site featuring the latest in Web research

Each of the above sites offers hundreds of links to school and district home pages for your surfing pleasure. Need an assignment for your students? Create a Web Site Evaluation Form and challenge your students to focus on the best of the best.

Thurgood Marshall Academic High School

San Francisco Unified School District

A science, mathematics, and technology magnet school with a "challenge-based" curriculum, providing a rigorous learning experience in an inner-city environment to all students, especially those who have historically been underrepresented in the fields of science and mathematics.

We believe in palpable, hands-on learning that simulates real world situations. Our school is using the "Project 2061" curriculum model, a movement for science education reform which incorporates large, cross-subject projects

Figure 5-2:
A Web page from Thurgood Marshall Academic High School in California — they'd get an *A* for style in Web publishing.

Here's a chance for a great learning activity! Given the guidelines listed earlier in this chapter, have your students create a "style manual" to be used later in the creation of your own home page. Their style manual should address such things as

✔ Style do's and don'ts

✔ Conventions for the type and amount of content you might include

✔ Ideas for common elements (elements that appear on each Web page and that unify your documents)

Need some design assistance? Rush down and kidnap your yearbook editor or advisor. Most of the elements of style used in designing your Web page are similar to those that yearbook staffs have been wrestling with for years.

Charting the Flow

In Chapter 4, I talk about linear, hierarchical, and Web structures for your school Web page, and elements of Web style to discuss with your students. If you've already absorbed that information, it's time to take action and begin to join structure and content. This is a great opportunity to use a flowchart or outline to show your students just how useful these tools are! Work with your students to create your outline by featuring major headings and sub-headings and indicating whether pictures or other resources are present.

Break out the crayons or colored pencils. Have students create a *storyboard* —
a sketch of the layout that shows appearance of your home page (and each
of the subpages) in your site. Use one sheet of paper per page; then, tack the
pages up on your classroom bulletin board and use yarn to connect the
pages and show the links. This method is a handy way to create your Web
site and move things around to where you want them before you begin to
write your pages.

Post these pages on a bulletin board for a few days and solicit some input
from others regarding their structure and organization, as well as their
content. You may also acquire some volunteers to help you with the artwork!

Chapter 6

Tools of the Trade

● ●

In This Chapter

▶ Grabbing the right tool

▶ Exploring what-you-see-is-what-you-get HTML editors

▶ Choosing cut-and-paste editors

▶ Using word processor add-ons

● ●

*I*n the early days of computing, we delivered (and attended) courses with names like "Computer Literacy" and "Understanding the Computer." Then, one day, somebody (or a group of somebodies) pulled his or her (or their) head(s) out of the back of an Apple II computer and had an inspired thought: "Why are we teaching about bits, bytes, and RAM when we should be teaching word processing?"

Conventional wisdom regarding computer instruction swiftly shifted from teaching about the *computer* to teaching about the *programs* the computer uses. We dutifully changed our course titles to reflect the new thinking. Course catalogs then had listings like "AppleWorks Made Easy" and "VisiCalc for the Teacher." We learned how to align text, how to fill cells without retyping information, and how to print labels. (I still have problems with that one!)

The winds of computer wisdom shifted again, and soon thereafter came the Great Evolution of Technology in schools. Suddenly, we were all asking the question, "After we learn about the word processor, *then* what do we do?" In little more than a techno-time generation (about two years), the emphasis shifted from teaching *about* computer programs to teaching *with* computers. Finally, the emphasis was on the *curriculum,* and the computer became a tool for assisting with the curriculum. Now we had course titles like "Science and the Middle School Classroom" featuring computer-assisted and computer-generated activities alongside models for integrating technology into the classroom.

Why don't we learn from our past and accelerate the process for our students? Think about the latest "great debate." Do students need to learn the predominant scripting language of the World Wide Web, Hypertext Markup Language (HTML), to fully understand the Web? Maybe not, although they probably should become somewhat acquainted with HTML. I think a continued focus on your subject area and the outcome of the lesson makes more sense.

Getting students (of all ages) into Web page production as quickly as possible doesn't require knowledge of HTML anymore. Some great programs, such as Claris Home Page 2.0 and Adobe PageMill 2.0 (trial versions of which I've placed on your *Web Publishing For Teachers* CD), now make Web page creation as easy as typing a letter. Save the HTML for later when you want to get really fancy with your pages or when your students get so good at this Web thing that they open their own businesses and out of sheer gratitude buy you your dream home in Florida overlooking the Atlantic. (Well, we can all dream, right?)

So, throw down those pencils and stomp on over to the teachers' lounge. (You know, that comfortable used-to-be-a-broom-closet place with the Coke machine?) Sit down and think a spell as you check out some of your options for the tools you and your students can use to create your Web pages. Your answer depends largely on your available time and resources (and how many quarters you have for the Coke machine).

Basically, you can use five types of tools to create a Web page:

- ✔ WYSIWYG *(What You See Is What You Get)* editors — these work like word processors and do all the HTML coding for you.

- ✔ Stand-alone "easy-paste" editors — they paste HTML tags into text with the click of a mouse.

- ✔ Word processors (with appropriate export utilities) — they let you use your word processor to write code and then export it.

- ✔ Conversion tools — they take documents created with other programs and convert them to HTML format.

- ✔ Hybrid tools — they let you manage an entire Web site, from tracking incoming *hits* (that's Web-speak for the number of times people visit your page) to supporting complex Web designs.

Whether you're using a Macintosh or a PC running Windows, you can find plenty of examples of all of these tools available in catalogs or available for downloading on the Internet. With students, I've found that the specific type of page-creation tool doesn't really matter, but I recommend that you stick to just one. All five types of tools are effective, but if you choose a WYSIWYG program, such as Claris Home Page or PageMill, you quickly find that your students are focusing on the *content* instead of on the process as you instruct them (which results in better content).

In the following sections, I share some suggestions (and reviews) for Web-page-creation tools. All these tools are available through FTP. *FTP* stands for *File Transfer Protocol,* which provides you with a means to transfer files from other computers *(FTP servers)* to your computer (and vice versa, if you are given access rights to post material to an FTP server). Some FTP files are shareware and carry fees, some are commercial, and some are freeware.

WYSIWYG Editors

Remember WYSIWYG? That stands for What Your Students Imagine When You're Grinning. (Um, sorry, but I couldn't resist.) It really means *What You See Is What You Get.* With WYSIWYG editors, you can get a good idea of what your Web page looks like without first launching a Web browser or posting your page to the Net.

Claris Home Page

WYSIWYG editors are great for learning how to use HTML. Although several WYSIWYG editors are available on the Net, two programs really stand out as "A students" in the world of WYSIWYG. One is called Claris Home Page (by Claris). Claris Home Page is a quick-and-easy Web page layout and design program. A 30-day demonstration version of Claris Home Page is on your *Web Publishing For Teachers* CD-ROM. If you and your students think that Claris Home Page is a good tool for you to use, follow the licensing and ordering instructions on the CD (and in Appendix D).

In this book, I've chosen to highlight Claris Home Page, mostly because

- ✔ It's cross-platform (works on PCs and Macs).
- ✔ It's easy to use.
- ✔ It's available to schools at special education prices (see the coupon in the back of this book!).
- ✔ It features both basic and advanced Web editing tools.

Adobe PageMill

You may also check out Adobe PageMill (http://www.adobe.com/prodindex/pagemill/main.html). Or, to make it even easier, I've included a trial version of PageMill 2.0 on the CD with this book! It's Claris Home Page's chief competitor and offers a few features that Claris Home Page doesn't have. (And Claris Home Page has a few features that PageMill doesn't have.) Watch for this WYSIWYG race to continue!

FrontPage

Microsoft FrontPage is a versatile tool for building Web pages easily. FrontPage is a cross-platform tool that combines site design with page editing and offers lots of higher-end capabilities — not the easiest tool to use, but maybe one the most fully featured. FrontPage excels in the creation of frames and tables and has a built-in spell checker. All its features, however, make for a steep learning curve. Find out about FrontPage at `http://www.microsoft.com/frontpage`.

Visual Page

Symantec's Visual Page is also an easy-to-use WYSIWYG editing tool. Although Visual Page runs only on Macs, it has the edge in frame editing and is a great tool for working with more advanced Web features (like multimedia and JavaScript). Visual Page lacks a spelling checker, but is still a dandy tool. Grab information about Visual Page at `http://www.symantec.com/vpagemac`.

Sunburst's School Version of Web Workshop

A simple tool designed especially for students in Grades 3–8. The good news is that it's very easy to use — the bad news is that the output is not in standard HTML, so editing files created with Web Workshop using other standard editors is not very simple. Check out Web Workshop at `http://www.snysunburst.com/webwork_index.html`.

AOL

America Online offers an online tool called AOLPress for building very simple Web pages that can be published on AOL. The cost of publishing your page is included in your regular monthly subscription, which means that if you already have an AOL account, you won't be paying anything extra to publish your page. It's not a high-end tool, but it is quick and easy. Check out the AOL online keyword: **www** (that's if you have an AOL account) or visit `http://www.navisoft.com` (on the Internet).

Surf before you create!

Before creating your own Web page, be sure to allow plenty of time to browse other sites for good ideas. The following Web addresses can serve as jumping-off points to help you find your way to the thousands of schools (and other sites) that are on the World Wide Web:

http://www.webcrawler.com/	Enter "school" or "k-12" as a search term.
http://www.yahoo.com/education/	The mother of all link catalogs
http://web66.coled.umn.edu/	More school Web sites than you can imagine
http://k12.cnidr.org:80/janice_k12/k12menu.html	Extremely well-connected Web site featuring Web research

Each of these sites offers hundreds of links to school and district home pages for your surfing pleasure. Want a great critical-thinking skill assignment for your students? Create a Web Site Evaluation Form and challenge your students to focus on the best of the best.

Cut-and-Paste Editors

Cut-and-paste editors are just one step below the WYSIWYG editors. You have easy access to insert HTML *tags* (commands), often by choosing them from a menu or a floating palette; but you usually have to launch a Web browser to preview your work, and you've also got to deal with raw HTML code (instead of just placing elements on the page).

Web Weaver

One of the better cut-and-paste editors is Web Weaver. Besides an easy-to-use interface and good menu organization, this shareware program offers features for novice and pro Web editors alike. Information about Web Weaver is available at the following site:

http://www.miracleinc.com

The powerful Web Weaver application, written by Robert C. Best, offers an easy way to remember HTML tags. Simply highlight the text that you'd like to format and choose the proper tag from a floating menu, such as those in Figure 6-1. (***Note:*** Web Weaver runs only on Macintosh computers.)

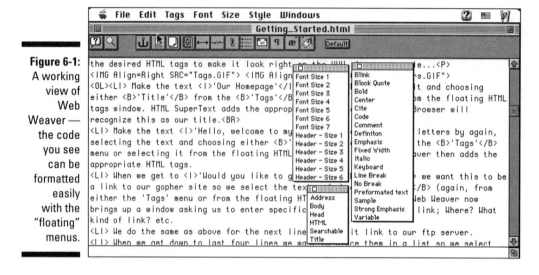

Figure 6-1:
A working
view of
Web
Weaver —
the code
you see
can be
formatted
easily
with the
"floating"
menus.

HoTMetaL Pro

Another very powerful cut-and-paste editor is HoTMetaL Pro. Check out the following site for the latest on this application:

```
http://www.sq.com/products/hotmetal/hmp-org.htm
```

HoTMetaL Pro is a feature-packed HTML editor that's available for Macintosh, PCs running Windows, and XWindow (UNIX) environments. Although HoTMetaL Pro has such features as a spelling checker and thesaurus, it eats up memory and has a steeper learning curve than most other cut-and-paste editors. Tags appear as graphics, however, making it less likely that you and your students may confuse tags with your text. Lots of folks use HoTMetaL Pro, though, and it's been around on the Net for more than three years.

Site Writer Pro

Site Writer Pro is a text-based editor for creating Web pages and managing entire Web sites. (Currently, only a Macintosh version is available.) It does all the basic stuff and also the forms, tables, and other, more advanced options. It also supports Netscape-specific tags including Center, Basefont, Fontsize, Background File, and color specifications. It comes with a built-in help feature. You can find Site Writer Pro at `http://www.rlc.dcccd.edu/Human/SWPro.htm`.

WebMaster Gold – Web Editor

A high-end, "propeller-head" (that's a geek to you non-geeks) program that's a must-have for many Webmaster types. WebMaster Gold is the professional version of WebMaster Web Editor and includes a host of exciting new features, such as an integrated document previewer (WYSIWYG, and you can preview it from within the program without opening your browser), document templates (ready-to-use page-creation templates), an image previewer (with an image library of 300 reusable images), point-and-click color selection, a spell checker, JavaScript scripts, and a great help function. You can find WebMaster Gold at `http://www.ozemail.com.au/~vtech/webmastr.html`.

Another program worth mentioning is NetObjects Fusion, which offers site management as well as Web development tools. This product comes with lots of templates and other things to get you started. Its WYSIWIG interface operates much like a page layout program. Snag it at the NetObjects site at `http://www.netobjects.com`.

Word Processor Utilities

A word processor is likely to be the tool that you use most on your computer. Word processors are also the tools most often available in schools. Many of the computing vendors who make word processors have begun to incorporate Web-specific tools into their programs to make the job of creating a Web page easier. ClarisWorks, a popular tool for K–12 students, has a handy set of HTML commands available for basic HTML coding. (See Figure 6-2.)

Figure 6-2:
ClarisWorks includes HTML shortcuts (like the hypertext link shortcut shown) to make editing super-simple.

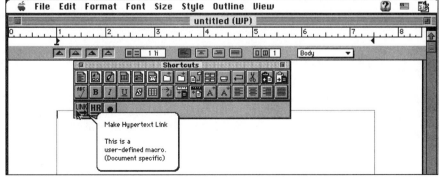

Add-on tools

Most word processors and desktop publishing programs are more powerful than stand-alone Web-creation tools, but are less able to handle graphics and links. Most of the tools in the list that follows are available for both Macintosh and Windows computers. Table 6-1 shows a few add-on tools that you can use with your page-creation programs.

Table 6-1	Add-On Tools	
Product	*Add-On Tool*	*Source*
Claris XTND	ClarisWorks 4.0	Built-in
Claris XTND	Web-It	`http://www_personal.umich.edu/~demonner/Primer_main/Primer_main/primer_main.html`
PageMaker	WebSucker	`http://www.msystems.com/mcohen/websucker.html`
PageMaker	Dave	`http://www.bucknell.edu/bucknellian/dave/`
Microsoft Word	ANT HTML	`http://www.w3.org/pub/WWW/Tools/Ant.html`
Microsoft Word	rtftohtml	`http://www.sunpack.com/RTF/rtftohtml_overview.html` (Other tools are also available at this site.)
WebWizard HTML	WebWizard	`http://www.jsp.fi/delta/deltaweb.htm`
Quark Xpress	BeyondPress	`http://www.astrobyte.com`
Lotus InterNotes	Web Publisher	`http://www.internotes.lotus.com`

BBEdit

This product is one of the first and the most fully featured "word processor-like" editing tools (and one of my all-time favorites!). BBEdit has both basic and very high-end Web publishing features, but not the most attractive interface. (BBEdit is kind of busy, and you may be overwhelmed by all the windows.) It's a Web workhorse, though, and lots of professional HTML junkies use it. Grab it at `http://www.barebones.com/`.

Hybrid Tools

Hybrid tools are tools that offer more than just basic Web page editing. Tools in this category offer the ability to manage Web sites, create *CGI* (Common Gateway Interfaces), and much more.

Let's Tango!

Tango is a high-end graphical development tool for building many kinds of Web-based applications. It's very good for integrating database servers with Web servers. Tango can help create such things as online shopping malls, product catalogs, event registration forms, and more. Tango enables you to monitor users on your site and build password-protected sites. Everywhere Development Corp. created Tango; you can find out more about Tango at http://www.everyware.com.

More Hybrids

Besides Tango, you can find a wealth of other tools that help you with specific tasks — from setting up your Web site (site management) to creating calendars and working on network security. Here's a sampling:

- ✔ **CalenderSet/CGI** (http://www.fsti.com/products/calendarset_cgi): Create calendars with hot-linked buttons for inclusion on any HTML Web page

- ✔ **Webmaster Pro** (http://www.heyertech.com): Web management toolkit

- ✔ **NetForms and NetCloak** (http://www.maxum.com): Tools for creating forms and building in security to your site

- ✔ **SiteMill** (http://www.adobe.com/prodindex/sitemill/main.html): Web site management software

- ✔ **Virtus Voyager and Walkthrough Pro** (http://www.virtus.com/products_wtp.html): An online 3-D browser and builder of 3-D "Web worlds"

Conversion Tools

In some instances, you and your students may want to take documents created with desktop publishing tools, such as PageMaker or QuarkXpress, and convert them to a Web-ready format. A number of conversion tools that can do a pretty good job with this task are available. The conversion process is not bulletproof, however, and you can expect to have to tweak the pages after they've been converted. Conversion, however, is easier than retyping and coding the entire document from scratch.

QuarkImmedia (`http://www.quark.com/aim001.htm`) is a cross-platform tool designed to allow the simultaneous creation of Web page and made-for-print documents. If you're a Quark user, this is a great tool.

Myrmidon is the friendliest and perhaps the most versatile conversion tool of them all. This Macintosh-only program turns every application's Print command into a powerful tool for publishing documents.

With Myrmidon, you can

- Convert any document into an HTML document ready for publishing on the Web.
- Use print spooling for almost any printer.
- Print to many different printers, trays, and fax modems all at the same time.
- Extract address information from documents and print envelopes.
- Create and send an e-mail message from within any application.

Myrmidon builds what the authors call "meta-printers" to perform customized operations for you. A meta-printer appears to your Chooser like any other printer, but it can manipulate data before printing. Just open your PageMaker or ClarisWorks document (it works with virtually any application) and choose Myrmidon from your Chooser; then print. The result is a properly coded, HTML-formatted document that is browser-readable. (I get goose bumps just thinking about how wonderful this program is!)

Grab this way-cool program from `http://www.terrymorse.com` or `ftp://ftp.terrymorse.com`. You can contact Terry at Terry Morse Software, `tmorse@terrymorse.com`. The program is shareware and is one of those must-have applications that all Mac users need.

No matter what type of tool you choose for yourself and your students, a great way to begin is by making logical connections between publishing for the Web and publishing a school newspaper, a yearbook, or even a football program. Brainstorm with your students on how each of these types of publishing is similar to, and different from, publishing your own Web page. Hyperlinks, for example, are the tools that enable you to navigate through a Web document, whereas indexes are your travel pointers in a printed publication.

Remember, too, that Web pages can be *internal* documents — useful for just your own school and accessible only through your school's *intranet* (its kind of like a local area network, except that you use Internet tools, such as Web browsers, to navigate it) — or *external* documents, useful for the whole planet. As you choose a tool (see Table 6-2), think about how you'll develop your Web site and how often you'll need to update the information in it. The text processors and conversion programs are great for folks who want to begin their Web-learning with HTML. But my pick-of-the-classroom, the WYSIWYG programs, are excellent for quick updates without messing up what you've already created!

Table 6-2	Web Page Creation Tools		
Tool (Type)	*Platform*	*Comments*	*Source*
Home Page (WYSIWYG)	M, 95, NT	Excellent for new Web page designers because of the simple but powerful interface. Lacks some very advanced features.	Claris. 800-544-8554 `http://www.claris.com` (educators' discount coupon in back of book, too!)
FrontPage (WYSIWYG)	M, 95, NT	Lots of whiz-bang features. Steep learning curve.	Microsoft. 800-426-9400 `http://www.microsoft.com`
PageMill (WYSIWYG)	M, W, 95	Nice high-end features for table design and frames production. Steep learning curve.	Adobe. 800-833-6687 `http://www.adobe.com`
AOL Press (WYSIWYG)	A	Great first editor — and it's free!	America Online. Go Keyword: **AOLPress** on AOL
QuarkImmedia (conversion tool)	W, M	Convert Quark-QuarkXPress page layout documents to Web-readable documents.	Quark. `http://www.quark.com`

(continued)

Table 6-2 *(continued)*

Tool (Type)	Platform	Comments	Source
BBEdit (text editor)	M	Extremely powerful, but steep learning curve.	BareBones Software. `http://www.barebones.com`
Communicator (WYSIWYG)	A	Appropriate for creating basic home pages using the built-in Composer tool.	Netscape. `http://www.netscape.com`
HotDog (text editor)	W, 95	Tag-based HTML editor. Very powerful, but not for beginners.	Sausage Software. `http://www.sausage.com`
HoTMetaL Pro (text editor)	95, NT, M	Excellent high-end features, and HTML editing is a breeze.	Soft Quad. `http://www.sq.com`
Myrmidon (conversion tool)	M	One click in the Chooser and it's HTML. Easy, but basic.	Terry Morse Software. `http://www.terrymorse.com`
PageMaker (conversion tool)	M, W	Save PageMaker documents in HTML formats.	Adobe. `http://www.adobe.com`
Visual Page (WYSIWYG)	M	Excellent for work with frames and tables. High-end features can be confusing.	Symantec. `http://cafe.symantec.com`
WebEdit Pro (text editor)	95, NT	Works with wizards to walk you through HTML coding.	Luckman Interactive. `http://www.luckman.com`

Key to Platforms: M = Macintosh; W = Windows 3.0; 95 = Windows 95; NT = Windows NT; A = all platforms

Part III
Weaving Together a Web Page

The 5th Wave   By Rich Tennant

"Fortunately, at this grade level Claris Home Page is very intuitive for them to use. Unfortunately, so is sailing mousepads across the classroom."

In this part . . .

*1*t's time to get busy and create some Web pages. In this part, I show you what you need to know to quickly plan and develop your Web page. To make things even simpler, I've included on the CD with this book a working demo of the powerful and easy-to-use Claris Home Page 2.0 that you can use for "what you see is what you get" editing. In addition to showing you the ropes in Claris Home Page, I've also included "raw HTML code" where appropriate so those of you who prefer to use other tools, such as a word processor, have a path to follow to create Web pages. With this chapter, you and your students can whip up a dandy Web page for yourselves, or for your school, in a cyber-flash.

Chapter 7

Starting Up Your Page Creation Tool

- -

In This Chapter

▶ Installation for the Macintosh/Power Macintosh

▶ System requirements

▶ Installation for Windows 95

▶ Installation for Windows NT

▶ Obtaining Claris Home Page

- -

I consider my job as your Internet coach to be serious business. That's why I've taken great pains to make sure that *Web Publishing For Teachers* is more *readable* than most off-the-shelf computer books and not jammed full with a bunch of technical language. With that in mind, this chapter (and the rest of Part III of this book) is written for those of you who are ready to take the next step in creating Web pages for yourselves or for your school. Before you slam the book closed and say to yourself, "I'm not ready for this advanced stuff yet," let me assure you that this material is *simple, easy to learn, and worth knowing*, especially for educators like you. Really.

 In this chapter, I cover the simple steps of installing Claris Home Page 2.0 (a demo version is on the *Web Publishing For Teachers* CD) on your Macintosh or PC running Windows 95 or Windows NT. Installing other Web page processors, such as Adobe PageMill 2.0 (which is also on the CD) is just as easy — they feature "installer" programs that walk you through the steps.

Installing Claris Home Page

 Great news! You can install Claris Home Page on your Mac or PC in less time than it takes you to walk the three miles across your school to the nearest restroom or telephone. The process usually involves running an Installer program (see Figure 7-1), like the one provided for you on the

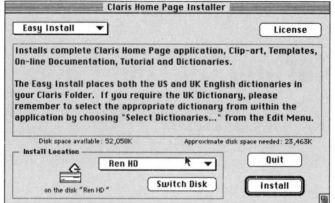

Figure 7-1:
The
Installer
makes
loading
Claris Home
Page onto
your
computer's
hard drive
a cinch!

Web Publishing For Teachers CD. If you're a computer whiz, you can probably just shove the CD into your computer and click Install. If you're like most of us and want a little more help, read on!

On the Macintosh

Here's a pleasant surprise: Claris Home Page should run on virtually every Macintosh in your school. Claris Home Page isn't too picky about what kind of Mac it's running on, but it does recommend that your Mac have

- ✔ A 68020 processor or above, or any of the Power Macintosh models (that means just about any Mac you have in your home or school)
- ✔ Operating System 7.1 or later
- ✔ 8MB of RAM (the more RAM you have, the better it works — but it still runs with 8MB)
- ✔ 2MB of free space on your hard drive (minimum install) and 6MB for a full install
- ✔ A CD-ROM drive
- ✔ A hard disk drive (internal or external)

Installing Claris Home Page on a Macintosh is as easy as double-clicking on the Installer program icon found on your *Web Publishing For Teachers* CD. The program decompresses the files on the disk and installs them in their proper place on your Mac's hard disk. Because the installer does all the work, you can't just copy the files from the *Web Publishing For Teachers* CD to your hard drive — use the Installer instead.

To install Claris Home Page:

1. **Start your Macintosh and hold down the Shift key until you see a dialog box that reads "Welcome to Macintosh. Extensions Off."**

   Holding the Shift key on startup causes your Mac to bypass all the bells and whistles in the extension files and allows for more efficient operation of your Installer program. This is a good thing to do before you install *any* program, by the way.

2. **Insert your *Web Publishing For Teachers* CD and double-click on the Installer icon.**

   The Claris Home Page startup and welcome screen appears.

3. **Click on Continue.**

   You see the Claris Home Page Installer dialog box.

4. **Click on Install.**

   The Installer goes to work, busily unstuffing and copying files from the CD to your hard drive. Watch the dialog box to find out what the installer's doing.

   After all the files are installed, a final dialog box gives you the good news about a successful installation.

5. **Click on Quit.**

6. **Restart your Macintosh before using the program.**

That's it! It's like MAGIC! Now, drag the icon for the *Web Publishing For Teachers* CD to the trash can to eject your CD. You're ready to go!

On your PC with Windows

You're in luck! Home Page runs on all of the new PCs and a few of the older ones, too. The only catch is that you must be using Windows 95 or Windows NT. Claris also recommends that your PC have:

- ✔ A 486 processor or better (a Pentium is okay)
- ✔ Windows 95 or Windows NT version 3.5.1 or later
- ✔ 8MB of RAM (with Windows 95) and 16MB of RAM (with Windows NT)
- ✔ 4MB of free space on your hard drive
- ✔ A 3.5-inch, high-density disk drive
- ✔ A CD-ROM drive

Installation is super-easy on your Windows PC. Just use the handy Installer program provided on your *Web Publishing For Teachers* disc! Don't attempt to copy the files directly to your hard disk by dragging the file icons to your desktop; it won't work. Use the Installer instead!

To Install Claris Home Page for Windows 95, follow these steps:

1. **Turn on your computer.**

2. **Click on the Start button and choose Settings.**

3. **Click on the Control Panel.**

4. **Double-click on Add/Remove Programs.**

   A dialog box appears.

5. **Click on Install.**

6. **Insert your *Web Publishing For Teachers* CD into your computer when you see the prompt.**

7. **Click on Next.**

   The Installer runs the setup program (SETUP.EXE) on the CD.

8. **Click on Finish.**

9. **Follow the instructions on the screen.**

Once the Installer has done its work, it creates a menu item for Claris Home Page in the Start menu. How does it know to do that? I dunno. More magic.

On a PC running Windows NT

Installing the NT version of Claris Home Page is a breeze. Follow these seven steps and you're on your way!

1. **Turn on your computer.**

2. **Start Windows NT and open the Program Manager.**

3. **Insert your *Web Publishing For Teachers* disc into your computer.**

4. **Choose Run from the File menu.**

   A Run dialog box appears.

5. **Type a:\setup in the command line box and click on OK.**

6. **Click on Next and follow the on-screen instructions.**

7. **When the installation is complete, click on Finish.**

After the Installer's completed its work, it creates a Claris Home Page program group. You'll see the Claris Home Page icon hidden inside. This is easy as pie (made with a frozen shell and pudding mix).

How to Obtain Home Page

The version of Claris Home Page on the *Web Publishing For Teachers* CD is an evaluation version that automatically self-destructs (that is, it expires) 30 days from the date of installation. But that's plenty of time for you to take a free trial run of Home Page and get acquainted with its basic operation.

To use the full (non-expiring) version of the program, you need to drop a dollar or two by ordering Claris Home Page through a catalog (I recommend the *Mac Warehouse* or *PC Warehouse* catalogs) or from your local software store. Claris also offers a special Education Version of the program — it's less expensive than those found in a store and it's fully featured, too. Jump over to the Claris Web site at http://www.claris.com to find out more.

To make purchasing Claris Home Page easy on your computing budget, I've included a coupon at the back of this book that offers special educational pricing. (Don't tell your non-teacher friends, though. They'll be jealous!)

A "school lab pack" of Claris Home Page doesn't exist, but there really doesn't need to be one. Claris Home Page is best used as a stand-alone program. Claris also offers special "bulk pricing" for schools (visit the Claris Web site at the URL mentioned earlier).

Well, there you go. You've got that puppy installed in your computer and you're ready to seize the day! Give yourself a pat on the back and march on to the nitty-gritty of creating a Web page with Claris Home Page in the chapters that follow.

Chapter 8

Web Page Building Basics

*Y*ou're in luck. Using a Web page creation tool is much easier than mastering outcome-based education, creating a Charter school, or chaperoning a school dance. In fact, you and your students really don't need much of a background at all in Web publishing (or even print-oriented desktop publishing) to achieve some pretty amazing results really quickly. (Web publishing programs are similar to desktop publishing programs except that the final layout and design aren't intended for print, but rather for online publication to the World Wide Web.)

After you've decided on the Web page tool that you're going to use, it's time to think about creating your Web page. (In this book I use the example of Claris Home Page 2.0; a demo version is your CD-ROM.) The basic steps are as follows:

1. **Launch your Web page processor (Claris Home Page, PageMill, or a generic word processor) and grab your storyboard showing your Web page design. (See Chapters 2 and 3 for more on Web page design.)**

2. **Enter the text (the written content) of your page while keeping your design in mind.**

3. **Add graphics and multimedia where appropriate.**

4. **Add links to other local Web pages or to Web pages that reside on other people's sites across the Internet.**

5. **Test your site like there's no tomorrow, and be sure to use different browsers to view your pages.**

6. **FTP your pages.**

   FTP stands for *File Transfer Protocol*. FTP provides you with a means to transfer files (the HTML code, graphics, and multimedia) from other "master" computers (FTP servers) to your computer and vice versa by using a software program or your school's network.

In this chapter, I take you through the process of launching a Web page creator (Claris Home Page 2.0 in this case). In subsequent chapters, I take you through the rest of the process.

One question it seems I'm always asked is, "Do I need to know HTML to create a Web page?" An appropriate answer, at this point, would be, no, not yet. This is a kind way of saying that Claris Home Page can do almost everything that you want it to do, but to *fine-tune* your work, you need to learn how to use other tools. So, although I've dedicated lots of space in this book to using Claris Home Page 2.0, I've also included HTML code directions in Appendix B. You'll thank me later! Now, I'm going to tell you more about this animal called HTML.

In the following sections, I give you information about how to launch Claris Home Page 2.0 and how to work efficiently with its toolbars and windows. If you're bold and want to fly without a net, jump to Chapter 9 to get busy Webbing right away. Be sure to mark the pages, though, because later on in this chapter I'll give you some important tips on saving and printing your work!

First, a Glimpse at What You're Missing: HTML

Web pages are created by using a simple page markup language called *HTML* (which stands for Hypertext Markup Language, which is an *FLA* — Four Letter Acronym). HTML was derived from *SGML* (Standard Generalized Markup Language — eek, another FLA!) as a way for Web site developers to create pages that can be accessed by a variety of different computers running a variety of different Web-page readers called *browsers*.

Working with HTML is much easier than programming in languages like BASIC or Pascal because most HTML commands are in "plain English," and the structure is pretty forgiving if you want to go back and make changes to your coding later on. Although getting the hang of HTML isn't that tough, trying to remember all the commands can be a pain. That's why programs like Claris Home Page were developed.

Just in case you'd like to see what you're missing, I'll show you a glimpse of what *raw HTML* code (automatically generated by Web page creation tools) looks like. HTML programs are called *scripts* and can also be written using any standard word processor and saved as ASCII text files. HTML scripting is kind of like creating a word-processing document and scattering around lots of special formatting commands for added flavor.

Return your seat back and tray table to their upright position, fasten your seat belt, grab the armrests, and prepare to land in the foreign territory of HTML code. Here's what some of it looks like:

```
<HTML>
<HEAD>
<TITLE>Munchkin Middle School </TITLE>
</HEAD>
<BODY>
<! Insert picture of our school in the next line.>
<IMG SRC="munchkin.gif">
<H1>Welcome to Munchkin Middle School!</H1>
This home page was created entirely by Mr. Templeton's
Seventh-Grade Science class in fulfillment of a science
            project about rocks and minerals... <P>
<BR>
Our school is located in Anywhere, France, and has 1,000
            students and 45 teachers....
</BODY>
</HTML>
```

There, it's not so bad, is it? (You can let go of the armrests now.) HTML is just lots of text with lots of commands, called *tags,* floating around a document surrounded by arrow brackets that look like this: < >.

With most Web page creation tools, all you have to worry about is the overall design and the text (content) of the page; the program makes sure that all the tags are in the right place and in the correct format for most Web browsers. It's like having a propeller-head assistant looking over your shoulder all the time. Wonderful!

Firing Up Claris Home Page

By now you've probably installed Claris Home Page on your Mac or PC and are ready to get busy! (If you haven't done so, read through Chapter 7 for the simple installation steps.) To fire up Claris Home Page:

1. **Look around your classroom.**

2. **Find a student who's been watching you install the program.**

3. **Glance at the student and give him or her a quick, toothy grin while you double-click on the Claris Home Page application icon.**

When you open Claris Home Page 2.0, a new, untitled Web page appears on the screen (see Figure 8-1).

Picking Your Preferences

Like all good programs, Claris Home Page allows you to decide whether you'd rather have Claris Home Page do nothing or display an Open dialog box when you start it up. To change your options:

1. **Choose Edit⇨Preferences.**

2. **Choose Display Open Dialog Box or Do Nothing from the At Startup pop-up menu in the General preferences menu.**

Is it ALL going to be this easy? Is there a final exam at the end? Yes and no. Now stop getting nervous about all this home page stuff and read on.

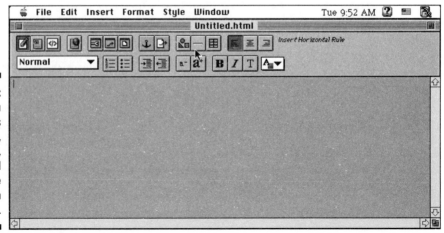

Figure 8-1: When you open Claris Home Page, a new, untitled Web page appears on the screen.

"O' Give Me a Home (Page)"

A new Claris Home Page document becomes a blank slate for creating your Web page. When Claris Home Page creates a new document, it opens in Edit Page mode. *Edit Page mode* is one of three modes the program uses to make Web page creation easy and efficient. I cover the other two, *Preview* and *Raw HTML code,* later in this chapter.

Working with a Claris Home Page document in Edit Page mode is a lot like composing with your favorite word processor. You can type text, insert pictures (images), copy, paste, save, and print just the way you would with most programs. However, because the Web is not yet "font-and-style-savvy," you can't use unusual typefaces (fonts), fancy character styles, or formatting commands, such as tabs and margins.

Unlike word processors, Claris Home Page features extra tools for inserting hypertext links (clickable connections to other Web pages) and links to other objects (such as graphics, JavaScript, and other items). The program also gives you easy-to-use menu options, keyboard shortcuts, and a handy toolbar to select HTML-friendly attributes for formatting the text on your Web page.

Opening an HTML Document

If you want to begin with a HTML document you have already created or one that you've saved from the Web, you can open the document easily with Claris Home Page. To see the HTML code behind any Web page, use the Document Source command (or another similarly named command) found in the View menu of most Web browsers. This command allows you to view, and save to your local disk, a copy of the HTML source code for the site. Copying ready-made HTML code is a clever way to learn the tricks of the trade.

After you've grabbed some source code and would like to view and edit it, it's easy to get things going. To open and edit any HTML document, just follow these steps:

1. **Choose File⇨Open (⌘+O on the Mac, or Ctrl+O in Windows).**

   You get the dialog box shown in Figure 8-2.

2. **Select the file you wish to open.**

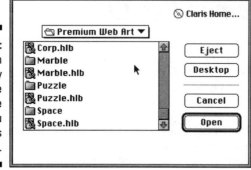

Figure 8-2:
You can
open any
HTML file
from the
File menu
with Claris
Home Page.

3. Click on Open.

After the page is open, Claris Home Page automatically displays the document in Edit Page mode, which you can use to create and edit your Web page. The Edit Page mode displays your Web page in a form that looks a little different than what you'd see on a standard browser— that's why there's also a Preview mode.

Like most other user-friendly programs, Claris Home Page allows you to change the way it opens a document. You can, for example, ask Claris Home Page to open documents displaying the raw HTML code instead of the Edit Page mode. To change the way your Open documents look:

1. Choose Edit⇨Preferences.

2. Choose General from the pop-up menu or click on the General tab.

3. From the Open Documents in pop-up menu (shown in Figure 8-3), choose Preview Page (the default option) or Edit HTML Source. (The figure shows the choice Edit Page.)

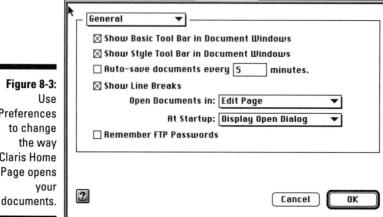

Figure 8-3:
Use
Preferences
to change
the way
Claris Home
Page opens
your
documents.

Just in case you get stuck in the wrong mode, it's easy to switch. To change to Edit Page mode from any other mode, select Edit Page from the Window menu on the Claris Home Page menu bar, or click on the Edit Page button in the Home Page toolbar, shown in Figure 8-4.

Figure 8-4:
Use the Edit
Page button
in the
toolbar to
switch to
Edit Page
mode.

Edit Page button

Cutting, Copying, and Pasting

Claris Home Page works very much like a word processor. The commands you regularly use to do simple things like cut, copy, and paste are virtually the same keystrokes your word processor knows and have largely the same effect on the formatting of your Web pages.

Web page creation tools allow you to cut, copy, and paste items including text, tables, hypertext links, images (pictures), and other elements (such as QuickTime movies or JavaScript) on your Web page. You can also use the cut, copy, and paste commands to move information between Web page or between Claris Home Page documents and other documents, just like you would with a word processor.

To cut, copy, or paste an element in Claris Home Page:

1. **Select the text, table, link, or graphic element you wish to copy or cut by using your mouse or keyboard.**

2. **Choose Edit⇨Cut (⌘+X or Ctrl+X) or Copy (⌘+C or Ctrl+C).**

    Claris Home Page takes a "snapshot" of the element and stores it on the computer's internal clipboard. (Remember, *cutting* information removes the original; *copying* leaves the original in place.)

3. **Click on the spot in your document where you'd like Claris Home Page to place the element.**

4. **Choose Edit⇨Paste (⌘+V or Ctrl+V).**

In some cases, there's an even easier way to copy and paste or move information into or out of Claris Home Page — it's called "drag and drop," and any Macintosh, and some Windows 95 and Windows NT machines, support this function. To use drag and drop:

1. **Select the text, image, or other element you wish to copy.**

2. **Click and hold the mouse button as you drag the image to its destination.**

3. **Release the mouse button.**

Changing Your Mind

If you realize that you've just typed something you didn't mean to or you want to delete any individual element (graphics, links, and so on) in your document, select it and press the Delete or Backspace key.

If you want to cancel the last action you performed, select Undo (⌘+Z or Ctrl+Z) from the Edit menu.

Step by (Web) step

The basic steps in creating any Web page are pretty much the same for any of your publications:

✔ Plan your content.

✔ Type your content into a word processor or specialized program for creating Web pages.

✔ Determine how to highlight (accent with bold, italic, or other style changes) text and insert formatting (HTML) tags, hyperlinks, and graphics (or other multimedia).

✔ Add graphic images to enhance your pages or to act as clickable links (but, remember, they *do* add to your readers' download wait).

✔ View your Web page off-line with your Web browser to preview how it will look to the reading public.

✔ Use FTP (file transfer protocol) to transmit your file to your Internet provider's computer. (See Chapter 19 for more information about file transfer.)

✔ Test your Web page by logging onto the Net, launching your Web browser, and entering your home page URL. (For more information on URLs, see Chapter 7.)

✔ Visit your Web page frequently to keep the content fresh and to update or add to your hyperlinks.

Using the Toolbars and Palettes

Claris Home Page features several toolbars and palettes you can use to complete tasks more quickly than searching for the corresponding option by pulling down menu after menu. Within Claris Home Page you can find a

✔ Basic toolbar

✔ Style toolbar

✔ Forms palette

✔ Image Editor palette

(I suggested adding a toolbar that helps with Lining Students Up for the Lunchroom and one to Ignore the Principal, but the Claris people were not amused.)

Toolbars are anchored across the top of your document window. Palettes float around wherever you want them to be.

The Basic toolbar (shown in Figure 8-5) provides access to many of the commonly used features in Claris Home Page. I'm not going to take up precious space in the book to go over the complete function of each item, because you can find out what each item in a toolbar does by placing the pointer (cursor) over any button in the toolbar. Poof! You'll see its name appear to the right of the toolbar.

Figure 8-5:
The Basic
toolbar
features
most of the
commonly
used
operations.

Macintosh

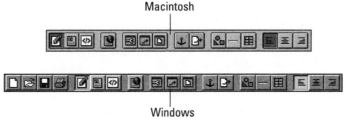

Windows

 To make a choice from the toolbar, just click on a button. You can also drag the Anchor, Horizontal Rule, or Table button right onto your page to insert those elements.

The Style toolbar (shown in Figure 8-6) has buttons you can use to format text. By using this toolbar, you can change the size, style, and alignment of your text. You can also format listings into bulleted or numbered lists.

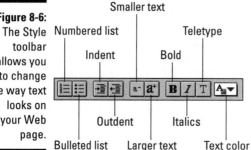

Figure 8-6:
The Style toolbar allows you to change the way text looks on your Web page.

Smaller text

Numbered list

Indent

Teletype

Bold

Outdent

Bulleted list   Larger text

Italics

Text color

If your on-screen "real estate" gets more crowded than your third-period class, Claris Home Page provides an easy way to show or hide the Basic toolbar or Style toolbar:

1. **Choose Edit⇨Preferences.**

2. **Choose General from the pop-up menu or click on the General tab.**

3. **Select or deselect the appropriate check box.**

You can also use this process to set the Show Toolbar preferences to display the toolbar in the Claris Home Page application window or in the document windows.

Claris Home Page has another tool palette, called a Forms palette (shown in Figure 8-7). To display the Forms palette, choose Show Forms Palette from the Window menu. To hide the Forms palette, choose Hide Forms Palette from the Window menu or click on the close box (the one with the X in it) in the upper-right corner of the palette. The Forms palette contains common HTML elements like lists, buttons, or pop-up menus you can embed into your Web page forms with the click of a mouse.

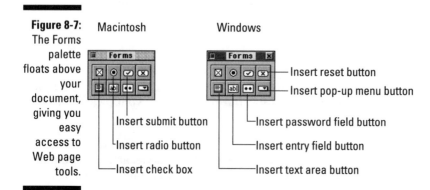

Figure 8-7:
The Forms palette floats above your document, giving you easy access to Web page tools.

Macintosh

Windows

Insert reset button

Insert pop-up menu button

Insert submit button

Insert password field button

Insert radio button

Insert entry field button

Insert check box

Insert text area button

To use the Forms palette, click on any of the icons and drag it onto your Web page. This action adds the corresponding element to your document (with one exception being the Insert Image icon — clicking on it displays the Open dialog box). To move the palette around on your screen, just drag its title bar. To make the palette vanish (but not permanently!) click the close box of the palette or choose Hide Tool Palette from the Window menu.

The Image Map Editor toolbar has buttons that are used to add special features to an image (see Figure 8-8). To use the Image Map Editor toolbar, double-click on the image to open the Image Object Editor, and then click on the Image Map button to open the Image Map Editor.

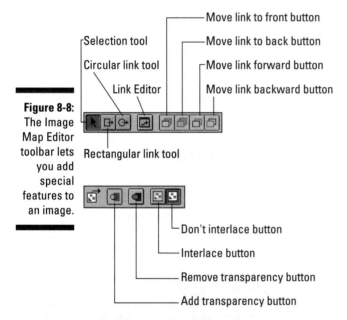

Figure 8-8:
The Image
Map Editor
toolbar lets
you add
special
features to
an image.

Figure labels:
- Selection tool
- Circular link tool
- Link Editor
- Move link to front button
- Move link to back button
- Move link forward button
- Move link backward button
- Rectangular link tool
- Don't interlace button
- Interlace button
- Remove transparency button
- Add transparency button

Editing Objects and Links

After you add elements such as tables, links, or images, you can use a built-in editor to change their characteristics. You can, for example, correct a faulty or expired URL or change the number of columns in a table by using Claris Home Page's *Link Editor* feature.

To open the Link Editor and edit a particular link:

1. **Select the appropriate link while in Edit Page mode.**

2. **Choose Window⇨Show Link Editor (see Figure 8-9).**

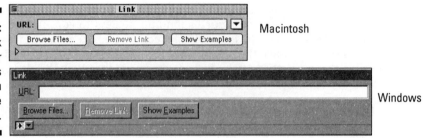

Figure 8-9:
The Link
Editor
expands
when you
click on the
triangle.

Macintosh

Windows

You can use any one of several methods to open the Object Editor to make changes to an element:

✔ Double-click on the element.

✔ Select the element and choose Window⇨Show Object Editor.

✔ Select the element and click on the Object Editor button in the Basic toolbar.

Enlarging or Shrinking Elements

In Claris Home Page, you can resize elements "on the fly." Here's how:

1. **Select the element (table, image, form, and so forth).**

   The element is highlighted with a border that includes one or more *handles* (the small black boxes located on the corners or the sides of an element).

2. **Drag the top or bottom handle to change the height of the element, drag a side handle to change the width of the element, or drag a corner handle to change the height and width of the element at the same time.**

Careful! Changing the size of a graphic can severely reduce its quality and proportions. Use this feature with great care!

Aligning Elements

You can change the horizontal alignment of text, images, and other elements in relation to the Web page. Choose Alignment from the Format menu or click the Indent or Outdent button on the Style toolbar.

Viewing Your Work

Claris Home Page provides several ways to check the appearance of your Web page after you've worked on it in Edit Page mode. They include

✔ **Preview Page mode:** Displays the page as it might appear in a browser

✔ **Previewing in a browser:** Displays the page from within your favorite browser

✔ **Edit HTML Source mode:** Displays the "raw" HTML code you've generated

Using Preview Page mode

When you switch to Preview Page mode (by clicking on the Preview Page button on the Basic toolbar or by choosing Preview Page from the Window menu), Claris Home Page displays your Web page the way it should appear in a browser. (Keep in mind, however, that the appearance of your Web page may vary depending on the browser used to display the page.)

You and your students can use Preview Page mode to test interactive elements of your Web page, such as links and forms, and preview elements, such as numbered lists.

Note: In Preview Page mode, all the editing capabilities and some menu options are disabled. You'll need to switch back to Edit Page mode to continue editing your page.

Previewing your Web page through a browser

Testing your Web page with the browsers your readers will actually use is critically important. Claris Home Page 2.0 allows you to flip easily between any browser, such as Netscape Navigator or Microsoft Internet Explorer, with the click of a button. First, however, you must be sure to save your Web page document (with ⌘+S or Ctrl+S).

To view your Web page in a browser, click on the Preview in Browser button on the Basic toolbar or choose Preview in Browser (with ⌘+R or Ctrl+R) from the File menu.

Working out with "mouse aerobics"

Ready to build some muscle into those clicking fingers? Okay, here we go. Have your students sit with their backs straight and feet flat on the floor in front of their computers. Is everyone poised with their right hands on a mouse? Good. Now turn on the computers and get ready for some mouse aerobics. All together now:

Point, click, and drag.... Point, click, and drag .... Point, click, and drag....

Drag and drop right. Drag and drop left. (Feel the burn?)

Now for some finger skills — Command or Control, then S. Command or Control, then P. Command or Control, then R. Command or Control, then Z.

Before you think I've gone totally crazy, let me say a word about kids, mice, and attention spans. Try the following little trick to get the attention of your students as you work with them to build their home pages.

Have each one of them grab a mouse and turn it over, so that the little belly button is exposed (on each mouse, of course). Ask your students to carefully lay the little mice back on the mousepads, with the mouse ball up!

I know it seems overly simple, but it works with both kids and adults as an effective attention-getter. I've used it a hundred times in staff development courses. Stop laughing! It works! Without mouse control, the attention is on you. (Now, there's some motivation to try it.)

Claris Home Page opens your Web page in Netscape Navigator by default. If you don't have Netscape Navigator on your system (you have Microsoft Internet Explorer, for example) or if you want to see how your Web page looks in a browser other than Netscape Navigator, you need to change the default selection.

Use the following steps to change the browser Claris Home Page uses to display your Web pages:

1. **Choose Edit⇨Preferences.**
2. **Choose Browser Preview from the pop-up menu or click on the Browser Preview tab.**
3. **Click on Set.**

   The Open dialog box appears.

4. **Select the browser application (program) filename and click on Open.**
5. **Click on OK to close the Preferences dialog box.**

Warning: If you're using the Windows version of Netscape Navigator, Claris Home Page opens a new copy of Navigator each time you choose Preview in Browser from the File menu. To avoid opening multiple copies, quit Navigator each time you are finished viewing a Web page.

Using Edit HTML Source code mode

When you switch to Edit HTML Source mode, you can see all the HTML code that Claris Home Page automatically generated. (This is a particularly satisfying activity that I highly recommend.) By using Edit HTML Source mode, you can edit, delete, add, or customize HTML code. (See Appendix B for a listing of the most commonly used HTML tags.)

 Be careful when editing your Web page in Edit HTML Source mode. Unless you are familiar with HTML code and its *syntax* (the rules for how HTML code looks and behaves), you and your students may accidentally mess up much of your hard work. It's a good idea to make a copy of your Web page before you change it in Edit HTML Source mode — that way you have a clean, mistake-free version to return to, if necessary.

To switch to Edit HTML Source mode, click on the Edit HTML Source button on the main toolbar or choose Window⇨Edit HTML Source.

 To change the display font of the code in Edit HTML Source mode, choose Edit⇨Preferences. Then choose HTML Editing from the pop-up menu (or click the HTML Editing tab) and choose a font or size.

Changing HTML Preferences

You can use several Claris Home Page options to change the default HTML code that the program automatically inserts into your Web page.

To make changes to the code that specifies HTML output, choose Edit⇨Preferences, choose HTML Output from the pop-up menu (or click on the HTML Output tab), and then change the appropriate option. The output options are listed in Table 8-1.

Table 8-1	HTML Output Options and Their Results
Output Option	*Result*
Header Comment	Adds information about your Web page to the beginning of the document. These comments can only be seen when viewing the document in raw HTML source code.

(continued)

Table 8-1 *(continued)*

Output Option	Result
Line Break Format	Allows you to change the format of the line break depending upon whether you're working with a Mac, Windows, or UNIX system. Don't mess around with this option unless you're sending the HTML code to a text editor (the program, not the person) that doesn't understand different line break formats.
Paragraph Alignment	Lets you toggle only between the <CENTER> tag and the ALIGN=CENTER parameter.
Generate </P> tags	Adds the optional closing </P> tag to every opening <P> (paragraph) tag.
Use Absolute Pathnames	Allows you to toggle between Relative and Absolute pathnames.
Generate X-SAS tags	A custom Claris Home Page tag that controls where the application window appears on your screen and what size the window is. It's also a way for Home Page to store various settings that need to be remembered the next time the page is opened.
Prefix Comments	Lets you add author name or other messages at the beginning of your HTML file.
<HTML> Tag Parameters	Adds <HTML> tag set automatically.
<HEAD> Tag Parameters	Adds <HEAD> tag Head section.
<BODY> Tag Parameters	Adds <BODY> tag in Body section.

Naming Your Creation

Just as a word processor does, your Web page tool prompts you to give your Web page a title the first time you save the document. The title you assign to your Web page will appear at the top of most browser windows.

The words that appear in each Web page title are examined by many Internet search engines as they hunt through all the data on the Web. (A *search engine* is a specific site that features fill-in-the-blank forms for *keywords* that it searches for throughout the Web.) If it's important that your readers are able to find your Web page through keyword searches, make sure that your title includes meaningful words your readers are most likely to think of when doing a keyword search.

Some unscrupulous Web site authors insert lots of extra keyword text into their titles in order to draw people to their sites. Then they color the text white so the keywords don't show up in the browser window. They figure by dumping a large collection of words into their titles, they can snag unsuspecting readers looking for something else. Don't try that at home (or at school). It's bad karma.

To give your Web page a title or to edit the current title:

1. **Choose Edit⇨Document Options (⌘+J or Ctrl+K).**

2. **Choose General from the pop-up menu, or click on the General tab.**

3. **Enter the title in the Document Title text box.**

4. **Click on OK.**

Saving Your Web Page

If you don't save frequently, all your work will vanish. (This will happen while the basketball team's bus blows a tire on their way to the big game. Nobody gets hurt, of course, but it's the stuff stories are made of.)

To save your Web page, just follow these steps:

1 . **Choose File⇨Save (⌘+S or Ctrl+S).**

   If you haven't yet given your Web page a title, the Enter Title dialog box appears. Enter a title and click on OK.

2. **After the Save dialog box appears, enter the filename for your Web page followed by the extension .htm for a Windows file or .html for a Macintosh file in the Save File As text box.**

   In order for your files to be seen as Web pages in Claris Home Page and in Web browsers, they must have .htm or .html extensions.

3. **Click on Save (Macintosh) or on OK (Windows).**

You can specify a default filename extension for new Web pages you create. (You should set the extension to .htm or .html.) Choose Edit⇨Preferences, choose General from the pop-up menu (or click on the General tab), and enter the extension into the Default HTML File Suffix text box. Remember to use the .htm extension if your DOS or Windows 3.1 friends will be working with the files. (Mac and Windows 95 folks don't have to worry about this one.)

There's an elf hidden inside Claris Home Page that automatically saves your documents. To put the little guy to work, choose Edit➪Preferences, and then choose General from the pop-up menu or click on the General tab. Tell the Claris Home Page elf how often (in minutes) you want Claris Home Page to save your files by selecting the Auto-save document every "# minutes" check box and entering a number.

The Claris Home Page elf dutifully auto-saves changes to your files as often as you specified and reminds you about titles and filenames for your Web pages if you've forgotten them.

Printing Your Web Page

Print your Web page just as you would any document from a standard word processor. You can print from within any of the viewing modes discussed earlier in this chapter; however, the way your page will look varies depending on which mode you were in when you chose to print.

To print your Web page:

1. **Select File➪Print (⌘+P or Ctrl+P).**

   Your system's standard Print dialog box appears.

2. **Click on Print (Macintosh) or on OK (Windows).**

   Claris Home Page prints the entire contents of your Web page file.

It's time now to take a coffee break and look back over all you've learned. If you master what's in this chapter, you can build a great no-frills Web page. The following chapters give you more information about working with text, adding graphics, and more. And, don't forget the M&Ms with your coffee (a standard teachers' lounge combo meal).

Page Creation Tips Worth Sharing

✔ Title your pages carefully. Descriptive titles are important to navigation, and Web browsers use these titles in a user's bookmark file. "Winterview High School" is better than "Home Page."

✔ Include your URL on each Web page. What if someone prints the page? What if they wish to return to the page later? Wouldn't it be nice to look in the footer of the page and see the URL? Enough said.

✔ Make quality a number-one concern. Build an editing team that checks for spelling errors, typos, grammatical errors, and pesky inconsistencies in content. Consider having your students create a checklist for quality content. Include items such as: Consistent look and feel, Used emphasis (bold, italics, and such) only where appropriate, or Tested all links.

✔ Have students create a tracking sheet to ensure that the Web page is regularly maintained.

✔ Add a date on every page. One of the merits of the Net is that the information is more up-to-date than you may find from other sources. Include a date on documents so everyone will know when and if a page or document was updated. Consider using the complete date, such as October 15, 1997, instead of numeric representations, such as 10/15/97, so that your international visitors wont get confused. If you're too chicken to use a date, try using a few "new" icons on the page.

✔ Insert copyright notices at the bottom of each page as appropriate. This reinforces the importance of copyright law to your students and to the readers of your page.

✔ Use teamwork to create your Web pages. After building a storyboard of your site and talking about common design elements, have small groups of students tackle one page. Then, put all the pages together and work on giving them the same style and appearance.

✔ Ask for feedback. Use a `MAILTO` tag (a link that automatically connects the user to your e-mail address — see Chapter 11 for more on the `MAILTO` tag) or create a feedback form.

✔ Get expert online help with validating your HTML code. There are a number of sites on the Internet that will automatically check your HTML code for mistakes (free of charge!). Here's a place to begin: `http://www.devry-phx.edu/webresrc/webmstry/langval.htm`.

✔ Test, test, test. Before you "go live," make sure to test your pages. If you're adding new pages, post them on your Web server and don't give out the URL or link them to your current page until you (and several others) have tested every link and button.

Chapter 9
Working With Text

*M*ove over Mr. Gutenberg, here comes Mr. Jackson's fourth-grade class! That's right, this chapter gives you and your students the *text tools* you need to put information into your Web pages.

Because most Web page creation tools let you work without seeing very much HTML code (it's generated automatically by the program), I've also included in each section examples of the syntax that's created behind the scenes (*syntax* being the rules that govern how HTML code is structured). These examples are for those of you who actually want to know *how* this HTML code stuff looks "under the hood" of your Web page. Most Web page creation tools feature a way to view the HTML ("raw code") you've created by using a keyboard command or by clicking a button. In Claris Home Page, you can simply choose Edit HTML Source mode from the Window pull-down menu.

If I were there to whisper my best advice in your ear right now, I'd tell you ***don't*** *eat the fishsticks in the cafeteria!* Seriously, I'd really remind you of something that's a bit hard to remember when you're up to your eyeballs in HTML. It's this: The *content* (your message) is more important than fancy animated thingies hopping around the page, or using all 12 HTML styles at once.

What you and your students publish is a reflection of your school (and personal) culture, your wisdom, and your zest for knowledge. So, as you and your students prepare to "do text," remind them to think first about the message, then about the way they'll convey it. Now about those *fishsticks. . . .*

Open for Business

Claris Home Page offers two ways to begin creating your Web page:

- ✔ By opening a new Claris Home Page file
- ✔ By opening an existing text or HTML file

The program automatically creates a brand-new home page document (file) when you launch it, so opening a new file is effortless.

Because you can use any standard word processor to *manually* enter HTML *tags* (that is, the code), the good folks at Claris made it plenty easy to open those HTML files within Claris Home Page. Remember to save your original word processor file in ASCII (text) format, however, or you may not be able to read it.

To open a text file created in other applications, choose Open (⌘+O or Ctrl+O) from the File menu. When you save the file in Claris Home Page, it is saved as an HTML document. Note that most standard word processors can open HTML documents, but they'll appear as plain old "vanilla" (unformatted) text.

Type It, Find It, Change It

Web page tools, such as Claris Home Page, let you work with text in some of the same ways that you would with a standard word processor. You can insert text, cut and paste text from another page or another document, and find and replace text. You can use several *levels* of headings (that's HTML-speak for the main heading, subheadings, and so on), change formats (bullets, outline, and so on), apply styles (bold, italics, and so forth), change the size of text and the way it's justified (right, left, or center), and change the text color.

Unfortunately, most Web page creation tools have their limits, and HTML can't do everything — at least not yet. You can't, for example, use different fonts or precisely control font size or style. (Although Claris Home Page does support some special HTML commands that Netscape Navigator can translate into different fonts, I don't recommend using them yet because there is no standard for font display across different Web browsers.) You can't change spacing between words or lines, use tabs, or change how words are hyphenated. (You can't use Claris Home Page to grade papers for you, either, but Claris is working on getting it to do that.) You're also limited by the fact that some browsers interpret your HTML commands a little differently from others; in fact, a Mac screen may look a little different in some browsers than a Windows 95 screen would look.

What's the moral of this story?

- ✔ Web page tools and HTML can't do everything to create the perfect Web page, but they can do a whole lot more than you'd think.

- ✔ Paying attention to the HTML code that Claris Home Page generates can help you learn enough code to tweak the contents of your site on your own.

- ✔ You need to have a means to test how your Web pages look with different browsers on different computers.

Entering text into your Web page

You and your students can add text to your Web page in any one of several ways:

- ✔ By typing it directly into the page (as shown in Figure 9-1)

- ✔ By copying and pasting it from another Web page or application

- ✔ By dragging it from another page in your Web site

  (On the Macintosh, you can drag and drop text from some applications as well.)

Claris Home Page Work Area

Figure 9-1: One way to add text to your home page is to open the Home Page document and type it directly into the page.

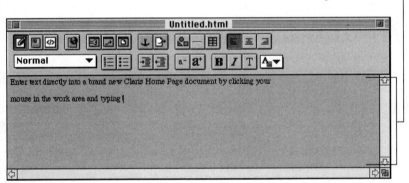

Here are some other essential things to know about working with text:

- ✔ When you enter text, the lines of text in a paragraph wrap around evenly, regardless of the size of the window. The text you type also wraps evenly in the reader's browser window, no matter what size the browser window is.

- ✔ You can delete text by selecting it and pressing Delete.

- ✔ You can undo your last action by choosing Edit⇨Undo (⌘+Z or Ctrl+Z).

✔ To end a paragraph, press Return and then press Enter. Claris Home Page automatically adds a blank line after each paragraph.

✔ If you want to make a paragraph break without adding the extra line, choose Line Break from the Insert menu.

✔ Stick to using no more than two or three type sizes on a page.

Unlike documents in most word processors, carriage returns in HTML files are basically irrelevant. Word *wrapping* (when the line turns down to create a new line) can occur at any point in your source file, and multiple spaces are collapsed into a single space.

Want to see what's happening behind the scenes? Claris Home Page adds the following HTML code when it inserts a blank line after a paragraph:

```
<P>
```

Here's the HTML code that Home Page inserts when you choose Line Break (a new paragraph without the extra line space):

```
<BR>
```

On a Mac, you can also press Shift+Return to insert a line break; on a PC running Windows, press Ctrl+Enter.

In case you need to see those pesky line break symbols, choose Show Line Breaks from the Edit Preferences menu (accessed with ⌘+J or Ctrl+J) found in the Edit menu. To hide line break symbols, choose Hide Line Breaks from the Edit menu.

Watch page length. Keep your Web pages to no more than two or three screens deep. Longer Web pages frustrate users who have to search for information and wait through the download time. Most designers believe that the first page (the home page) should be only one screen long.

Not all HTML code (tags) are supported by all World Wide Web browsers. If a browser does not support a tag, it just ignores it, often giving some not-too-pleasing results.

Finding and replacing text

Finding text in your Web page is much simpler than finding that student who grabbed the potty-pass from your blackboard an hour ago and still hasn't returned. Web page tools let you find and replace strings of text, including text characters, words, phrases, and keyboard symbols (such as a dollar sign or ampersand).

To find and replace text in Home Page:

1. Choose Edit⇨Find/Change (⌘+F or Ctrl+F).

The Find/Change dialog box appears (see Figure 9-2).

Figure 9-2:
Use the
Find/
Change
dialog box
to search
for and
replace
text.

Find/Change
Find: [   ]
Replace With: [   ]
⦿ Partial Word   ⊠ Case Sensitive
○ Entire Word   ☐ Search Backwards
⊠ Wrap Around
(Replace) (Replace All) (Replace and Find) (Done) (**Find**)

2. Enter the text you want to find in the Find text box.

3. If you want to replace the found text, enter the replacement text in the Replace With text box; if you want to delete the found text, leave this box blank.

4. Choose the options you want to use.

5. Click on Find or on one of the other buttons in the Find/Change dialog box.

Zoom! Claris Home Page does its thing!

Wanna search for something else? Choose Find Next from the Edit menu.

Webbing with (Paragraph) Style

You can use Claris Home Page 2.0 and other Web page creation tools to apply standard HTML formatting styles to *paragraphs* and to individual *characters* or words easily. Make sure that you're in Edit Page mode. (Choose Edit Page from the document window or click on the pencil-and-paper icon at the far left of the basic toolbar.) Choose a format and *poof!* Claris Home Page adds the appropriate HTML tags to the text or paragraph for you.

You and your students can use paragraph formats to add various levels of headings, and various types of lists, quotes, and bylines to your Web pages. (See Figure 9-3 for a sample of the six HTML headline styles.)

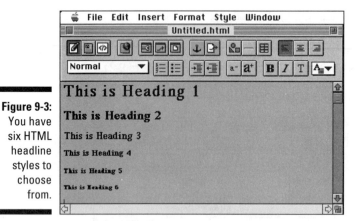

Figure 9-3:
You have
six HTML
headline
styles to
choose
from.

When you apply a *paragraph format,* the change affects all the text within the paragraph. In most cases, if text within the paragraph already has a character style, it adopts the paragraph format in addition to the character style. For example, if you make the first word in a paragraph italics and then make the paragraph into a heading, the paragraph becomes a heading with the first word set in italics.

Cybersleuthing with "reverse engineering"

Don't give me detention if I share a little secret with you. Most Web browsers allow you to take a peek behind the scenes and see the source code (actual HTML scripts) that created the page.

You can learn much from analyzing HTML and watching the way some of the more creative folks on the Net finesse their graphics. The folks in Cybertown call the process of looking under the techno-hood of other people's Web documents and dissecting what's there *reverse engineering.*

To view behind-the-scenes action while using the Netscape Navigator browser, choose View➪Source. With Internet Explorer and other browsers, the View Source command can usually be found in one of the menus on the program's menu bar. The source code automatically downloads into a text file on your computer and pops up on your Mac or PC in a SimpleText or Write window.

Be aware that each Web browser interprets HTML code in slightly different ways. Text-only browsers, for example, can't display graphics, so they show some kind of text instead of your wonderful graphics and colorful icons. Plus, some graphical browsers don't (yet) support some of the more recent Web page bells and whistles, such as tables, colored backgrounds, and other flashy, yet useful, options.

If you choose to copy code that's more than just basic syntax from someone's document — um, I mean if you choose to reverse engineer — it's a good idea to ask the Web page author's permission before including his or her code on your page. Someday, you may find that this is the most useful tip in the whole book.

To apply a paragraph format:

1. **Select the paragraph or group of paragraphs you want to format.**

2. **Choose the style from the Format menu or click on the style box (the one that says "Normal" in the basic toolbar).**

(For more information on using toolbars, check out Chapter 8.)

Here's a handy table to help you understand what some of the formats look like on the page. Table 9-1 lists each format and the HTML *syntax* each format generates. (The syntax is listed in pairs because the HTML code generated requires both an opening and closing tag to denote the beginning and end of each formatting style.)

Table 9-1	HTML Text Formats and Code	
Formats	*Effect*	*HTML Code*
Normal	Default style — removes all other special formatting.	No code.
Headings 1 through 6	Enlarge or reduce the size of text. Heading 1 is largest text size.	`<H1>...</H1>`
Preformatted	Creates that ugly monospace font that makes it easier to line up text exactly.	`<PRE>...</PRE>`
The following tag pairs are used to format paragraphs into lists of items:		
Bullet List*	`<UL>...</UL>`	
Numbered List*	`<OL>...</OL>`	
Definition List*	`<DL>...</DL>`	
Directory List*	`<DIR>...</DIR>`	
Menu List*	`<MENU>...</MENU>`	
Address	Formats page author's name or e-mail address so that readers can find it easily. Usually goes at the bottom of the page.	`<ADDRESS>...</ADDRESS>`
Alignment	Aligns text left, center, or right.	`ALIGN="TOP"` (also **LEFT**, `CENTER`, or `RIGHT`)
Blockquote	Indents both the left and right sides of the paragraph.	`<BLOCKQUOTE>... </BLOCKQUOTE>`

* Within each of the formatting tags above, you must denote individual list items by using the `<LI>` tag.

What's My (Browser) Style?

There are two types of style commands (or *tags*) in HTML: style tags that are *browser specific* and those that are *browser independent*. Browser-specific HTML commands depend on each browser to interpret the style and display it according to whatever rules have been set for that browser. Browser-independent HTML style commands look the same no matter what type of computer or which browser you're using.

Browser-specific style commands

Because some HTML commands are proprietary to the browser (Netscape, for example, supports a command that allows for the display of different fonts, but the others generally do not), it's important to be aware of which commands might result in different results when read by different browsers. Although there is an HTML standard out there (it's called HTML 3.2 and is developed and maintained by a consortium of companies called W3C), each browser programmer, it seems, just can't resist putting in a extra few bells and whistles to attract users to its particular browser.

A list of "special effects" that you can use to give your page some style follows. (Changing the style of text on your Web page generally requires using your Web page tool to highlight the text and choosing a style from an on-screen list.) Remember, however, that using these tags is a bit risky because you never know exactly how other browsers (those not as hearty as Netscape Navigator or Microsoft Internet Explorer) will read and interpret your script.

Several browser-specific styles are available. To select a style using Claris Home Page 2.0:

1. **Select the character(s) that you want to format.**

2. **Choose a style from the Style menu.**

    Table 9-2 shows you what effect each style has on your text. (**Note:** Some of these styles are found in the Other submenu of the Style menu.)

Table 9-2	HTML Text Style and Code	
Style	*Description*	*Raw HTML*
Emphasis	Each browser treats this text style differently. Some browsers display it as italics; some as underlined text.	`<EM>...</EM>`

Style	Description	Raw HTML
Strong	Used for strong emphasis in text. Some browsers display it as boldface; others as underlined text.	`<STRONG>... </STRONG>`
Code	Used for sample code or an Internet address. Appears in most browsers as Courier or another similar monospace font.	`<CODE>...</CODE>`
Sample	Used for illustrative text or examples. Appears similar to Code text.	`<SAMPLE>...</SAMPLE>`
Keyboard	Used to indicate something to be typed by the user. Appears in monospace (Courier) font on graphical browsers.	`<KEYBOARD>... </KEYBOARD>`
Variable	Used to name a variable. Some browsers show this text as italics or underlined.	`<VAR>...</VAR>`
Citation	Used for citations for bibliographies. Usually shows text as italics.	`<CITE>...</CITE>`
Deleted	Indicates that the text has been deleted from the document.	
Strikethrough	Creates ~~strikethrough~~ text.	`<STRIKE>...</STRIKE>`
Superscript	Creates superscript text.	`<SUP>...</SUP>`
Subscript	Creates subscript text.	`<SUB>...</SUB>`

Browser-independent style commands

Because you can never be certain how browser-specific tags will display, you should use browser-independent tags for text that must be boldface, italic, or set in monospace in order to have your presentation make sense.

A list of four styles that display on virtually every browser (text or graphical) follows with their respective HTML codes (one of the styles, underline, is supported by many, but not all, browsers):

- Boldface `<B>...</B>`
- Italic `<I>...</I>`
- Teletype (similar to a typewriter font) `<TT>...</TT>`
- Underline (not supported by all browsers — yet) `<UL>...</UL>`

Using the Document Statistics window

One of my favorite Web pages (done by someone in an unnamed western U.S. state) is so graphically rich that it's absolutely stunning. The problem is that with my 28.8 modem connection, it takes more than two minutes to load all the graphics on the page (not good). Members of the Nintendo Generation, who can do their homework and eat lunch in the same period of time, would never wait that long for a page to load.

To make sure that your Web page isn't a slow-poke that turns off the Web surfers out there, Claris Home Page provides a nifty tool called the Document Statistics window. It can give your Web page creation team an estimate of how long it will take surfers to download your Web page (or sections of your page) to their browsers. (You can check the estimated download time for a page you're building any time you are working with your page in Edit Page mode.)

Of course, the Claris exactness gurus are quick to say that the Document Statistics window displays estimates of download time under *ideal* conditions. Network congestion, a busy server, or other unpredictable conditions can significantly increase the download time of your Web pages. Just be aware that the Document Statistics window is a great yardstick for beginning to check the tolerance level of your Web page.

To use the Document Statistics window:

1. **Click and drag with your mouse to select a section of your Web page (or the entire Web page).**

2. **Choose Document Statistics (⌘+K or Ctrl+K) from the Edit menu. You'll see a window like the one in this sidebar.**

You can find a wealth of information in the Document Statistics dialog box, including how many characters (letters, spaces, or numbers) are in your Web page, the total number of bytes for all images in your Web page or for all images in the section you selected, and even how long impatient people will have to wait to see what you've created. Neat, huh?

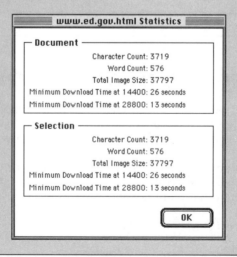

As with other text styles, you can apply these four styles by selecting the character or characters and then choosing the desired style from the Style menu (shown in Figure 9-4).

Figure 9-4:
The Style menu allows you to choose features for selected text.

Style	
Reset	⌘T
✓Plain	
Bold	⌘B
Italic	⌘I
Underline	
Strikethrough	
Superscript	
Subscript	
Teletype	
Raw HTML	
Other	▶
Font	▶
Size	▶
Color	▶

If you're frustrated by the lack of different type styles in HTML and are feeling creative, try designing the titles or headlines yourself and save them as a graphic (GIF or JPEG) file.

Formatted Web pages can be used as presentation tools. Simply place your content in HTML format and use an overhead projector or classroom TV to display the results. After the class is over, post the Web pages online (on your intranet) so kids can review them later.

An exception to the browser-compatibility rule occurs with text-only browsers, such as Lynx. The Lynx program interprets virtually any special character instruction as underlined text because the computers (typically "dumb terminals") can't handle boldface or italic type formats.

Claris Home Page also has a style called Raw HTML that looks like a type of a typewriter face. Use this as a default when all else fails. (See Figure 9-5 for a sampling of text styles.)

Zapping Character Styles

To remove a style from your text, select the text and choose Plain from the Style menu. To remove all character styles from your text, select the text and choose Reset (⌘+T or Ctrl+T) from the Style menu.

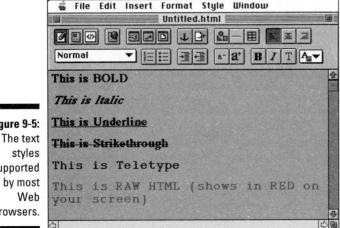

Figure 9-5:
The text
styles
supported
by most
Web
browsers.

Making a List and Checking It Twice

Think about the lists you make each day — grocery lists, outlines, to-do lists. Each list contains multiple items, but their formats are different.

Lists are a great way to organize information. Because people *browse* the Web (that is, pop in and out of sites), placing information in lists helps users recognize the value of your information quickly. You can use lists to organize student names, display menu items (subject areas), define terms, and more.

One of the neatest features of HTML is its capability to create and display items in a list. HTML list tags create preformatted lists that can be displayed as numbered lists, bulleted lists, or in other ways.

The HTML standard supports five kinds of lists that virtually any Web browser can display:

- Ordered or numbered lists (labeled with numbers)
- Bulleted lists
- Glossary lists (a highlighted term followed by a definition)
- Menu lists (lists of paragraphs)
- Directory lists (short lists of one- or two-word items)

Napkins, magazines, and matchbooks

Some of the greatest thoughts in history were first penned on (school lunchroom?) napkins, envelopes, tablecloths, and even matchbook covers. An idea popped into an author's head and ended up on a torn corner of an old magazine. When the ideas were flowing, the author didn't focus on how the text looked, but on what it said.

Later, though, someone took the ideas and crafted them into a form that was more readable, attractive, and organized. This step was essential to ensure that the author's message was useful and easy to absorb.

Web page organization and design help to

✔ Draw the reader into your page

✔ Highlight important information

✔ Provide easy navigation through the information that you've presented

Encourage your students to use text formatting sparingly and only when needed for emphasis. Too much "style" is *not* a good thing!

Creating a list

Creating a list on your Web page is easy. Lists typically are used when you are providing your readers with Web links, people's names (or e-mail addresses), products in a catalog, and so on. As with most other HTML tags, lists begin and end with a tag that identifies the type and format of the list that you'd like to use.

I suggest that you and your students experiment with the different kinds of lists and discuss which are most appropriate at what times. All of the lists are created by using the same method, except for the glossary lists, which are described later. (Most Web page creation tools require you to select the text by using your mouse and to choose the list format from a pull-down menu.)

To create a bulleted, numbered, menu, or directory list in Claris Home Page 2.0:

1. **In Edit Page mode, enter the list items, starting each item on a new line.**

   To enter Edit Page mode, click on the Edit Page icon (it looks like a pencil and paper and is located on the far left of your Claris Home Page toolbar) or chose Edit Page from the Windows menu. As you end each line, press Return (Mac)/Enter (PC).

2. **Select the list.**

3. **Choose Bullet List, Numbered List, or Other from the Format menu.**

   The Menu or Directory formats are located in the Other submenu.

   **4. Click Preview Page (second icon from left on your Claris Home Page
   toolbar).**

   That's all there is to it! The text will appear formatted on your Claris
   Home Page screen. (See Figure 9-6 for some sample list styles.)

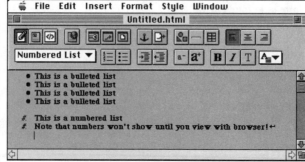

Figure 9-6:
Here's what
the bulleted
and
numbered
lists look
like on most
Web
browsers.

Glossary lists are used to highlight vocabulary and definition material. This
format is handy for creating a list of key terms for your students as they
create Web pages. To create a glossary list:

   1. Enter the first term in the glossary list.

   2. Select the term.

   3. Choose Other from the Format menu.

   4. Choose Term (it's a submenu in the Other menu).

   **5. Press Return (Macintosh) or Enter (Windows), and Claris Home Page
   automatically changes the format to definition.**

   6. Enter the term's definition.

   The term's definition is automatically formatted as a definition paragraph.

   7. Press ⌘+Return (Macintosh) or F8 (Windows) and type the next term.

   **8. Repeat Steps 5 through 7 for each glossary term and definition you
   want to create.**

You can view the results of any of your list stylings in the Preview Page
mode or in a browser.

We don't need no stinking bullets!

A bullet usually displays on your browser's screen as a small round dot or asterisk (depending on your browser). Netscape Navigator (and a few other browsers) can also read some tags that let you choose what your bullet will look like. You can actually choose between a solid circle, a hollow square, or a solid square shape by using the following code:

`<UL TYPE=disc>`
Displays a standard round, solid bullet

`<UL TYPE=circle>`
Displays a hollow square bullet (someone obviously failed geometry!)

`<UL TYPE=square>`
Displays a solid square bullet

The "UL" refers to an unnumbered list. The attribute (the part after the equal sign) sets the bullet appearance.

Claris Home Page doesn't support these bullet types directly, so you have to enter the bullet tags as raw HTML code (you can use either the Edit HTML Source button on the menu bar or select Edit HTML Source from the Window menu).

Adding additional list entries

You can add items to an existing list without having to reapply the list's style. Just do this:

1. **Click at the end of the line that is located above the spot where you want to enter the new item.**

2. **Choose List Entry from the Insert menu.**

3. **Type the new list item.**

On a Mac, you can also press ⌘+Return to insert a list item. In Windows, press F8.

When you create a numbered list in Edit Page mode, you see a number symbol (#) or an X in front of each entry. Nope, you're not going crazy (yet). The actual numbers or letters appear only when you view your page in Preview Page mode or in a browser.

Reordering items in a list

What a drag! But wait, it's not that bad. You can change the order of items in your list by selecting each item's text and dragging it to a new position in the list.

To reposition a single list item:

1. **Select the entire line, including the carriage return at the end.**

2. **Triple-click on the item you want to move.**

   If you want to move more than one item at a time, hold down the Shift key while you select the items.

3. **Drag the selected item or items into the left margin of the new location.**

   If you change the order of numbered list items, they're automatically renumbered in correct order.

TIP

Netscape Navigator: Leader of the Pack

It's common practice for the folks who create Web browsers to keep an eye on HTML developers and then write code to match. Not content to be part of the pack, the folks at Netscape would be classified by teachers as, well, gifted overachievers. They decided to jump ahead of the current HTML standards development and create their own new features and tags before they were written into the standards.

As with any gifted student who skips beyond the assigned curriculum, Netscape has both overjoyed and angered HTML developers. As far as Netscape's competitors go, I say they just have to "get over it." Netscape browsers are used by the vast majority of Web surfers, and the popularity of the browser Netscape Navigator continues to grow.

Unfortunately, Claris Home Page doesn't have a built-in ability to use these special tags (commands) used by Netscape browsers. That means you have to enter these tags as raw HTML code by using the Claris Home Page Edit HTML Source option in the Windows menu on the menu bar.

Some additions to HTML that work only on "Netscape-aware" browsers are:

✔ `<nobr>...</nobr>` Indicates text that must stay together with no line breaks

✔ `<center>...</center>` Centers text horizontally on the page

✔ `<font>` and `<basefont>` Creates drop caps and adds emphasis to documents by varying the font size

✔ **Bullet form commands** Allow you to specify the kind of bullets you prefer (circles, squares, disks)

✔ **List control** Controls the style (such as Arabic versus Roman numerals) and the starting numeral for digits used to number a list

✔ **Special characters** The tag `&reg` gives you a registered trademark (™) symbol; `&copy` gives you a copyright (©) symbol

✔ `<isindex>` Adds words or phrases to searchable databases on your server

✔ `<list>` Gives you flexibility in changing list types on the fly

✔ **Image control** New commands that can be added to the `<IMG>` command to control the alignment and size of images and borders on images

✔ `<hr>` Controls the thickness of a horizontal rule

And there are more! For additional information, check out the new specs at http://www.netscape.com/.

Numbering lists with style

Claris Home Page offers five number styles you can use for a numbered list. Note that these styles are supported only by newer browsers (Netscape 3.0 and higher, for example). Here are the number styles from which you may choose:

- ✔ 1, 2, 3 (number series)
- ✔ A, B, C (alphabetical, uppercase)
- ✔ a, b, c (alphabetical, lowercase)
- ✔ I, II, III (Roman, uppercase)
- ✔ i, ii, iii (Roman, lowercase)

To change the number style of a list:

1. Select the numbered list.

2. Choose Number Style from the Format menu.

3. Select a number or alphabetic style.

Whoosh! The list is automatically transformed into the number style of your choice. Remember, in Edit Page mode, you see number symbols (#'s) or X's in the list in place of the numbers that will actually appear on a browser. You must view your page in Preview Page mode or in a browser to see the actual numbers or letters.

Wonder what sort of raw HTML code the magical Claris Home Page generates for these list styles? Here's what the code looks like:

Numbering Scheme	HTML Tag Generated
1, 2, 3 (number series)	`<OL TYPE=1>`
A, B, C (alphabetical, uppercase)	`<OL TYPE=A>`
a, b, c (alphabetical, lowercase)	`<OL TYPE=a>`
I, II, III (Roman numerals, uppercase)	`<OL TYPE=I>`
i, ii, iii (Roman numerals, lowercase)	`<OL TYPE=i>`

Colorizing Text

Most Web page creation tools let you easily change the color of all or some of the text on your Web page. Before you start going "rainbow" on me, let me remind you (so that you might remind your students) that the use of color on a Web page is primarily for effect and to accent your content. There's no law that says that you must have colored text (or colored backgrounds, for that matter). Black text on a white background still provides the most legible text. Think about readability as you plan for colorizing your Web page, and your visitors will be much happier.

Colors assigned to selected pieces of text are treated as character styles and will override the color you assign as the default for text on your Web page.

To change the default color for *all* the text on a Web page:

1. Choose Edit⇨Document Options.

The Document Options dialog box appears (see Figure 9-7).

Figure 9-7:
The Document Options dialog box allows you to change the color of your text or background.

```
┌──────────────────── Untitled.html Options ────────────────────┐
│  ┌─ Basic      ▼ ─────────────────────────────────────────┐   │
│  │          Text: ■      Normal Link: ■      Active Link: ▨ │   │
│  │    Background: ▨       Visited Link: ■                   │   │
│  │                                                         │   │
│  │    Background Image:  [ Set... ]  [ None ]              │   │
│  │    ┌─────────────────────────────────────┐ ┌────────┐  │   │
│  │    │                                     │ │        │  │   │
│  │    └─────────────────────────────────────┘ └────────┘  │   │
│  │                                                         │   │
│  │      Document Title: │                                 │   │
│  └─────────────────────────────────────────────────────────┘   │
│  [?]  [ Use Defaults ]                  [ Cancel ]  [[ OK ]]    │
└───────────────────────────────────────────────────────────────┘
```

2. Choose Basic from the pop-up menu or tab.

3. Click in the rectangular color box next to the word Text.

A dialog box named Color appears.

On a Mac, you see the standard Color Picker dialog box. Choose a color by clicking in the color circle or by using the color slidebar.

If you're using Windows, you'll see a Color dialog box. Click Custom Colors to choose from the color rectangle.

Note that some computers can view only a limited number of colors, so it's a good idea to stick with primary colors (red, blue, green) and, of course, black and white, for text.

4. Select the color you want for the text.

5. Click on OK.

6. Click on OK again to close the Options dialog box.

Smoke and mirrors and colors

The Home Page method of inserting colorful text is really nifty, especially when you understand what you'd have to do if you were actually creating the raw HTML code.

Because browsers display text in basic black, there's an HTML tag called BODY TEXT that helps you bring color to your page. Here's what the syntax looks like:

`<BODY TEXT="#nnnnnn">`

Looks simple enough? It is, until you realize that in order to insert a number into the code you've got to know the value of the color *in hexadecimal format* — a system of letters and numbers used to specify colors in HTML. (Now that's something we all carry around in our heads, right?)

An example of how that format looks is in the next column:

Color	Hex value
Black	#000000
White	#FFFFFF
Red	#FF0000
Green	#00FF00
Blue	#0000FF
Magenta	#FF00FF
Cyan	#00FFFF
Yellow	#FFFF00

(***Note:*** All those 0's up there are zeros, not the letter *O*.)

To find out more about colors and color numbers (and hexadecimal codes), point your browser to `http://www.bnl.com/colors.html`.

If you want to change all the options back to their original (default) settings:

1. **Choose Document Options (⌘+J or Ctrl+J) from the Edit menu.**

2. **Click on the Use Defaults button.**

3. **Click on OK.**

   Your links revert to their default color, any text not assigned a specific color character style reverts to the text default color, and any image background disappears.

To change the color of *selected* text:

1. **Select the text.**

2. **Click on the Text Color icon on the toolbar (it's the one on the lower-right with the letter "A" on it) or choose Color from the Style menu.**

3. **Choose one of the predefined colors or choose Other for more options.**

   If you choose a predefined color, the color is applied to the text you selected.

   If you choose Other, a standard color dialog box appears.

4. **Click on the color you want.**

5. **Click on OK to apply a new color to the text.**

The Golden (Horizontal) Rule

After you have all your text flopped down on the page, you next have to figure out how to make it more readable. You can use various text styles (see Chapter 10), or you can use horizontal rule lines to help guide the reader's eye and keep text separated on your Web page. (You usually find horizontal rules just after a headline, such as in a newspaper masthead, or between groups of hypertext links. See Figure 9-8 for an example.)

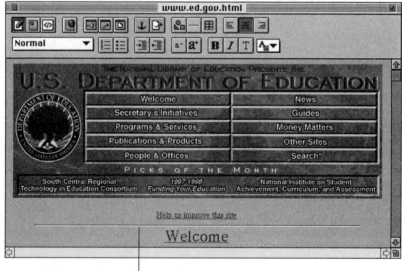

Figure 9-8: Use a horizontal rule to help your readers differentiate between parts of your Web page.

Horizontal rule used to divide segments of a Web page

To create a horizontal rule:

1. **Click your mouse where you want the rule line to appear.**

2. **Choose Horizontal Rule from the Insert menu, or click on the Insert Horizontal Rule button from the menu bar.**

   Claris Home Page inserts a default horizontal rule that's the size commonly used by many Web page designers.

To change the size of a horizontal rule:

1. **Double-click on the horizontal rule.**

   This brings up the Horizontal Rule Object Editor.

2. **Enter a new value for the dimensions of the line.**

   For Height, enter a new size in pixels.

   For Width, choose Percent or Pixel, respectively, to enter a size in either pixels or a percentage of the overall browser window width.

You can also use your mouse to change the height of a horizontal rule. Click on the rule to select it and drag the handle on the bottom of the rule to change the rule's height.

Don't Blink!

If you happen to remember the early days of BASIC programming, you may recall a command called FLASH. Using the command caused the text on your screen to blink incessantly, something that was at first kind of neat and then quickly became very annoying. There is an equivalent in HTML — it's called the <BLINK> tag, which would be coded like this:

```
<BLINK>This annoying text is blinking.</BLINK>
```

I'm telling you about this tag merely so you can have something to talk about when you wax nostalgic at your next computer club meeting. I implore you, though, don't ever use it on your Web page. It's incredibly obnoxious, and other Webmasters who catch you using it will point at you and call you "Blinky."

Chapter 10

Getting the Picture with Graphics

● ●

In This Chapter

▶ Options, options, and more options

▶ Adding images to your page

▶ Doing the graphic conversion

▶ Building backgrounds

▶ Editing images

▶ Going to the library

● ●

*O*ne of the most powerful things about the Web is its capability to display images that enhance text and make your pages more exciting to look at and interesting to read. The images you use can include anything from simple line art to color photos, and they can be used in a number of ways:

✔ To add visual appeal

✔ As clickable links to another Web page

✔ As links to a Common Gateway Interface (CGI) (see Chapter 14 for more information on CGI)

Most Web page creation tools or HTML (the document markup language used to create Web pages) give you lots of options for using images on your Web page. For instance, you can edit the *transparency* of an image to make parts of it (such as the background) disappear, or you can use an image to create a background pattern for your Web page. (For more on transparencies, see the section "Creating See-Through Images" later in this chapter.)

One of the reasons that I use Claris Home Page 2.0 examples in this book is because Home Page comes equipped with a handy library of clip art that makes it easy to add ready-made, eye-catching graphics to your Web pages, as shown in FIgure 10-1. (You can also create your own libraries of images.) I show you how to access these clip-art images later in this chapter in the section "Checking Out a Home Page Library."

Clip art images

Figure 10-1:
Claris Home
Page has a
library of
clip-art
images you
can use to
enhance
your
school's
Web page.

But, I must warn you about the downside of adding graphic images to your pages. It usually slows down the process of downloading Web pages because additional data must be transmitted. The moral of this is that you must use images with care. ***Remember:*** Some folks out there (mostly schools!) are still using slow dial-up connections to the Internet.

Make sure that the graphics are relevant and necessary to convey the message. Although pictures of your school mascot are cute and may get a giggle, is the download time to see them really worth the wait? Work with your students to assess the relevance of each and every graphic on your Web pages.

As you add images to your Web page, you can use the Document Statistics window (explained in Chapter 9) to check how long it will take visitors to download your page. You can get an estimate of the download time of any graphic, or group of graphics, on your page. Follow the 20 Seconds Rule. Web site testers say that if the wait for graphics to download is more than 20 seconds, it increases the chance that the user will surf off to a different site.

Your Web page creation tool also allows you to change an image so that your visitors can see more of it as it downloads on their browsers. (This process is called *interleaving;* more info on that later in this chapter.) This helps them to see what they're getting right away and then make the decision to either wait until the entire masterpiece loads or to click off to another place.

To insert an image into your Web page by using Claris Home Page 2.0, you have to do two things:

1. **Enter the proper HTML code into your Web page (or let Claris Home Page do it for you).**

2. **Upload (copy) the image to your Web server by using FTP (file transfer protocol) or some other file transfer method.**

   (Check out Chapter 19 for the skinny on FTP.)

Web browsers read HTML scripts and go searching for the graphics files that you've pointed to. So, it's absolutely essential that you name the file correctly and make sure that the image is in the correct format that can be read by all Web browsers. I'll talk more about storing your graphics files later in this chapter.

Adding an Image to Your Page

To add an image that's stored on your Web server to your Web page, just follow these steps:

1. **Place the insertion point (cursor) in the page where you want the image to appear.**

2. **Choose Image from the Insert menu.**

   An Open dialog box appears.

3. **In the Open dialog box, select the GIF, JPEG, BMP, or PICT image file you want.**

4. **Click on Open.**

   The image then appears on the Web page.

You can also *drag and drop* (select and drag to a new location) your image from within another program that also supports drag and drop (such as ClarisWorks or Microsoft Word), from your scrapbook or clipboard, or even from your desktop. If your file's on the desktop, just click on the file icon to select the file and drag it to where you want it to appear in your Claris Home Page document. Be sure you're in Edit mode before dragging and dropping!

To add an image that's stored on *someone else's* Web server (a *remote* image) to your Web page, just follow these steps:

1. **Place the insertion point (cursor) in the page where you want the image to appear.**

2. **Click the Edit HTML Source button (the one with two arrow brackets) on the toolbar or choose Edit HTML Source from the Window menu.**

   The HTML generated by Claris Home Page appears on your screen.

3. **Enter the location and name of the graphic using the following format:**

   <IMG SRC="www.servername.com/picture.gif">

4. **Click on the Edit Page icon (the one showing a pencil) to return to Edit Page mode.**

   You'll see the URL for the image, but you can't test it until you're logged into the Internet and running your browser.

Lots of possible formats exist for graphics, but only GIF and JPEG are supported on the Web. Fortunately, Claris Home Page 2.0 automatically converts most BMP and PICT files to GIF format on the fly (as you copy them) and places them in a special folder called "default images" created by the program manually.

If you're using a word processor or other Web page creation program like Adobe PageMill, you may have to convert your images to these "net-friendly" formats. For more information about formats see the "Converting image files" sidebar later in this chapter.

By the way, for you purists out there, GIF is pronounced *jif*, like the peanut butter, not *giff* as in gift. (The folks at Unisys, owners of the GIF patent, asked me to set the record straight.)

When you add an image to a Web page, Claris Home Page creates a pointer to the folder (or subdirectory) where the image file is stored. So before you begin adding lots of graphics to your Web page, make sure that you've first set up a folder (which will later be moved to your Web server) in which to store your images.

If you get wild and move the folder where the image files are stored to another place on your Web server or onto another machine, you have to edit the *pathname* (file location), or the reading browser can't find the file. Use Edit HTML Source in the Windows menu (or click on the Edit HTML Source button in the toolbar) to edit filenames. You can also use the Link Editor (found in the Windows menu). For more on the Link Editor, see Chapter 11.

When you insert an image into your document, Claris Home Page automatically generates an HTML tag called the <IMG> (image) tag that looks like the following in raw HTML ("imagename.gif" is the filename of the graphic you want to use):

```
<IMG SRC="imagename.gif">
```

Converting image files

Since the dawn of the computer age, programmers have worked hard to make it easier for you to display images on your computer screen. This hard work has paid off, and there are now several formats for graphics. However, only GIF (CompuServe's Graphics Interchange Format) and JPEG (Joint Photographic Experts Group) are supported by all Web browsers.

The reason all those Web graphics pop up so reliably on your browser is that the industry has adopted the GIF and JPEG standards (formats that everybody uses) for images on the Web.

Claris Home Page automatically converts PICT files on the Macintosh and BMP files on Windows into GIF format.

You can also convert images to GIF or JPEG format by using an image editing program, such as Adobe PhotoShop, or a conversion program, such as Lview Pro on your PC or Graphic Converter or GIF Converter on the Macintosh.

Because these programs are more efficient at the conversion process than is the Claris Home Page automatic conversion, you may also be able to produce smaller, more manageable files.

Graphics are automatically converted into GIF *(graphics interchange format)* images by Claris Home Page 2.0, but you can also convert other graphics by using one of the handy tools I've stuffed into your *Web Publishing For Teachers* CD.

HTML provides support for many different kinds of multimedia, including the graphic images on your pages. Not all browsers *support* (that is, *read*) images, and those that can't usually just ignore the HTML code and skip right past the graphics to display only the surrounding text.

Using the Image Object Editor

After you've added an image to your page, you can use the Image dialog box to change the attributes of the image. (See Figure 10-2 — the Image dialog box is expanded or collapsed depending on how you last left it.)

You can open the Image dialog box in any one of three different ways:

- ✔ Double-click on an image.
- ✔ Click on an image, and then choose Show Object Editor from the Window menu on the toolbar.
- ✔ Click on an image, and then click on the Object Editor button in the toolbar.

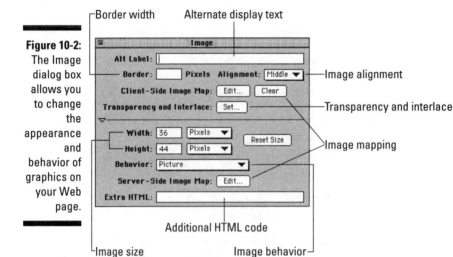

The Image dialog box (also called an Object Editor) has several options for image editing.

To change the attributes of an image:

1. **Select the image.**

2. **Change the settings in the Image dialog box.**

3. **Apply the new settings by pressing Tab or clicking on the Close box in the Image dialog box.**

Table 10-1 lists the various options within the Image dialog box and the effect of each option.

Other people's graphics

You and your students may be tempted to "appropriate" images from other people's Web pages for use on your own Web page. It's easy enough: Just click and hold on the graphic in your browser and choose the "Save Image as..." choice. Voilà. It's on your hard drive.

Of course, just because you *can* do this doesn't mean you *should*. Make sure that you discuss copyright and "intellectual property rights" with your students. *Always* ask permission to use a graphic taken from someone else's Web page. It's the right thing to do.

Table 10-1	Image Object Editor Options
Setting	*Result*
Alt label	Sets text that appears in the place of a graphic if the browser your Web page visitor is using can't "see" the graphics or if the visitor has the view graphics option turned off.
Border	Changes the thickness in pixels of the border around an image (a setting of 0 [zero] makes the border around the image invisible).
Alignment	Changes how an image is aligned with the text (at the top, middle, bottom, left, or right).
Image Map	Creates or removes an interlaced image, adds or removes a transparency, adds *hotspots* to an image map, and edits links.
Transparency and Interlace	Allows you to make the background of images transparent and to interlace images for faster loading.
Width	Changes the width of an image.
Height	Changes the height of an image.
Reset Size	Restores a resized image to its original size.
Behavior	Changes what an image does when you click on it. You can set the image "behavior" as a normal image, a form button (used to submit or reset an interactive form), or an image map for creating hyperlinks. (See Chapter 11 for information on image maps.)
Extra HTML	Adds additional HTML attributes to your table. (This is where you add HTML code that Claris Home Page doesn't generate directly.)

Want to see the HTML code that Claris Home Page would generate for a graphic image? Here's the code that's generated for an image called school.gif set at 100 x 100 pixels with a 6-pixel border and aligned to the middle of accompanying text. Its alternate name (the name you see if your browser doesn't display graphics) is Picture here:

```
<IMG SRC="school.gif" ALT="Picture here" WIDTH=100
        HEIGHT=100 BORDER=6 ALIGN=middle></P>
```

Going digital

It's nice to think about all the great pictures you'd like to include on your school's Web site. But to actually make your thoughts into reality, you've got to find a way to get the pictures into *digital format* (that's the basic format your computer knows and loves). You can use any of four options to *digitize* your images:

- **Scan them.**

  Scanners have become quick and easy to use. If you're scanning for the Net, make sure that your scanner can scan in color and (preferably) comes with software that converts the scanned image into PICT, JPEG, or GIF format on the fly as you're working. Flatbed scanners — the ones with a flat surface onto which you place your picture, book, or other image source — work much better than hand-held scanners (which require you to move the scanner over the source image).

- **Digitize them with a digital camera.**

  Today's digital cameras are much more affordable than they used to be and cut out the middle person in the process — you can digitize the image yourself! Just point and shoot (with the camera, of course) and then connect the camera directly to your Mac or PC. A couple of mouse clicks later and you've got a usable image. No photo developing or scanning needed! You'll find that these cameras quickly pay for themselves. Lots of schools now use Apple's QuickTake 200 camera that works with both Macs and PCs. You can find out about these cameras at `http://www.apple.com`.

- **PhotoCD them.**

  Kodak offers an option by which photo developers translate your negatives into digital format and then save them to a CD that you can read with your computer's CD-ROM drive. The good news is that you have a handy archive for your images; the bad news is that the PhotoCD option is more expensive than the other options in the long run. And if you use a PC instead of a Mac, you have to add some software to your system to read the disks.

- **Borrow them.**

  You can also use graphics on your Web page that come from other pages on the World Wide Web. If you've got copyright permission (don't forget to ask first!), simply insert the graphic image's URL (its Internet address) and filename into your Web page script and you're in business. (Specific directions about linking to remote images can be found under "Adding an Image to Your Page" in this chapter.)

Setting the Image Size

Most Web page tools allow you to decide whether images on your page are rescaled as your Web page visitors resize their browser windows, or if the images remain in fixed dimensions as your visitors rescale their windows. Depending on the graphic, it's generally a good idea to use the default setting in which graphics resize automatically when a visitor's browser window is resized.

To resize an image with Claris Home Page 2.0 or to determine how the image size will adjust to the size of a browser window:

1. **Double-click on the image to open the Image dialog box.**

2. **Choose a setting type from the Width or Height menus.**

   Choose the Percent setting if the image width or height should appear as a certain percentage of the browser window width or height.

   Choose the Pixels setting if the image width or height always appears as a specified size, measured in pixels, regardless of the browser window's size.

3. **Enter the number of pixels or percentage for the image's width or height.**

4. **Press Return (Macintosh) or Enter (Windows).**

You can use your mouse to change the width and height of the image proportionately. Select the image, hold down the Shift key, and then click on and drag the lower-right corner handle of the image.

Think about designing for 472 pixels. Most browsers default to displaying around 500 pixels on Macs or Windows PCs. Just to make sure that everything you place on your page "fits," no matter the window size, shoot for 472 pixels. (In Claris Home Page and other Web page processors, you can use the graphic editing tools to set pixel size.)

Include width and height information in the HTML code for the graphics. There's a really easy way to set the final size of a graphic — here it is: `<IMG SRC="Sample.GIF" WIDTH="200" HEIGHT="75" >`. The numbers supplied are measured in pixels.

Changing the Background Color

Color adds visual interest and appeal to your Web page — and it's something you can apply to your page without too much effort. In fact, you can easily change the color of your text (see Chapter 9) or the color of your Web page's background by using the following steps. (This takes some planning on your part, however. You want to be sure to choose background colors for your text that offer high contrast and, therefore, good readability.)

To change the color of your Web page background in Claris Home Page 2.0:

1. **Choose <u>D</u>ocument Options from the <u>E</u>dit menu.**

   The Document Options dialog box appears.

2. **Choose Basic from the pop-up menu or click on the Colors and Background tab.**

3. Click on the Background color box.

A dialog box appears in which you can make your color selections (see Figure 10-3).

4. Select the color you want to use as the new background for your Web page by clicking in the appropriate area.

5. Click on OK to close the Color dialog box.

6. Click on OK to close the Document Options dialog box.

Poof! The background color of your Web page changes.

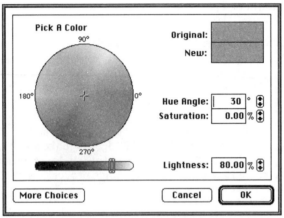

Figure 10-3:
The color of the background of your Web page can be changed with this Color Picker dialog box.

Adding Background Images

To insert background artwork to appear behind the elements in your Web page, follow these steps:

1. Save the background artwork file in GIF or JPEG format.

2. Upload (send) the artwork file to your Web server.

3. Identify the artwork within the `<BODY>` **of your script with this HTML code:** `<BODY BACKGROUND="imagename".GIF>ICON`

The `<BODY BACKGROUND>` tag isn't supported by some older browsers, therefore visitors accessing your page with older browsers won't see the background art.

Be certain to use background art that is subtle enough to allow foreground text to be readable. Also, be aware that loading background art, like any other art, slows down access time to your Web page, so use background art and color sparingly.

TECHNO TERMS

The mysterious HTML colors codes

Users of Netscape Navigator Version 1.1 or greater can add a splash of color behind their Web pages by using the powerful `<BGCOLOR>` HTML tag. (Users of Internet Explorer and other browsers may see different colors when you are using this code, so it's important to test your colors by viewing your page with different browsers before posting it to the Web.) Here's the HTML code, for example, to set background color to black, text color to white, clickable links to appear in red, and already-clicked-on links to appear in blue:

```
<body bgcolor="000000"
  text="ffffff" link="ff0000"
  vlink="0000ff"
  alink="0000ff">
```

The numbers in these HTML codes are derived from the hexadecimal (a special numbering system) equivalent for colors. To see more colors or read more about how these "hex" equivalents are derived, visit Yahoo! at `http://www.yahoo.com` and use the search terms hex and color.

The following is a list of some basic (and more exotic) colors and their hexadecimal equivalents:

Color	Hex Equivalent
Black	000000
Navy blue	0000FF
Speckled cornflower	003D84
Light speckled cornflower	0063A4
Dark speckled green	874000
Speckled teal	008F93
Speckled medium blue	00A0DD
Neon green	00FF00
Neon blue	00FFFF
Dark purple	1C0B5A
Dark gray	262626
90% gray	333333
85% gray	404040
80% gray	4D4D4D
Speckled grass green	4DA619
Purple	53005D
75% gray	595959
70% gray	666666
65% gray	737373
Speckled purple	7C005F
60% gray	808080
55% gray	8C8C8C
Light speckled green	92C000
50% gray	999999
45% gray	A6A6A6
40% gray	B3B3B3
30% gray	BFBFBF
Dark red	C40026
Medium red	C5004C
Dark pink	C50067
Gray	CCCCCC
20% gray	D9D9D9
Dark orange	DC6000
Off-white	E6E6E6
Light orange	EC9800
Bright red	FF0000
Bright purple	FF00FF
Speckled dark yellow	FFEB00
Neon yellow	FFFF00
White	FFFFFF

Online services and custom home page design

You won't be completely left out of the action if you access the Internet via an online service and want to create your own home page. Both America Online and Prodigy have fill-in-the-blank forms that you and your students can use to create simple home pages without knowing any HTML language.

Prodigy's Home Page Creator offers several template designs (which you can use at no extra charge) that make creating a home page very simple. AOL's Personal Home Page uses a similar fill-in-the-blank method, but it allows more flexibility in the integration of graphics and sound and includes a few more templates.

Of course, you can't get really wild or build your own CGI scripts by using these services, and when you are ready for more bells and whistles to play with, you'll be wishing you could enter your own HTML code. But for beginners who just have to have their own home pages *now*, these online service home-page designers provide a simple way to weave your own basic Web page.

Tiling Your Background Image

If you and your students want to get really fancy, you can change the background of your Web page to appear as any graphic image. (Note that this can decrease the readability of the Web page dramatically, so use this technique sparingly.)

Browsers can create an effect called *tiling* — the browser reads the graphic image and then pastes it repeatedly onto the Web page background in rows. This means, unfortunately, that you can't take one huge image and paste it into the background of your Web page. The best you can do (without using some big-time voodoo commands not supported by some browsers) is to create one large background image and then cut it up into sections and "fake" the background. The resulting image and text can then be made into clickable images by creating an image map. (See Chapter 11 for more on this.) It's tedious, but it works.

To test out how a tiled background may look:

1. **Choose Document Options from the Edit menu.**

2. **Choose Basic from the pop-up menu or click on the Colors and Background tab.**

3. **Click on the Set button located next to Background Image.**

    An Open dialog box appears.

4. **Select the image file you want to use from the list of files on your hard drive.**

5. **Click on Open.**

The path (location) of the image file and a thumbnail representation of the image appear in the Document Options dialog box.

6. **Click on OK to close the Document Options dialog box.**

To remove an image from the background of your Web page:

1. **Choose Document Options from the Edit menu.**

2. **Choose Basic from the pop-up menu or click on the Colors and Background tab.**

3. **Click on the None button to the right of Background Image.**

If you've gone and messed up your color settings, you can use the following steps to reset them:

1. **Choose Document Options from the Edit menu.**

2. **Choose Basic from the pop-up menu or click on the Colors and Background tab.**

3. **Click on Use Defaults.**

This procedure zaps all the background images from your Web page and resets the color of all links.

Creating See-Through Images

You can make a single color in an image transparent so that the background of the Web page shows through. This feature comes in handy to make the rectangular background and outline of an image disappear.

To make the background of an image transparent:

1. **Make the image background a single color.**

Use an image-editing program (such as Adobe PhotoShop or ClarisWorks) if necessary (for example, with most scanned images and photographs).

2. **Add the image to your Web page.**

3. **Select the image and open the Image Editor (refer to Figure 10-2) or double-click on the image.**

4. **Click on the Set button next to Transparency and Interlace to open the image file in the Transparency and Interlace Editor.**

   (You can see the Transparency and Interlace Editor in Figure 10-4.)

5. **Click on the Interlace button in the toolbar.**

6. **Move the pointer over the image until the pointer turns into an eyedropper.**

7. **Select the color of the image you want to make transparent by clicking on the color while using the eyedropper pointer icon.**

   All pixels of the selected color become transparent.

8. **Close the Transparency and Interlace Editor and save the changes to the image.**

The color you selected in the image becomes transparent so you can see the background of your Web page through that color.

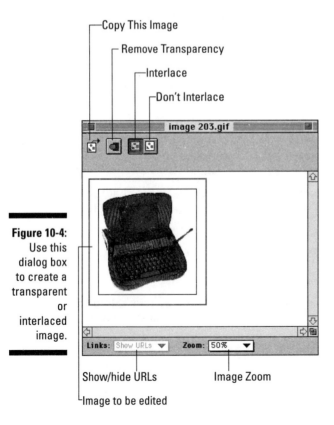

Figure 10-4:
Use this
dialog box
to create a
transparent
or
interlaced
image.

To remove a transparency from an image:

1. **Open the image in the Transparency and Interlace Editor.**

2. **Click on the Remove Transparency button in the toolbar.**

✔ Professional Web designers often use nifty color stripes that run down the left-hand side of a page. They accomplish this by creating a single line graphic 472 pixels wide and 1 or 2 pixels high that fades from a bold color to white (or black). Then they paste this graphic into the background of the page. (In Claris Home Page, for example, you'd paste it into the Basic Preferences dialog box.)

✔ Design for the default page size (generally a 14-inch monitor). One frustrating element of designing for the World Wide Web is that you as a designer don't have control over the Web page delivery environment. Your readers can resize their windows, which may alter the amount of text on each line of your page. In general, it's best to design for the default screen size and anticipate that users may resize the screen, making it smaller or larger.

Tying Your Interlaces

When browsers download images, the images usually appear line by line, from top to bottom, on the screen. If an image is especially large and takes a long time to download, your visitors likely will growl, tap their fingers, and then bail out to another page. The anticipation is agonizing at 28,800 bps modem speed and downright torture at 14,400 bps.

To avoid the problem of lengthy waits while files download off the Web, Claris Home Page makes it easy for you to create what's known as an *interlaced* image. When a browser downloads an interlaced GIF image, a rough outline of the entire image is displayed first, and then the detail is gradually added. The Web page visitor can make a decision much more quickly about staying at your school's home page or surfing off in another direction.

Several graphics programs are available on the Web to help you create interlaced images (you can find them at `http://www.downloads.com`), but you won't need them if you're using Claris Home Page 2.0. To create an interlaced image with Claris Home Page 2.0:

1. **Double-click on the image to open the Image Object Editor.**

2. **Click on the Set button next to Transparency and Interlace (refer to Figure 10-2) to open the image file in the Transparency and Interlace Editor.**

The image appears in the Transparency and Interlace Editor (see Figure 10-4).

3. **Click on the Interlace button in the toolbar.**

4. **Close the Transparency and Interlace Editor and save the changes to the image.**

The image file is stored and displayed as an interlaced image.

To change the image back to a noninterlaced image:

1. **Repeat Steps 1 through 3 listed previously to create an interlaced image.**

2. **Click on the Don't Interlace button (see Figure 10-4).**

3. **Close the editor and save the image.**

To make Claris Home Page automatically convert PICT and BMP images into interlaced GIF images:

1. **Choose Preferences from the Edit menu.**

2. **Choose Images from the pop-up menu or click on the Images tab to display a new set of options.**

3. **Select Make Interlaced GIF.**

4. **Click on OK.**

Storing Your Image Files

Claris Home Page allows you to specify the folder (or subdirectory) where your GIF files are stored when you add PICT or BMP images to your Web page. The program also prompts you for a filename and location each time it converts a PICT or BMP image to a GIF file. (See the sidebar entitled "Converting image files," earlier in this chapter.)

If you store your image files folder in the same folder that contains your Web pages, each relative *path* to the images is always maintained, even when you move your Web site onto your Web server. The path can be broken, however, if you move either an image file, or the folder containing the image file, or the Web page that references the image. If you do this, you must reinsert the image into the Web page to set the new path. (For information about paths, see Chapter 11.)

If you need to store your graphic images file folder somewhere other than within the Web site folder in your system, you can specify an absolute path to the image files that won't change when you move your Web page files to a new location. For example, the images you add to your Web pages may already reside in a special image folder on the Web server that you're going to use for your Web pages.

To set the default location where Claris Home Page stores the converted GIF files:

1. **Choose Preferences from the Edit menu.**
2. **Choose Images from the pop-up menu or click on the Images tab to display a new set of options.**
3. **Click on Set.**
4. **If you're on a Macintosh, navigate to the folder where you want to store the created images and click on Select "folder name." If you're in Windows, enter the directory path where you want to store the created images.**
5. **Click on OK.**

To ask Claris Home Page to prompt you for a filename and location each time it converts an image file:

1. **Choose Preferences from the Edit menu.**
2. **Choose Images from the pop-up menu or click on the Images tab.**
3. **Select Prompt for File Name/Location.**
4. **Click on OK.**

When Claris Home Page converts a file, it prompts you to assign a filename and a location for the converted file.

To specify absolute paths to the location where you want your images to be stored:

1. **Choose Preferences from the Edit menu.**
2. **Choose HTML Output from the pop-up menu or click on the HTML Output tab.**
3. **Click on the box labeled Use Absolute Pathnames.**
4. **Click on OK.**

Claris Home Page generates a complete, exact pathname that's not relative to the location of your Web page each time you insert an image. In other words, the pathname points to a specific location (subdirectory) as opposed to a relative one.

Checking Out a Home Page Library

Claris Home Page has a terrific feature, called a *library,* that serves as a convenient storage place for frequently used Web page elements. You can store your school logo, frequently used navigation buttons, clip art, tables, and forms — even pieces of raw HTML code. If you don't want to use the Claris Home Page 2.0 built-in library, you can grab graphics from the Web (with permission of the graphic image's author) or from any number of clip art disks available from your favorite Mac or PC catalog.

To display the elements of an *entry* in the open area at the bottom of the library window, select the entry listed in the top section of the window. An *entry* is what Claris Home Page calls any element stored in the library.

Using a library

The folks at Claris have provided you with a library of common clip-art images just to get you started. Using the library is pretty simple:

1. **Choose Open Library from the File menu.**

   A Library dialog box or an Open dialog box appears.

2. **Double-click on the library you want to open.**

3. **Position the Clip Art Library window (see Figure 10-5) on your screen so you can see the library's contents and your Web page simultaneously.**

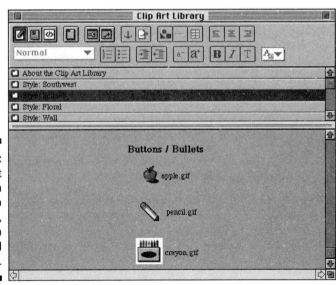

Figure 10-5: The Clip Art Library can be used to store text, buttons, clip art, and more.

To copy one element of a library entry onto your Web page, drag the element from the bottom section of the library window to your Web page.

To copy multiple elements of a library entry to your Web page, hold down the Shift key down while you drag them onto your Web page.

To copy all the elements in a library entry to your Web page, drag the icon of the entry in the top section of the library menu onto your Web page.

Editing a library

Claris Home Page allows you to edit contents of a library very easily. You can rename library entries, make new entries, add elements to an entry, add entries from other Claris Home Page libraries, and delete entries in a library.

You can even change the order of entries in a library by dragging its icons to new positions in the top section of the library window. (Good programming, Claris!) You can also edit text elements in the bottom section of the library window by using the same tools and methods you use to edit text on your Web page.

To make a new library entry:

1. **Choose New Entry from the Library menu or click on the New Entry button in the toolbar.**

   An untitled entry appears in the top section of the window that appears. You may have to scroll through the list of entries to find the new entry.

2. **Click on the Untitled new entry and enter a name for the new entry.**

   Give it a descriptive name so you'll remember what it is later!

3. **Save the new Library entry by clicking on the close box.**

You can also drag an element directly into the top section of the Clip Art Library window to make a new entry.

To add elements to the entry:

1. **Select the entry in the top section of the Clip Art Library window.**

2. **Paste the elements into the bottom section.**

   Elements can come from your computer's scrapbook/clipboard, from within other programs (graphics, text), or from other Web pages.

To add entries from another library:

1. **Open both the original and additional library.**

2. **Position them side by side.**

3. **Drag the entry from the original library to the top section in the new library window.**

To delete library elements, simply

1. **Select the library elements in the bottom section of the library window.**

2. **Press Delete.**

To rename a library entry, just

1. **Double-click on the entry name in the top section of the library window.**

2. **Enter a new name.**

Creating a new library

Libraries can contain graphics, frequently used HTML code, or practically anything else you'd find on a Web page file.

To create your own library, just choose File⇨New⇨Library. (Windows files are saved with the extension .hlb.)

Going Interactive

Images can be more than just nice pictures on your Web page. You can make them *interactive* so that the reader can click on them to perform a particular action.

Interactive images on your Web pages can include:

- ✔ Buttons designed in a way that visitors can click on them to send fill-in-the-blank form data to your Web server

- ✔ Hypertext links that allow visitors to click on a spot on your Web page to go to an anchor in the same Web page or to a different page or even to another Web site

✔ Image maps whose various parts visitors can click on to activate different links (You can find out more on the subject of creating interactive images in Chapter 14 and more on image maps in Chapter 11.)

Wow! We've come a long way since trying to figure out how to format a floppy, haven't we? Now we're placing interlaced graphics from our library into HTML-formatted Web pages stored on our own server at our own domain. Time for a well-deserved coffee break and a quick Dr. Seuss story or two for your kids — just to keep you humble.

Chapter 11

Dropping Anchors and Linking Links

In This Chapter

▶ Building internal links

▶ Building links to other people's pages

▶ Dropping anchors to specific destinations

▶ Testing your links

▶ Making image maps

*O*ne of the really great things you can do on a Web page is share your favorite Web addresses with others. Luckily, instead of typing out long *URLs (Uniform Resource Locators,* the fancy name for Internet addresses), you can set up your Web page to include clickable *hypertext links.*

Links (also known as *hyperlinks*) are those usually blue underlined text items that, when clicked, whisk you away to somewhere else on the Net. You can include hypertext links in your Web pages to allow your readers to move easily from one page to another within your site, or to other locations on the World Wide Web.

Most Web page tools, such as Claris Home Page 2.0, allow you to create several kinds of links, including:

✔ Links within your own Web site

✔ Links to other Web sites

✔ Links to FTP sites (sites packed with downloadable files and programs)

✔ Links to e-mail addresses

You can make text, images, or specific parts of an image (called an *image map*) into links. You can also create links that reference frames, which I talk about in Chapter 13.

In order to place these links in your Web page, Claris Home Page generates HTML code containing *anchors*. These anchors denote what specific piece of text on your page is linked to another site, page, or address.

The bottom line on links is that they can be created, just like most other functions on your Web page, with just a few steps by using Claris Home Page.

What's the Address?

Every link needs to have an address. This address is referred to as a URL. Claris Home Page automatically inserts the URL when you create a link to another page in your Web site or to an anchor within a Web page.

Links can use *relative paths* or *absolute paths*. *Relative paths* look like this:

```
<A HREF="pagename.html">
```

Relative paths are links that refer to files you've saved on your own fileserver in the same directory as your home page. Since the linked file resides on your own Web site, there's no need for extended pathnames (directory information) in order to access the file.

You'll use *absolute paths* to refer to Web pages stored on other servers somewhere else on the Net or those that are saved in different directories on your Web server's hard disk drive. An absolute pathname contains more path information than a relative path. Here's an example:

```
<A HREF="servername.com/MyFiles/pagename.html">
```

It's best to have the contents of your Web pages in place before you begin creating links. Sketching out a flow chart of your pages can help you keep track of where you want to add links and where those links should lead.

Linking to Other Pages in Your Web Site

With most Web page creation tools, you don't need to type the URL of a Web page within your own Web site to link to it.

To create a link to another Web page you've created within your own site using Claris Home Page 2.0 follow these steps:

1. Select the text or image you want to act as a link.

2. **Choose Link to File from the Insert menu or click on the Insert Link to File button (the one showing a document page and right-pointing arrow) on the toolbar.**

   The Insert Link to File button is ninth from left. It looks like a piece of paper with an arrow pointing away from it.

3. **Select the filename of the Web page file you want to link to.**

4. **Click on Open.**

   The text becomes underlined, and the color of the text or the image border changes to indicate the link. (To find out how to change the color of the text or underlining in a link, see Chapter 9.)

When you link to another page within your Web site, here's the HTML code that Claris Home Page generates (the "pagename" would actually be the name you specify):

```
<A HREF="pagename.html">
```

After Claris Home Page knows where the destination page is, you can easily link that page to other elements on your current page.

To create an additional link to the same Web page:

1. **Select the new text or image you want to make into an additional link.**

2. **Choose Show Link Editor from the Window menu.**

   The Link dialog box appears (see Figure 11-1).

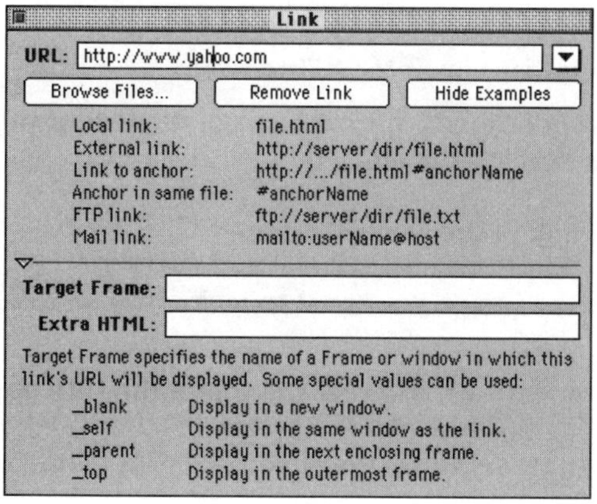

Figure 11-1:
Use the Link Editor to create links on your Web page.

3. **Click on the downward-pointing triangle icon to the right of the URL box to reveal a pop-up list of recently linked URLs.**

4. Choose the most recent URL listed at the top of the URL pop-up menu.

You can also click on the Browse Files button to locate a Web page file if it's within your site.

That's all there is to it. Your link is now set to whatever you chose from the pop-up menu.

Linking to Other Web Pages and Resources

Most hyperlinks on Web pages link visitors to other Web pages (or other resources) that are located on other people's Web servers somewhere else on the Internet. To link to another Web page or resource, you must know the exact URL for that Web page or resource, and you must enter it correctly into the Link Editor. (Just one typo and the link won't work.)

To create a hypertext or image link to another site:

1. Select the text or image you want to point to another site.

2. Choose Link to URL from the Insert menu or click on the Link Editor button (the one showing a document window and curvy right-pointing arrow) on the toolbar.

The Link Editor appears.

3. To see some examples of the correct *syntax* (HTML code format) for URLs, click on Show Examples.

4. Type the URL of the link's destination in the URL text box.

5. Press Return (Macintosh) or Enter (Windows).

The text becomes underlined, and the color of the text or the image border changes to indicate the link.

To create an additional link to the same location:

1. Select new text or the image you want to make into an additional link.

2. Choose the most recent URL listed at the top of the URL pop-up menu.

Easy as pie! Your link is now set to whatever you chose from the pop-up menu.

Table 11-1 provides a list of HTML code that most Web page creation tools generate when you create links in your pages.

Table 11-1	Hypertext Links and Their Codes
To Link To This	*Here's the HTML*
A Web page within your Web site	`file.html`
A Web page outside your Web site	`http://sitename/dir/` `file.html`
An anchor on the same Web page	`#anchorname`
An anchor on a page within your Web site	`file:html#anchorname`
An anchor on a page outside your Web site	`http://.../` `file.html#anchorname`
An anonymous FTP site	`ftp://sitename/dir/file.txt`
An e-mail address	`mailto:e-mailaddress`

You can use links to send an electronic message to a specific *e-mail address*. When links to e-mail addresses are used, the browser opens an e-mail message window where you can type and send a message addressed to that e-mail address.

Anchors Aweigh!

Because a hyperlink is really just a cross-reference point, it is also possible to use links to jump around *within* a page or to jump to a specific point somewhere on another page within your site. Most Web page tools make it easy to create a link to a *specific point* (called an *anchor)* on your Web page. These anchors can jump your visitors to specific points on the same page that the link itself is on or to anchors on other Web pages.

You need to do two things to create a link to an anchor: Create an anchor at the place on your Web page where you want your readers to end up when they click on a link (destination point), and create a link to the anchor from the text or image that the reader would click on to jump to a destination (origin point).

Specifying an anchor — the link destination

Here are the steps to creating a link to an anchor (destination point) in Claris Home Page 2.0:

1. Position your cursor where you want to place the anchor in your Web page and click.

2. Choose Anchor from the Insert menu, or click on the Insert Anchor button (it looks amazingly like a boat anchor) on the toolbar.

A dialog box appears with a default name for the anchor (see Figure 11-2).

Anchor Name

Please name this Anchor:

Anchor Name Here

[Cancel]   [**OK**]

---

3. Click on OK (or you can enter a new a name for the anchor and *then* click on OK).

Be descriptive in the wording of your links. Say "QuickTime movie of our school's courtyard" and not "Click here to see a movie." Avoid using very short labels or, heaven forbid, single characters for links — they may be hard for users to click on with a mouse.

4. Choose Save from the File menu so you can link with the anchor you've created.

Claris Home Page then generates HTML code that looks pretty simple but accomplishes a complex task.

Here's an example of the HTML code for the link and the anchor point:

```
<A NAME="anchorname"></A>This is the destination text.</P>
```

In this example, "anchorname" is the name for the anchor point. Because you can have different anchor points within the same page, name it something descriptive like "aboutourschool" or "footballschedule." The text that follows ("This is the destination text.") is optional. To include multiple anchor points in one page, just visit each destination point and click on the anchor icon. Be sure to name each destination (anchor) point with a unique name.

Linking an anchor to text or an image

After you've created and named the anchors in your Web pages, you then need to create links to them (starting points) by using the following steps:

1. **Open the Web page that contains the anchor you want to link to.**

   You can also link to anchors within the same page.

2. **Open the Web page that contains the point from which you'd like to link.**

   Reposition the two windows side by side on your screen. (It'll be one window if you're linking to an anchor on the same page.)

3. **Select the text or image you want to make the link to the anchor.**

4. **Choose Link to URL from the Insert menu, or click on the Link Editor button (the one showing a document window and curvy right-pointing arrow) on the toolbar.**

   The Link Editor opens (see Figure 11-1).

5. **Enter the anchor's name preceded by a number symbol (#) in the URL text box in the Link editor or choose the anchor's name from the pop-up menu. (Click on the triangle to the right of the URL menu to see the pop-up menu choices.)**

   The text becomes underlined, and the color of the text or the color of the image border changes to indicate that the text or image is now acting as a link.

What's going on behind the scenes? Claris Home Page generates the following code for a "starting point" that jumps to an anchor:

```
<A HREF="#anchorname"></A>This is the origin text.</P>
```

The "#" sign is very important, so don't forget it. If the jump was to an anchor on another page on your site, the link may look like this:

```
<A HREF = "http://otherserver.com/#anchorname"></A>This is
          the destination text.</P>
```

Don't you just love shortcuts (even if the sign says, "Don't walk on the grass!")? Here's a great shortcut to create a link to an anchor:

1. **Open the page where you want to place the link and open the page containing the anchor.**

   Note that both pages must be named and saved before proceeding.

2. **Resize each window so that the two windows are side-by-side on your screen.**

3. **Click on the anchor icon and drag it to the position where you want the link to appear.**

4. **Release the mouse button.**

    Claris Home Page inserts a text link to the anchor.

By default, the text of the link is `filename#anchorname`, where `filename` is the name of the file containing the anchor and `anchorname` is the name of the anchor.

If you want to change the default text to different text:

1. **Select the link.**

2. **Type the new text for it within the text of the link.**

Changing an anchor name

You can change the name of an anchor at any time or add extra HTML code to it. Be aware, however, that any links you've made to the anchor must be re-created using the new name you assigned to the anchor.

To rename an anchor:

1. **Double-click on the anchor icon in your Web page.**

    The Anchor Object Editor appears. (Make sure that you're in Edit Page mode, or your double-click won't access the Anchor Object Editor.)

2. **Rename the anchor by entering the new name in the dialog box.**

Testing, Testing

After you have created links, you and your students should test them to make sure that they work. The way you test a link depends on what kind of link it is and how you want to test it.

- ✔ To test a link to a Web page or anchor within your own site in Edit mode, Command-click on the link (Mac), or Alt-click on the link (Windows).

- ✔ To test a link to a Web page or anchor within your own site in Preview mode, select Preview Page from the Window menu; then click on the link.

- ✔ To test a link to an external Web page or resource, choose Preview in Browser from the File menu to display your Web page containing the link in the default browser; then click on the link.

- ✔ Check your links regularly. Links change faster than the winds of education reform. Develop a process for you and your students to check links and log the date and time whenever you check links.

Copying or Deleting Links

You can copy and paste links between pages of your Web site, rather than re-create them multiple times, by using these steps:

1. **Select the link text or image.**

2. **Copy and paste as you would normally, or drag the link from one page to another.**

   Claris Home Page copies the entire link, including the link's address.

To delete a link, but not the text or image associated with the link:

1. **Select the link text or image.**

2. **Choose Show Link Editor from the Window menu.**

3. **Click on Remove Link.**

To delete the text or image, in addition to the link itself:

1. **Select the link.**

2. **Press Delete.**

Creating Links within Images

When you turn an image into a single hypertext link, the entire image becomes a clickable link that leads to a single destination. When you create an *image map,* however, you can link different parts of one image to separate destinations. You can post a picture of your school, for example, and have your reader transported to different locations on your Web page, depending on which part of the picture the reader clicks on.

There are two types of image maps, *client-side* and *server-side*. Server-side image maps are complex to build. They require knowing about CGI programs, Web servers, and writing complex code. Client-side image maps, however, reside entirely within the Web page that the image map is on, so you don't kneed to know anything about HTML code, CGI, or Web servers. Claris Home Page 2.0 and other Web page creation tools, such as Adobe PageMill (on the CD with this book), have features that make it easy to generate client-side image maps.

So what's the difference? Client-side image maps work only in newer browsers, such as Netscape Navigator 3.0 and Internet Explorer 3.0. If you wish to support older browsers, you can learn to build server-side image maps, or you can use several individual graphic images placed closely together to simulate an image map.

To create either kind of image map, you need to assign hotspots to the image. *Hotspots* are areas on an image map that viewers can click to open different URLs.

Because creating a server-side image map is way too complex for this book, I concentrate on walking you through the steps to create a client-side image map.

To create a client-side image map, you first need to change the *behavior attribute* of the image and then make parts of the image into linkable hotspots.

1. **Select the image and open the Image Object Editor by double-clicking on the image.**

   The Image dialog box appears (as shown in Figure 11-3).

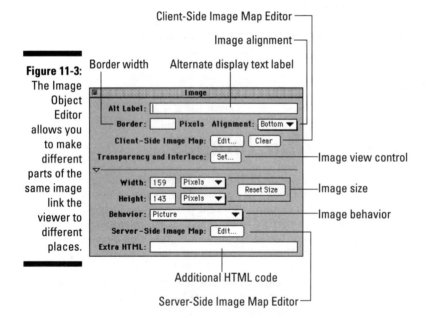

Figure 11-3:
The Image Object Editor allows you to make different parts of the same image link the viewer to different places.

2. **Click on the Edit button next to Client-Side Image Map.**

   The Image Map Editor appears (see Figure 11-4). The Rectangular and circular area on the graphic in Figure 11-4 represent hotspots. (These won't appear automatically on your graphic.) The URL information you see overprinted on each shape represents destination URLs (the location each link takes you).

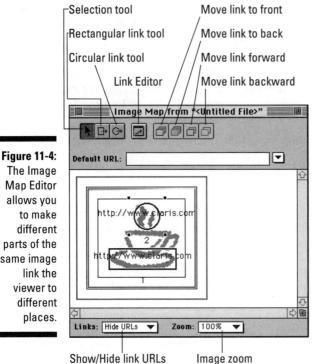

Selection tool   Move link to front

Rectangular link tool   Move link to back

Circular link tool   Move link forward

Link Editor   Move link backward

Figure 11-4:
The Image
Map Editor
allows you
to make
different
parts of the
same image
link the
viewer to
different
places.

Show/Hide link URLs   Image zoom

3. Select the Rectangular Link or Circular Link tool in the Image Map Editor toolbar.

The shape you choose depends upon the area within the image you wish to cover. If you have an area that is very irregular in shape and can't be delineated by Claris Home Page's Circular Link or Rectangular Link tools, you may wish to search the Net for other image map tools. A good place to find tools for your Mac or Windows PC is http://www.download.com and search for "image map."

4. Draw a rectangle or circle over the area of the image that you want to make into a hotspot.

The pointer changes into a crosshair pointer as you move it over the image area.

You'll also notice that the Link Editor automatically opens when you select a hotspot.

5. Enter the filename or URL of the link destination in the URL text box.

6. Repeat Steps 3 through 5 to create other hotspots in the image.

Claris Home Page numbers each hotspot as you draw it. (The number appears below the URL inside the shape you've drawn.)

If you can't see the URL names or numbers, click in the pop-up menu to the right of Links (lower-left corner of the Link Editor window) and change the value to "Show URLs."

If you draw hotspots that overlap each other, the hotspots in front (those with lower numbers, a.k.a. the ones you created first) take precedence over the ones in back. Use the Move Link buttons to change the order that layered hotspots are used (that is, to move hotspots forward or backward within the image map).

7. Save your image map and close the Image Object Editor.

The image map file is stored in the Converted Images folder.

8. Save your Web page.

It's also easy to make the areas of an image map that aren't covered by hotspots link to a specific file or URL. When a viewer clicks on the image map but does not click on a particular hotspot, a "default URL" link is activated. To specify a default URL for the image map, type the URL in the Default URL text box (located at the top of the Image Map Editor window) or choose the URL from the pop-up menu next to the Default URL text box.

Remember, these instructions work only for *client-side* image maps. To do server-side maps, your Web server must be running an *image map CGI program.* Then you must assign a link to the image that references the image map CGI program and the map file that Claris Home Page creates and stores in the same folder as the original image file. Claris Home Page generates NCSA-compatible image map files. If you'd like to find out more about writing CGI scripts, see *Perl 5 For Dummies,* by Paul Hoffman.

If you've read through this chapter, at this point you and your students have placed your images on the page, tweaked them, and linked your text and images to places somewhere out there in cyberspace. For the brave among you, you've also created image maps and worked with others to write CGI scripts. Isn't this a great feeling?

I've got to take this opportunity to remind you (again) that it's the *content* that's most important on your Web page. It's really easy to while away hundreds of hours tweaking and editing your pages. Granted, that's fun (and rewarding), but get the content done first! Okay, I'm off my soapbox now.

You can find out how many times your page is accessed (the number of "hits" on your page) and who's accessing it by using some nifty pieces of software. (These software programs generally reside on a Web server.) Surf to http://www.downloads.com and use the search term "tracking" for more information.

Chapter 12
Turning the Tables

● ●

In This Chapter

▶ Creating a table

▶ Using the Table Object Editor

▶ Resizing and other stuff

● ●

*A*t times, you and your students may find yourselves with lots of data on your Web pages that screams for organization. There's a nifty HTML format called a *table* that answers your call. Webmasters use tables for displaying images, creating menus, and much more. You and your students can also use tables to help contain and control the information on your Web page.

Just What Is a Table?

A table is basically a rectangular arrangement of rows and columns on the screen. The *matrix* (or setup) of rows and columns is made up of single blocks of information called *cells*. Within a cell, you can insert text, images, lists, form elements, and even other tables. Anything that can be placed into an HTML document (yes, even sound and multimedia elements) can be placed into a table cell.

If you don't feel like learning to create tables (which, incidentally, is a cinch if you're using most Web page creation tools), you can also go back to organizing columns of data the old-fashioned way by using the ⟨PRE⟩ . . . ⟨/PRE⟩ (preformatted) HTML text tag pair to line things up on your page. The ⟨PRE⟩ tag (see Chapter 9 for more on this) works only with text and it displays your table in monospace (the default is usually the ubiquitous Courier) font, which (if you don't mind my saying so) is pretty ugly.

Figure 12-1 shows how the fictitious Beacon Hill High might use a table to organize school data.

Figure 12-1:
A table, such as the one shown in the center of this figure, is a great way to format information for easy navigation.

Setting a Table with the Table Object Editor

Web page tools, such as Claris Home Page 2.0, make table creation very simple. Like many other functions, this one involves pointing, clicking, and selecting. To create a table, follow these steps:

1. **Locate the place on your Web page where you want a table to appear, place the insertion point (cursor), and click with the mouse button.**

2. **Choose Table from the Insert menu or click on the Insert Table icon (the one that's divided into six boxes) on the toolbar.**

   A table with two rows and two columns appears, along with the Table dialog box, also called the Table Object Editor (see Figure 12-2).

You can also open the Table dialog box in any one of three other ways:

- ✔ Double-click on a table border.
- ✔ Click on a table, and choose Show Object Editor from the Window menu.
- ✔ Click on a table, and click on the Object Editor button in the toolbar.

To enter data into your table, just click into a cell and type away, or use the Table dialog box to add additional rows and columns, change the size of borders, or set other attributes (see Figure 12-2) to the table and the elements it contains.

Figure 12-2:
The Table
dialog box
lets you
change the
appear-
ance and
behavior
of the
elements
inside your
table.

Set size of rows/columns

Set width of table border

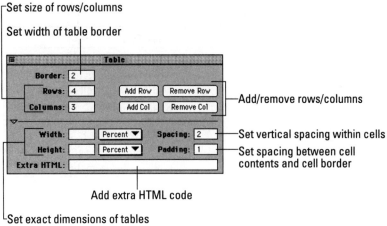

Add/remove rows/columns

Set vertical spacing within cells

Set spacing between cell
contents and cell border

Add extra HTML code

Set exact dimensions of tables

This is WAY too easy, isn't it?

You should see the magic that Claris Home Page performs behind the scenes with HTML and your Web page. To see what the HTML code that Home Page generates when you create a table looks like, see Table 12-1.

Table 12-1	HTML Table Code and What It Does
HTML Code	*Does This*
`<TABLE>`	Tells the browser to expect to begin a table — this is important!
`<TABLE BORDER>`	Places a border around the table — optional.
`<CAPTION>...</CAPTION>`	Adds a caption placed outside the table — optional.
`<TH>...</TH>`	Indicates a table header — optional.
`<TR>`	Indicates a table row.
`<TD>...</TD>`	Indicates table data — each `<TD>...</TD>` tag pair represents one column. (Enter the data for each cell between the `<TD>...</TD>` tags.)
`<TD ALIGN=LEFT>...</TD>`	Works the same as the plain old `<TD>` table data tag but also aligns text — optional. (CENTER and RIGHT alignment can also be specified here.)

(continued)

Table 12-1 *(continued)*

HTML Code	Does This
`<TD VALIGN=TOP>...</TD>`	Works the same as the plain old `<TD>` tag but also positions text at the TOP, MIDDLE, or BOTTOM of cell — optional.
`<TR>`	Adds another row.
`<TD>...</TD>`	Adds more data.
`</TABLE>`	Close tag that indicates the end of the table — this is important!

Changing a Table with the Table Object Editor

After you've added a table to your page, you can use the Table dialog box (the Object Editor) to change the appearance and *behavior* of the table. (If only it were that easy to change the behavior of students!) You can do things such as create invisible borders or `ALIGN` text within cells. The Table dialog box appears automatically when you create a table, as mentioned in the previous section of this chapter.

Remember, you can get to the "hidden" features in any Table Object Editor by clicking on the little right-pointing triangle icon at the bottom of the Table dialog box. When additional features are displayed, the triangle points downward.

To change the attributes of a table:

1. **Select the table (or cell) by dragging over it with your mouse.**

2. **Change the settings as desired in the Table dialog box.**

To apply the new settings, press Tab or click on the close box in the Table dialog box.

Table 12-2 shows what the Table Object Editor is capable of doing.

Table 12-2	Table Object Editor Options
Table Settings	*Will Do This*
Border	Changes the thickness of the borders of the table. (Set border to 0 [zero] to make the table's borders invisible.)
Rows	Changes the number of rows in the table. (Rows are added to and subtracted from the bottom of the table. The maximum number of rows is 50.)
Columns	Changes the number of columns in the table. (Columns are added to and subtracted from the right side of the table. The maximum number of columns is 20.)
Add Row	Adds a row directly below the selected cell or table.
Remove Row	Deletes the selected row or the bottom row of the selected table and its contents.
Add Columns	Adds a column directly to the right of the selected cell or table.
Remove Columns	Deletes the selected column or the last column to the right of the selected table and its content.
Width	Changes the width of the table.
Height	Changes the height of the table.
Spacing	Changes the amount of space *between* cells (by making the border thicker).
Padding	Changes the amount of space *around* the data within cells.
Extra HTML	Adds other HTML attributes to your table. (Use this to set other attributes for the <TABLE> tag.)
Alignment	Changes the alignment of elements within the cell.
Row Span	Changes the number of rows that a cell spans.
Col Span	Changes the number of columns that a cell spans.
Header Cell	Makes the selected cell a table header cell for you to label a row or column.
Extra HTML	Adds other HTML attributes to a particular cell. (This is where you can specify additional parameters for the <TH> or <TD> tags.)

Claris Home Page also allows you to use the Table Object Editor to change the attributes of *individual cells* in a table. To do this just:

1. Select any table cell by clicking on it.

2. Change the attribute as desired by using the Table dialog box.

Adding Text to a Cell

You can add text to a cell in any number of ways:

- ✔ Just click into the cell to select it and start typing to enter text!
- ✔ You can copy and paste text from one cell to another.
- ✔ You can copy and paste text from another application (that supports the copy-and-paste function) into your table.
- ✔ You can copy and paste text from an open Web page into your table.
- ✔ You can drag text from one cell to another.
- ✔ You can drag text from an open Web page into your table.

If, on the other hand, you want to delete text in a cell, simply select the cell and press the Delete key.

Adding "Cellular" Images

No, I'm not talking about *those* cells; however, after years of looking at cheek tissue and onion cells under a microscope, I may have gone a bit batty.

It turns out that most Web page creation tools make it easy to insert a graphic image into a cell. To do so with Claris Home Page 2.0, follow these steps:

1. **Select the cell by clicking in it.**

2. **Choose Image from the Insert menu.**

   The Open dialog box appears.

3. **Select the image you want to insert.**

4. **Click on Open.**

   That's all there is to it! The graphic appears in the cell.

When you insert an image into a cell, the cell expands downward if the image height is larger than the cell height. The width of the cell, however, does not change automatically to accommodate the image, so you may need to adjust it.

There are a number of other ways to insert an image into a cell:

- ✔ You can copy and paste an image into your table from other cells.
- ✔ You can copy and paste an image into your table from other Web pages.

✔ You can also copy and paste an image into your table from other applications that support copy and paste.

✔ You can select and drag an image from other cells to insert a copy of it.

✔ You can select and drag an image from open Web pages to insert a copy of it.

Growing Your Table

Most Web page creation tools provide a number of ways to change the overall size of your table and the size of the table's cells:

✔ By changing the width or height of a table in relation to the browser window

✔ By changing the number of rows or columns in a table

✔ By changing the table's dimensions using the mouse

✔ By changing the size of individual cells

To change the size of a table and the rows and columns within the table, use the Width and Height settings in the Table Object Editor (the Table dialog box). The larger the width and height numbers, the larger the table. The overall table size will adjust when you make changes to the cells. Individual cell sizes will adjust when you resize the whole table.

To resize a table in relation to the browser window:

1. **Double-click on the table border to open the Table dialog box.**

2. **Choose a setting type (pixels or percent) from the Width or Height pop-up menus (refer to Figure 12-2).**

3. **Enter the number of pixels or a percentage for the table's width or height.**

   If you selected Default for the width or height, you don't need to enter a value.

   It takes a bit of playing around and experimentation to get a sense of what changing the pixel and percentage numbers does to your table. I'd recommend using percentage most of the time; it somehow seems easier (for me at least) to judge how much of the table, in percent, would be covered by a cell or cells.

4. **Press Return (Mac) or Enter (Windows).**

Using your mouse is the easiest method to resize your table. Just select the table and drag its *bottom* handle to change the height of the table, drag the *right-side* handle to change the width of the table, or drag the *lower-right* corner handle to change the width and height at the same time.

Spanning Cells

You can expand a cell so that it spans two or more rows or columns (see Figure 12-3). When you make a cell span more than one row, it expands downward. When you make a cell span more than one column, it expands to the right.

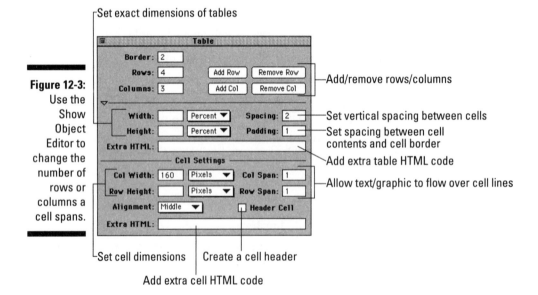

Figure 12-3:
Use the Show Object Editor to change the number of rows or columns a cell spans.

To change the number of rows or columns that a cell spans, try these steps:

1. **Click inside the cell to select it.**

   A heavy line appears on the inside of the cell.

2. **Choose Show Object Editor from the Window menu or click on the Object Editor button (the one with a little wrench) on the toolbar to open the Table dialog box.**

3. **Enter the number of rows or columns you want the cell to span in the box next to Rows and Columns.**

4. **Press Tab or click on the close box of the Table dialog box.**

There's an even easier way to change the number of rows or columns that a cell spans! Try clicking on the cell to select it and dragging the bottom handle to change the number of rows it spans. Or drag the right-side handle to change the number of columns it spans, or drag the lower-right corner handle to change the number of rows and columns it spans at the same time. Told you it was easy!

Aligning Table and Cell Elements

Any element that is in a table cell can be aligned to the border of the cell or to other elements in a row of cells. You can also align text elements to the left, right, or center of a cell.

To align elements vertically:

1. **Click in the cell to select the element.**

2. **Choose Show Object Editor from the Window menu or click on the Object Editor button (the one with a little wrench) on the toolbar to open the Table Object Editor.**

3. **Choose a setting from the Alignment pop-up menu.**

   Choose Top to align elements at the top of the cell.

   Choose Middle to align elements in the middle of the cell.

   Choose Bottom to align elements along the bottom of the cell.

   Choose Baseline to align text along the baseline of each character.

The *baseline* is an imaginary line between the main part of a letter and its *descender* — for example, the descender is the "leg" on the letter *g*. This setting is generally used in tables in which each cell contains a single line of text. When you are viewing your page in Claris Home Page, however, the text will look like it's top aligned. Preview the page in your browser to see how it will actually look to a reader.

Now you know the secret of tables! Table manners, of course, require that your tables don't overwhelm the page and that the elements in the table should somehow be related to each other and fit into the design of the page.

It's also common to use a table as a placeholder for text that jumps the visitor to other spots on your page. (See Chapter 11 for information on links that jump readers to other spots on your Web page.) Hmmm . . . does that mean it's okay to put your anchor on the table? Not in *my* house you don't!

Part IV
Jazzing Up Your Web Page

"What do you mean you're updating our school's Web site?"

In this part . . .

*H*ere are a bunch of tips and techniques for using
Claris Home Page 2.0 and other tools to add "fancy
stuff" to your Web page. In this chapter, I explore frames,
forms, sound files, QuickTime, VRML, Java, and
JavaScript. (I know I've tossed out lots of nerd-speak.
Don't worry, though. You'll understand it in no time!)
Some of the fancy stuff I've included, by the way, will
require you to enter your own HTML code because Claris
Home Page (and most other "Web page processors")
don't yet support an easier way to do everything. So, I
tried to make it easy for you to "go techno" and write
your own HTML code using any standard word processor.

Chapter 13

Getting Framed

• •

• •

*T*here was a time when things were much simpler. A *table* referred to the place in the lunchroom where you ate your meals. A *web* was the thing that a spider spun. *Surfers* were found only at the beach. And, *frames* were the things that you put around pictures before you hung them on the wall.

Now, the Internet has introduced a whole bunch of jargon that has made life just a bit more complicated. Fortunately, savvy folks like us absorb the ubiquitous Internet media hype just enough to have mastered these terms. *Tables* and *frames* as you know (or will find out by reading this chapter and Chapter 12) are parts of a Web page that are visited by Web surfers.

Just so you don't get cocky, though, here are a few more terms you probably don't yet know but can impress your friends by using at your next party. As my sixth-grade teacher was fond of telling us, make it a point to refer to each of these terms three times and these words "will become yours."

- ✔ **arachnerd** *n.* a person who spends more time on the Internet than eating, sleeping, and *living.*

- ✔ **e-loot** *n.* 1. the electronic equivalent of what's *not* in my wallet 2. *v.* stealing money from someone using the Internet (as in "Those kids just e-looted the Federal Reserve out of $10 million!").

- ✔ **RT** *n.* means *real time* as opposed to meeting someone in cyberspace (as in "I'll meet you next week, RT.").

- ✔ **beanie-spinner** *n. see* arachnerd.

- ✔ **cyber-patties** *n.* a rather graphical reference to those sites you and your students might visit that have no redeeming value.

✔ **Web-widow/Web-widower** *n.* an indication you're one if you don't see your spouse for several days, then he/she emerges from in front of the computer and asks you for the URL for the search engine he/she might use to find your kids.

What's a Frame?

The term *frame* is Web-speak for a design element used to divide your Web page into segments that contain separate chunks of text, graphics, and other media. Each chunk may be located on a different Web page and with frames each of these chunks is visible simultaneously.

Browsers usually display just one Web page at a time, but with frames you can, for example, make standard menu items (like an index) remain on the screen while the content changes on your Web page. In this case, you'd use one frame for the Web site menu and another for the rest of the content. For the example in Figure 13-1, I created three frames. Can you find them?

Okay. I won't leave you in suspense. One frame (a vertical one) is on the left and is a clickable menu, the second (a horizontal frame) is the school logo, and the third (a vertical frame) is the remaining text.

Figure 13-1:
Frames
allow you to
segment
Web pages
with each
segment
ready for
independent
navigation.

You can place as many frames on a Web page as you wish and once they're there, your Webmaster can change their size, orientation, and contents with the click of a mouse. You can even embed frames within frames (if you want to get really fancy).

Making Frames

A new frame document contains a single frame inside which you can display one Web page. You can also add horizontal frames, vertical frames, and frame lists (frames within a frame) to display more than one Web page at a time.

 Right up front, I have to give you one caution: If you decide to use frames, be aware that they are a relatively new feature of most graphical Web browsers such as Netscape Navigator and Microsoft Internet Explorer and aren't supported on some older versions of browsers. If many of your visitors use older versions of Netscape Navigator or other browsers, they won't see your document in frames. Instead, they will see the explanatory message that Claris Home Page automatically adds to frame documents for readers who use browsers that don't support frames.

Opening a frame document

Claris Home Page 2.0 automatically opens two frame documents when using the Edit Frames mode. This is a special mode available only when you are working with frame documents. There are a few other modes you may also want to select:

- ✔ Use Preview Page mode to view the message that appears in browsers that don't display frames. (This message gives the reader an explanation of why the frames aren't visible.)

- ✔ Switch to Edit Page mode to edit the explanatory message that appears in browsers that don't display frames.

- ✔ Use the Edit HTML Source mode to directly edit the HTML source code of the frame document.

To begin a new frame document in Claris Home Page 2.0, all you really need is an idea of what individual pages you'd like to include in as frames. Then, try this:

1. **Create several individual Web pages and store them on your hard drive in the same folder (subdirectory).**

2. **Create a new, blank page.**

3. **Choose File➪New Frame Layout.**

    Claris Home Page automatically opens a Frame Wizard dialog box like the one in Figure 13-2.

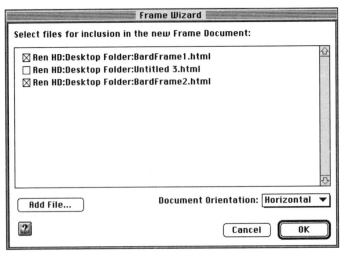

Figure 13-2:
Use the
Frame
Wizard
dialog box
to select
the pages
you want
to appear
in your
frames.

4. **Use the Add File button or click in the check box next to each page you'd like to have appear in one of the frames in your new document.**

   Choosing two files displays as a two-frame Web page, four files a four-frame Web page, and so on.

5. **Choose Vertical or Horizontal from the Document Orientation menu.**

6. **Click on OK.**

   The Web page now displays your frames with the names (pathways and locations) of the Web pages you've linked together via frames.

 You'll be able to see the contents of your frames *only* when you preview your Web page in your Web browser. Some of your changes won't appear until you save your document and the Web pages are displayed in the frames.

 Want to create a clickable link that jumps the user back out of frames into "standard Web format"? Just append _top to the end of the URL (for example, http://www.whatever.com/main.html_top) and it'll get the user free and clear.

Adding more frames to your page

If you've already created a page with several frames and you would like to add horizontal or vertical frames to your Web page in Claris Home Page 2.0, follow these steps:

1. **Choose Subdivide Vertically or Subdivide Horizontally from the Frame menu or click on the Subdivide Vertically button or Subdivide Horizontally button.**

   The single frame is divided into two horizontal or vertical frames.

2. **Choose Subdivide Vertically or Subdivide Horizontally again to add the next vertical or horizontal frame.**

It's also easy to add a new frame in a specific place in a Web page instead of subdividing an existing frame:

1. **Select a frame.**

2. **Choose Add Frame from the Frame menu.**

   Once you've added the frame, you can change its orientation by clicking on the outermost frame to select it and choosing Horizontal or Vertical from the pop-up Frame List menu.

   If you want to add a frame without choosing a Web page to display in the frame, choose Add Blank Frame from the Frame menu.

Deleting a frame

Or, if you decide you want to delete a frame, simply:

1. **Select the frame.**

2. **Press the Delete or Backspace key.**

Making frames within frames

If you're feeling really frisky and want to embed frames within other frames, you're in luck. Claris Home Page calls embedded frames a *frame list*.

To create a frame within a frame (a frame list):

1. **Click on the border of the frame to select it.**

2. **Select Subdivide Vertically or Subdivide Horizontally from the Frame menu, or choose the appropriate icon from the menu bar.**

   If you want to split the frame into two horizontal frames, select Subdivide Vertically.

   If you want to split the frame into two vertical frames, select Subdivide Horizontally.

3. **Continue selecting Subdivide Vertically and Subdivide Horizontally to divide the frame any way you like.**

Is framed the way *you* want to be?

A big controversy on the Net these days concerns the use of frames. Naysayers say that frames aren't the greatest design tool because they:

✔ Restrict valuable screen real estate

✔ Slow down the browser

✔ May confuse visitors if not used correctly

The yay-sayers, however, say that frames:

✔ Make Web site navigation easier

✔ Allow you to provide a common, easy-to-use interface between pages in your site

I suggest jumping on the Net and viewing lots of pages with frames (begin at http:\\www.netscape.com) and see what makes sense for you and your visitors. One way to please everyone is to take the time to create both a "frames" version of your page and a "non-frames" version — allowing the visitor to make the choice on your opening page.

Taming Frames with the Frame Object Editor

After you've created a Web page and added frames to it, you can use the Frame Object Editor to change the appearance and behavior of your frames. Use the Frame Object Editor to name a frame, associate frames to Web pages, and apply other attributes to frames.

Claris Home Page gives you three ways to open the Frame Object Editor:

✔ Double-click on a frame.

✔ Click on a frame, then choose Show Object Editor from the Window menu.

✔ Click on a frame, then click on the Object Editor button in the basic toolbar.

See the triangle in the middle of the window (the one under the Browse Files button)? Clicking on it expands the Frame Object Editor to display more options that allow you to name your frame (for later reference), specify the exact size and shape of the frame, and add extra HTML code to make your frame behave differently.

You can change the following frame attributes (each of these options is shown in the Frame dialog box — see Figure 13-3):

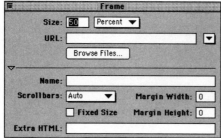

Figure 13-3:
The Frame dialog box allows you to set the attributes of one or more frames.

- ✔ Size (the size of the frame)
- ✔ URL (the URL you want displayed in that particular frame)
- ✔ Name (you need to name the frame so that the Link Editor can find it later)
- ✔ Scrollbars (to specify whether you want a scrollbar in the frame)
- ✔ Margin Width and Margin Height (to adjust the height and width of margins)
- ✔ Fixed Size (to lock the frame, making it unchangeable by the viewer)
- ✔ Extra HTML (to add code to further customize a frame)

As you make changes in each frame with the Frame Object Editor, press Tab or Return (Macintosh) or Enter (Windows). The changes will show up immediately.

Using the Frame List Editor

Use the Frame List Editor to edit *frame lists*. For example, you may want to use the Frame List Editor to change the orientation and size of a frame list.

To open the Frame List Editor, double-click on the border of a frame list. The editor looks like Figure 13-4.

From the Frame List dialog box, you can do the following:

- ✔ Change the size of the frame list
- ✔ Change the orientation of frames (to vertical or horizontal)
- ✔ Change the position of frames
- ✔ Change how the frame document will resize between browsers (in percentage of browser window size or in pixels)

Figure 13-4:
The Frame
List Editor is
used to edit
frames
embedded
within other
frames.

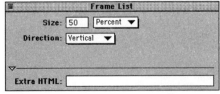

To change the size of the frame list in Claris Home Page 2.0:

1. **Enter a new number in the box marked Size.**

2. **Choose percent, pixels, or stars from the Size pop-up menu.**

   If you choose *percent,* the frame or frame list dimensions are the
   specified percentage of the frame layout document.

   If you choose *pixels,* the frame or frame list is the specified amount of
   pixels tall if it has a horizontal orientation, or the specified amount of
   pixels wide if it has a vertical orientation.

   If you choose *stars,* the frame or frame list uses all of the remaining
   space in the frame layout document. For example, if you have two
   frames, and you set the first frame to 40 percent and the second frame
   to Stars, the second frame uses the remaining 60 percent of the document. If more than one frame in a document has the Stars size attribute,
   the remaining space is divided up between them proportionately based
   on the value in the Size text box.

To change the orientation of frames, select horizontal or vertical from the
Direction pop-up menu.

To change the position of frames, you can click and drag them from one area
of the screen within your Web document to another.

Linking Frames with Web Pages

After creating the frames, your next task is to link each frame with the Web
page that will be displayed in the frame. Remember, each frame can contain
a reference to a Web page that you've written (one that is saved on your
own Web server) or a reference to a Web page that's on someone else's
server somewhere else on the Internet.

Are those *stars* in my frames?

The Claris Home Page 2.0 Frame List Editor includes a curious feature called *stars*. The stars setting automatically assigns all the available left-over space in a frame document to any new frame that's added.

For example, if you have a frame document with two frames in it, and you size the first frame at 30 percent and size the second frame to Stars, the second frame automatically uses the remaining 70 percent of the frame document.

If more than one frame in a frame document is assigned the Stars size attribute, the remaining space is divided up between them proportionally based on the value in the Size text box.

To link frames with Web pages in Claris Home Page 2.0:

1. **Double-click on the frame to open the Frame dialog box (see Figure 13-5).**

2. **Enter in the URL text box the URL of the Web page you want displayed in the frame.**

3. **Press Return (Macintosh) or Enter (Windows).**

   The URL of the Web page appears in the frame.

4. **Select the other frames in your frame document and repeat Steps 2 and 3 for each to link them with Web pages.**

5. **Save the Web page containing the frame document.**

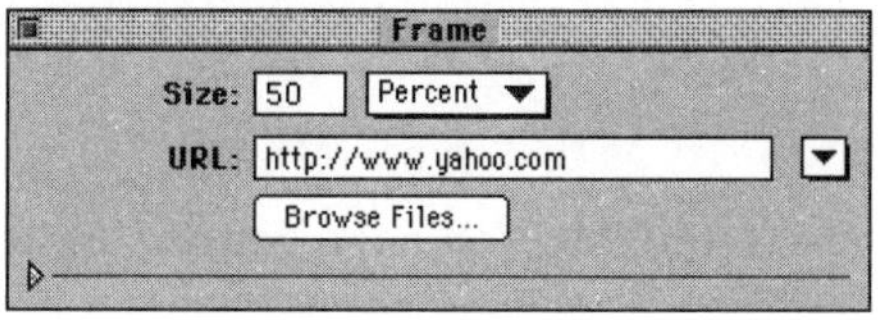

Figure 13-5:
Use the Frame dialog box to enter the URL of the Web page you want displayed in the frame.

Keeping the Original Page on Display

When a reader clicks on a hyperlink in a frame, the target page appears in the frame and the original page containing the link usually disappears from the frame.

If you want to keep the original page that contains the link in the frame, you must specify a separate frame to display the target page. This is useful for displaying a table of contents for a Web page in one frame and the actual Web page in another.

To specify a frame other than the original one to display target Web pages in Claris Home Page 2.0:

1. **Associate the Web page that contains the link with a frame in your frame document (follow Steps 1 through 3 described in the section "Linking Frames with Web Pages").**

2. **Save the frame document.**

3. **Select the frame in which you want the target Web page displayed.**

4. **Make sure the Frame object editor is open (you can double-click on the frame to open it).**

5. **Enter a URL into the URL field for the first Web page you want readers to see before they activate (click on) a link in the frame other than the original frame.**

6. **Enter a name for the target frame in the Name text box (see Figure 13-6).**

   You'll use this name to associate the link with the frame later.

   If you don't see the Name text box, click on the triangle at the bottom of the dialog box to reveal more options.

7. **Press Return (Macintosh) or Enter (Windows) and save the frame document.**

   The name of the frame appears as text in each frame.

8. **While in Edit Page mode, open the Web page containing the links.**

9. **Select the first link.**

10. **Open the Link Editor.**

    Choose Show Link Editor from the Window menu or click the Link Editor button in the basic toolbar.

11. **Type the name that you gave the frame in Step 6 in the Target Frame text box.**

    If necessary, click on the triangle icon to expand the Frame Object Editor.

Figure 13-6:
Type a
target
frame name
in the Name
text box for
later use
when you
link frames
together.

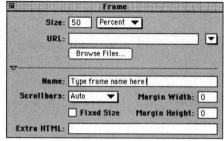

12. **Press Return (Macintosh) or Enter (Windows).**

13. **Save the Web page.**

If you haven't yet created the links in the Web page, you can use this shortcut:

1. **Choose Document Options from the Edit menu.**

2. **Choose Advanced from the pop-up menu.**

3. **Enter the name of the target frame that you specified in Step 6 in the preceding steps, in the Default Target text box (Macintosh) or in the Default Target Frame text box (Windows).**

Now all the links you create in the Web page will automatically reference the target frame.

Making a frame page into an index

A common option with a Web page frames layout is to use one of the frames as an *index* (a list of things that are displayed in other frames).

To create an index Web page to display in the index frame, do this: Choose Document Options from the Edit menu, then select Advanced from the pop-up menu, and then enter the name of the most frequently targeted (index) frame into the "Default Target Frame" blank.

When everything's entered properly, the index page will remain ready and clickable throughout the visitor's time on your site.

Are You Framed?

Testing your frames requires saving your Claris Home Page document and viewing (opening) the document from within Microsoft Explorer, Netscape Navigator, or another browser because you can't view the finished product in Claris Home Page's Preview or Edit modes.

In case you're wondering what's going on behind the scenes as your Web page tool creates frames, here's what the Raw HTML code would look like for a page with three frames (with no visible border separating them) including a header, a menu running down the left-hand side, and the balance used for body copy. The text between the <NOFRAMES>...</NOFRAMES> tags indicates what message "frameless" browsers will display for the reader:

```
<FRAMESET rows="113,82%" border=0>
<NOFRAMES><BODY>
<P>This page is designed to be viewed by a browser that
          supports Netscape's Frames extension. This text
          will be shown by browsers that do not support
          the Frames extension.</P>
</BODY>
</NOFRAMES>
   <FRAME SRC="header.html" name="View in Browser" scrolling="no">
  <FRAMESET cols="21%,78%">
   <FRAME SRC="menu.html" name="MenuFrame" marginWidth="100">
   <FRAME SRC="body.html" name="ContainerFrame">
  </FRAMESET>
</FRAMESET>
```

Well, you're framed! Now you can set about frustrating all those frame-haters out there. Don't get me wrong, however. I like frames. When used judiciously, they can be a sterling organizational tool.

As you and your students plan your Web site, consider making *both* a framed and frameless version of your home page to accommodate the millions of "frameless" folks out there.

Chapter 14

Creating Interactive Forms

● ●

In This Chapter

▶ Filling in forms

▶ Creating your own forms

▶ Buttons, fields, and boxes

▶ What goes on behind the scenes

● ●

*T*he mere mention of the word *form* causes most educators to repeat, over and over, "Use a Number 2 pencil, and be sure to make your marks heavy and dark." We use forms for standardized tests (remember those "bubble sheets"?), grade reporting, attendance gathering, certification renewal, and much more.

Forms, as it turns out, can also be a terrific way to collect information from people who visit your Web page. Through the magic of HTML and a good Web page authoring tool, you and your students can create your own forms and post them to your Web site.

Filling in Forms

Interactive forms allow you to get information from people who visit your site. The process typically goes something like this: The visitor logs on to your site and fills in information in the blanks you provide. When complete, the contents of the form are *posted* (submitted) somewhere for processing and are either sent to an e-mail address or stored on a *server* (a computer that keeps files as a central resource for other computers) for later use.

If your form content is sent to a Web server that processes requests for information, the information can be checked and processed in real time, and a reply can be generated (which probably requires another form!) and then returned to your visitor. You can also send the information to yourself or to someone else via e-mail. Mailing the results back to you requires just dropping a letter into your e-mail box. You and your students can then use your built-in processor (your brains) to make the information meaningful.

Forms can be used for many things. In the form shown in Figure 14-1, a school polled the community to find out if the community supported a bond bill for educational technology. Suddenly, those boring forms became an essential element in the political process and a great interdisciplinary activity!

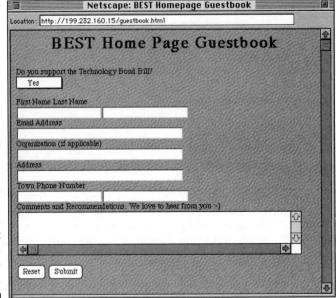

Figure 14-1: Forms are a useful way of capturing information about visitors to your Web site.

Creating a Form

Several Web page creation tools, such as Adobe PageMill, Microsoft Front Page, and Claris Home Page, allow you to create forms easily. (You'll find demo versions of PageMill 2.0 and Home Page 2.0 on the CD that comes with this book.) All you have to do is come up with a basic design and purpose; then let the point-and-click features help you with the rest.

You can create one form per Web page when using Claris Home Page. (PageMill and Front Page also limit the number of forms per page.) Your form can contain lots of things besides just text, such as images and tables. Making a form is simple — all you have to do is add each part of the form separately and arrange the parts on the page.

Form parts can be text areas, text fields, pop-up menus, buttons, or check boxes that visitors can select, as well as "submit" buttons that visitors can click on to send their input to your Web server. (You can also include a button for resetting visitors' input when they make mistakes, and a blank field for adding a password, in your form.)

All form parts can be changed the same way you change the other stuff on your page. You can copy, move, resize and delete them by using the same methods you use for other elements.

Adding form parts

It's almost as easy as 1, 2, 3 (and 4, and 5) to add form parts (also called *elements*) to your Web page.

1. **Place the cursor in the spot in the page where you want the form part to appear.**

2. **Click the mouse button once to set the insertion point.**

3. **Choose Insert⇨Forms.**

4. **Select a forms part by choosing Insert⇨Forms⇨Pop-up Menu or bring up the Forms palette (see Figure 14-2) by choosing Show Forms Palette from the Window menu.**

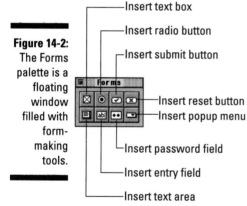

Figure 14-2:
The Forms palette is a floating window filled with form-making tools.

— Insert text box
— Insert radio button
— Insert submit button
— Insert reset button
— Insert popup menu
— Insert password field
— Insert entry field
— Insert text area

5. **Select the part and open its Object Editor by selecting Show Object Editor from the Window menu or by double-clicking on the part.**

   Figure 14-3 shows the Object Editor for a text element.

6. **Enter the name (arbitrary, but important to remember later when you learn to program buttons and fields) and other "vital statistics" for the part (such as size and length) in the Object Editor.**

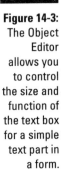

Figure 14-3:
The Object
Editor
allows you
to control
the size and
function of
the text box
for a simple
text part in
a form.

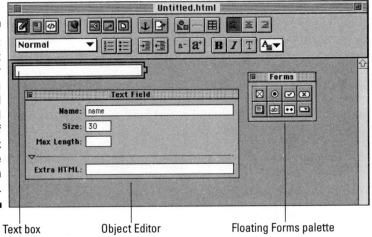

Text box   Object Editor   Floating Forms palette

The name of the part is used by the *CGI script* (a special program written and stored on your Web server) to locate the visitor's input. Names are used to identify variables from your form and can be used by the CGI scripts to sort, extract, and reformat data from a form. The name matters less if you're having the output of your form sent to your e-mail address.

7. **Press Return (Macintosh) or Enter (Windows) to accept your changes.**

Adding a text field

To create a *text field,* choose Insert⇔Forms⇔Text Field. The entry box shown in Figure 14-4 appears.

Figure 14-4:
A text field
contains
only one
line of text.

Enter your last name:

An alternative method of creating a text field is to click on the text field icon in the floating Forms palette.

Text fields can contain *only one line of text,* can be 1 to 500 characters wide, and can only be resized horizontally. These fields are generally used for brief information, such as a name, phone number, or parts of an address.

You can set the maximum number of characters that your visitors can enter in the Maximum Length text box by double-clicking on the field and changing the number in the Object Editor.

It's always a good idea to add a label next to a text field to show the visitor what kind of information to input, or to provide a default value to be input if the visitor doesn't enter anything in the field. In Figure 14-4, for example, I created the instructions "Enter your last name" to help visitors to the Web page.

Here's what's happening behind the scenes in HTML code to create a text field for entry of a last name up to 30 characters long:

```
Last name:<INPUT TYPE="text" NAME="last" VALUE=""
         SIZE=30></P>
```

Adding a text area

Sometimes one line of text isn't enough for people to say what they have to say. Claris Home Page *text areas* allow your visitors to enter multiple lines of text. The size of a text area is measured in rows and columns, with each row equivalent to one character in width and each column equivalent to one character in height. A text area can be 1 to 100 rows wide and from 5 to 500 columns high. (If you create a 100 x 500 text area, those folks standing in Times Square looking at the Jumbo-Tron screen will have nothing on your Web page readers.)

The size of a text area does not limit the amount of text that your visitors can enter; if more text is entered, the text area scrolls to accommodate it.

To create a text area, choose Insert⇨Forms⇨Text Area. A blank form area appears in your Claris Home Page work area (see Figure 14-5).

Figure 14-5:
A text area is a scrolling window in which multiple lines of text can be entered.

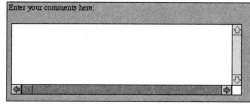

The code that Claris Home Page generates for a text area that measures 4 rows wide by 20 columns tall looks like this (the text area entry can be anything you choose):

```
<TEXTAREA NAME="Description" ROWS=4 COLS=20>
The text you've entered in the text area appears here.
</TEXTAREA>
```

Claris Home Page lets you enter the text and display it in Edit mode as it will appear in the text area window. This is what-you-see-is-what-you-get formatting, so format the text to make it appear as you wish (including hard paragraph returns).

Creating a password field

You can add a field to your form that allows the Web page visitor to enter a password. Passwords allow you to limit access to information on your Web site. You will, for example, want to password protect Web pages that contain personal information about you and your students. For added security, the password field displays the entry as a series of bullets as the user enters the password.

To create a password box, follow these steps:

1. **Choose Insert⇨Forms.**

2. **Choose Password or click on the Password icon in the floating Forms palette.**

   The Password box is basically just a text field box that turns your text into bullets (see Figure 14-6).

Figure 14-6:
A password field asks the Web page visitor to enter a password. It then displays text as bullets for security.

To use your password, click here:

••••

Claris Home Page generates the following HTML code as it creates a password box that accepts a password of up to four characters:

```
Enter password:<INPUT TYPE="password" NAME="Password"
         VALUE=""
SIZE=30 MAXLENGTH=4>
```

I typed in the words "Enter password" before choosing Password from the Insert⇨Forms menu. SIZE specifies the actual length of the password box; MAXLENGTH is the maximum number of characters allowed in the user-entered password.

Using radio buttons or check boxes in a list

Both radio buttons and check boxes give your Web page readers the ability to select from a variety of options. You may, for example, want students accessing the page to indicate their grade level and check off a list of their favorite subjects. Radio buttons allow the reader to select only one choice from a list of options. (See Figure 14-7 for sample radio buttons.) Check boxes allow the reader to select as many choices as desired from a list. (Radio buttons got their names because they resemble old-fashioned radio knobs.)

Figure 14-7:
Radio buttons enable Web page visitors to choose from a list of options.

Choose your favorite subject:

Science   ◉

Social Studies   ○

Other   ○

You need to assign the same button name to every radio button in a list so they can work together. In addition, you must assign a unique button value to each radio button or check box to differentiate it from the others in the list.

To build a list of radio button or check box choices:

1. **Type the list and place the insertion point before the first item in the list.**

2. **Choose Forms from the Insert menu and then choose Radio Button or Check Box.**

   You can also choose the Radio button icon from the floating Forms palette.

   A radio button or a check box appears in your Web page at the insertion point.

3. **Select the radio button or check box and open its Object Editor.**

4. **Type a name in the Button Name text box and press Return (Macintosh) or Enter (Windows).**

   Make sure that this name is the *same* for every radio button in a list if you want the other buttons to clear and only one button at a time to be able to be selected.

5. **Type a unique name in the Button Value text box for the radio button or check box and press Return (Macintosh) or Enter (Windows).**

   Make this value *different* from every other button in the list.

6. **To make a radio button or check box selected by default, select Checked.**

   The default choice is selected unless the visitor selects a different button or check box in the list.

   Only one radio button in a list can be the default button.

7. **Repeat Steps 2 through 6 for each radio button or check box you want to add to the list.**

Claris Home Page automatically generates the following code for a three-button list in which the user would be asked to choose one item:

```
<P>Choose your favorite subject:</P>
<P>Science <INPUT TYPE="radio" NAME="radio464346"
VALUE="1"></P>
<P>Social Studies <INPUT TYPE="radio" NAME="radio466603"
VALUE="2"></P>
<P>Other  <INPUT TYPE="radio" NAME="radio467296"
VALUE="3"></P>
```

Creating a pop-up menu or scrolling list

Pop-up menus and scrolling lists allow visitors to choose from a list of items. They're really useful for choosing predictable input like the names of states or other categories that might be too long to type reliably or too time-consuming to create. With pop-up menus, visitors can choose one (or more) items at a time from a pop-up menu and make multiple selections in a scrolling list.

Figure 14-8:
You can use pop-up menus to allow users to choose from a list of pre-determined options.

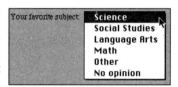

To create a pop-up menu or scrolling list:

1. **Choose Insert⇨Forms.**

2. **Choose Popup Menu from the Forms dialog box.**

3. **Select the pop-up menu and open its Object Editor by double-clicking on it.**

4. **Assign a name to the part in the Name text box.**

   The name of the part is used by the CGI script to locate the visitor's input.

5. **Type a number in the Items Visible text box.**

   Type 1 if you want the part to be a pop-up menu. If you want it to be a scrolling list, type a value greater than 1 to specify the number of list items you want to be visible in the list.

6. **Click on the Edit Items button.**

   The Define Popup List dialog box appears. (See Figure 14-9.)

7. **Enter the names of the items you want to include in the pop-up menu or scrolling list.**

   If you want to allow the visitor to select more than one item in a scrolling list, click in the Allow Multiple Selections check box.

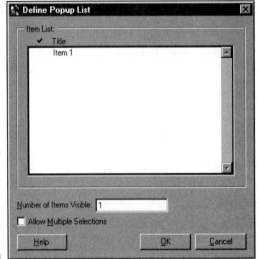

Figure 14-9:
Enter items
in your
pop-up list
in the Edit
Items dialog
box.

8. To make a particular item the default choice, click next to it in the Define Popup List dialog box.

A checkmark appears next to the item in the dialog box to indicate the default choice.

9. Click on OK.

You can make multiple items in a pop-up menu or scrolling list default items. Make sure that Allow Multiple Selections is selected, click next to all of the items, and for scrolling lists, make sure that the Number of Items Visible value is large enough that all the default items will be visible when the visitor isn't working with the list.

The HTML code generated by Claris Home Page for a simple pop-up list with four items looks like this:

```
<P>Your favorite subject: <SELECT NAME="name">
    <OPTION>Science
    <OPTION>Social Studies
    <OPTION>Language Arts
    <OPTION>Math
    <OPTION>Other
    <OPTION>No opinion
</SELECT></P>
```

I typed the words "Your favorite subject" before I chose Popup Menu from the Forms menu.

Adding a submit button

After your visitors enter data into the form, they need a way to SEND the data to you or your server. Most sites use a *submit* button. That's simply a button or graphic programmed to e-mail or copy the file for use with a CGI script.

Forms can have more than one submit button, with each button specifying a different way that the information is processed.

To insert a submit button, you can use either of two methods:

- ✔ Choose Insert⇨Forms⇨Submit Button.
- ✔ Choose Submit Button from the floating Forms palette (you can get the Forms palette by choosing Show Forms Palette from the Window menu).

When you add a submit button to your page, the default text Submit appears in your page. You can change this text if you want your visitors to see something different.

To assign an identifying name to the button for use in a CGI script:

1. **Select the button.**
2. **Open its Object Editor by double-clicking on the button.**
3. **Type a name in the Action Name box.**

   The default name is Submit.

Because submit buttons must be attached to a CGI script or e-mail address to work properly, you won't be able to test CGI functionality in either the Edit Page or Preview Page mode. Use your Web browser instead to test your submit buttons.

You can also turn an image into a submit button, so that when the visitor clicks on the image, the form is submitted.

To use an image as a submit button, double-click the image to open its Object Editor and choose Form Button from the Behavior menu, or choose Submit Button from the floating Forms palette. (Show the Forms palette by choosing Show Forms Palette from the Window menu.)

An outline appears around the image indicating that it is a submit button.

Adding a reset button

Sometimes folks make boo-boos when entering text into a form. They can either go back and retype the information, or you can make their lives easier by adding a *reset* button so visitors can clear their form entries and return the form to its default values. Similar to adding a submit button, you use the Insert⇨Forms⇨Reset Button to add a reset button to a form.

In order for a reset button to do more than just look pretty on your Web page, the button must work in tandem with a CGI script. For information about CGI scripting, see the next section, "Specifying a GCI script for your Web page." After you've got both the script and button assembled, you have to test the button in Browser mode (not Edit Page or Preview Page mode) to see the results.

When you add a reset button to your form, the default text Reset appears in it. (See Figure 14-10). You can change this text if you want the visitor to see something different.

Figure 14-10:
Users click on submit buttons to send their forms and reset buttons to clear their form.

Enter your information and click SUBMIT to send your form. Click RESET if you make a mistake.

Enter your name:

Choose your favorite subject: Science

Submit   Reset

Specifying a CGI script for your Web page

To process forms (as opposed to just mailing the data to your e-mail account), you need to "tell" your forms, via HTML code, what to do with the information the user has submitted. This is done with CGI script, which instructs your Web server to access other programs that take the data your visitor has entered into the form you've created and reformat, store, or return custom information.

You could use a CGI script to enter visitor data automatically into a FileMaker Pro (or some other) database. Most Web providers have libraries of ready-made CGI scripts you can use, or, you can write your own. You'll need special access to the Internet Service Provider's server to enter the CGI script. Most Web page creation tools, including Claris Home Page 2.0, allow you to specify a CGI script for each Web page that contains a form.

To specify a CGI script for your Web page:

1. **Choose Edit⇨Document Options.**

2. **Choose Advanced from the pop-up menu or click on the Advanced tab to display the document options information.**

3. **Enter the name and path for the CGI script file on the server in the Form Action text box.**

Figure 14-11:
The Form Action box in the Document Options menu allows you to tell the form where the CGI script resides.

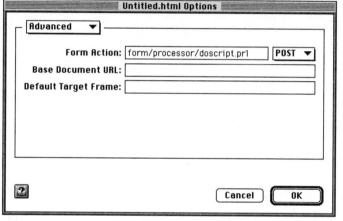

4. **Choose GET or POST from the Form Action pop-up menu to specify how you want the form data sent to the server.**

   The *POST* command is the default and the one most frequently used in HTML form processing. For more information about the GET and POST commands, pick up a copy of *Perl 5 For Dummies* by Paul Hoffman.

5. **Click on OK.**

Behind the Scenes

Here's an example of the script created by Claris Home Page that you might use for a simple form asking for a visitor's name and some free-form comments about your school's Web site. When the visitor clicks on the Submit button, the information is mailed to your e-mail address.

```
<HEAD>
<TITLE>Web Page Input Form</TITLE>
</HEAD>
<BODY>
<P>What's your name? <INPUT TYPE="text" NAME="name"
          SIZE="30"><BR>
<
<H1>What do you think of our page?</H1>
<P>Please enter your comments in the box below, then click
          the Submit button to send the comments to our
          webmaster.</P>
<FORM METHOD="post" ACTION="mailto:myname@school.edu">
<TEXTAREA NAME="comment" ROWS=6 COLUMNS=40></TEXTAREA>
<P>Thanks for your comments!</P>
<INPUT TYPE="submit"><INPUT TYPE="reset"></P>
</FORM>
</BODY>
```

When the information arrives in your mailbox, it's in "raw" form. The HTML code above, for example, would mail you something that looked like this:

```
<name=John+Smith&comment=I+really+like+your+web+page%21
```

Note that HTML uses a plus sign "+" for blank spaces. The "%21" is the ASCII translation of an exclamation mark. Okay. It's not very pretty, but it works. It's pretty simple to write a macro in your word processor or an AppleScript (Mac users) to put this stuff into readable form.

All in all, forms can be lots of fun. It doesn't take a genius to look ahead at the prospect of students taking everything from SATs to drivers' tests on the Web by using Web forms. Now if they could just invent an intelligent computer agent that would fill in the forms for us, we'd all be set!

Chapter 15

Sound Advice on Adding Sound

● ●

In This Chapter

▶ Plugging in sounds with plug-ins

▶ Using sounds effectively

▶ Adding a sound file to your page

● ●

*L*oad up one of those great educational videos into your VCR; then sit back and stick your fingers in your ears. Not very exciting, huh? That's because the sounds you hear on a videotape can add meaning to the content, raise the excitement level, or create a special mood.

In a world punctuated by *interaction* and *multisensory environments,* Web pages, no matter how visually exciting, still lack depth in some ways. Adding sound to a Web page can create the same effect as hearing, as well as seeing, a videotape.

In this chapter, I give you just enough information to begin to incorporate audio into your Web page. You can also use Java (a programming language often used to increase the functionality of the Web) and a scripting language called VBScript (and other multimedia tools as well) to add audio to your Web pages. But delving into those subjects could fill a book of its own!

On the *Web Publishing For Teachers* CD you'll find tools such as Cool Edit for Windows and Sound Machine for Macintosh that provide hours of fun with editing and tweaking your sound files. Use these tools before you incorporate the audio into your Web site.

For a great on-screen reference with directions on how to prepare and create sound files, check out `http://www.realaudio.com`.

Claris Home Page doesn't have any built-in HTML coding for adding sound to a Web page, but it's really pretty simple to add sound on your own anyway.

You can add sound to your Web pages that will work in any of three ways:

    ✔ Post files, which your readers can download and read with "helper applications," that play your sound independently of the browser

✔ Add HTML code that "kick starts" a browser plug-in and makes the plug-in play a sound file automatically

✔ Add HTML code that causes a sound to be played as surfers enter your Web site

Because there are several file formats for sound on the Web (QuickTime, WAV, MIDI, and AIFF to name just a few), your Web visitor must be equipped with either of two tools in order to hear your wonderful audio:

✔ A browser plug-in that is compatible with the sound file you've chosen

✔ An application designed for this function, such as RealAudio, which you can find at `http://www.realaudio.com` (see Figure 15-1), or that you can access through your browser's "helper application" function that plays your sound independently of the browser.

Figure 15-1:
The RealAudio player is a helper program popular for playing audio files with your Web browser.

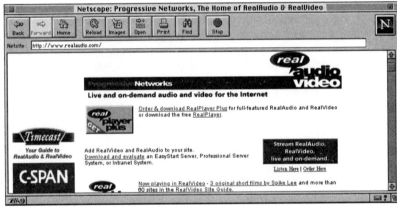

In the next section, I explain how easy it is to get the tools I just mentioned and to configure your Web browser to use them.

Plugging In an Audio Program

Before you can bring the world of sound to your Web page visitors, you need to grab a little program from the Internet and add it to the bag of tricks accessed by your Web browser. This program, one of a genre of programs called *plug-ins,* adds the capability to listen to music on a Web page, as well as deliver music, live cybercasts, audio-based multimedia shows, and more — all integrated with your Web browser. Several plug-ins play audio; my favorite is RealAudio from Progressive Networks in Seattle.

To get your own copy of RealAudio, use your browser to surf to http://www.realaudio.com. There you'll find RealAudio and its close cousin RealVideo, as well as a host of other audio-related Net goodies. The most current version of RealAudio is available at this site and is free to download. (A professional and more fully featured program is also available for a slight charge.)

The RealAudio plug-in supports both 68K and PowerMacintosh computers, as well as Windows 95, Windows NT, and Windows 3.1 platforms. (Sun, UNIX, and NEXT are also supported!)

To run the plug-in, you must have Netscape Navigator 2.0 or later installed. (If you're using Microsoft Internet Explorer, you can find similar tools for playing sound files on the Web. Check out Microsoft's tool-rich site at http://www.microsoft.com.) It's also recommended that you have at least a 28.8 modem to send and receive digital sound files. (A faster modem is better, of course, when moving data such as sound across the Net.)

To download the RealAudio program on any Macintosh:

1. **Use your Web browser to navigate through the RealAudio Web site (use the URL mentioned earlier in this section) until you find the plug-in that works with your Macintosh or PowerMacintosh computer.**

2. **Click on the link to download the file.**

   Navigator automatically downloads the plug-in to your computer.

3. **Quit Netscape Navigator.**

4. **Double-click on the RealAudio Installer icon; then follow the instructions on-screen.**

   Remember to check "yes" when the program asks if you want to install RealAudio plug-ins.

5. **Quit the Installer when it's finished and restart your computer.**

On your Windows PC (486/66 CPU minimum is required), do this:

1. **Use your Web browser to navigate through the RealAudio site to find the plug-in that works with your version of Windows.**

2. **Download the executable file to a temporary directory.**

3. **Quit Navigator.**

4. **Double-click on the file setup executable file to run the installation program. (Express setup should work well.)**

   Remember to check "yes" when the program asks if you want to install RealAudio plug-ins.

5. **Quit the Installer when it's finished and restart your computer.**

Now that you've downloaded and installed the plug-ins, you're ready to test things out. Note that the installer actually installed two programs, RealAudio Player (a helper application that processes incoming audio files) and a RealAudio Netscape Plug-in (a Netscape plug-in that supports "within the page" audio).

Sounding Off on the Web

Before I divulge the secrets of incorporating audio into your Web site, it's time for a little field trip. There are a few sites you should visit so you can think about the appropriateness of using audio on your own site. Just because you *can* include audio on your school's Web site, doesn't mean that you *should*. Like any other design element, you should use audio for a specific purpose, not just because you can.

Some sites, such as that for National Public Radio (NPR), use sound to inform its readers (or listeners in this case). At the NPR site, you can find both *stored* and *real-time* audio files with the latest news and commentary. (Stored files download to your computer, then play. Real-time files play "on the fly" in real time — they're also called *streaming audio*.) You can find the NPR site at `http://www.realaudio.com/contentp/npr.html`.

Other sites are designed mostly to entertain, such as the AudioNet Sports Network site that features live audio broadcasts (on the Net) of your favorite sports events. (Now we're going to be spending all our time cheering and screaming at our COMPUTERS!) You can find the AudioNet site at `http://www.audionet.com/sports/`. (See figure 15-2.)

Figure 15-2:
The
AudioNet
site
features
live
broadcasts
of sporting
events.

Schools can think about using sound in lots of different ways. You may, for example, use sound to

- Deliver a message from your principal
- Post a school "joke of the day" (besides the cafeteria mystery meat)
- Highlight the recitation of a soliloquy by a student
- Play classical music in the background of your home page to supply your readers with some "culture" (and your students, too, as they create the page)
- Play your school's fight song or anthem
- Share samples of the best numbers from your latest school musical
- Publish for the world the admonitions of the driver on Bus Number 244

Hear this: information on sound formats

There are a zillion ways to store sound digitally for playback on the Net. Unfortunately, no one standard for audio on the Internet has emerged (although RealAudio and QuickTime are picking up steam). The standard must be cross-platform and readable (or, in this case, audible) by Web users everywhere.

Sound formats include:

- **Mu law (pronounced mu-law).** Most common and readily available sound format on the Net. It's mono, so the sound quality isn't great, but the files tend to be small. The file extension most used by mu-law folks is .au.

- **AIFF: Audio Interchange File Format.** Developed by Apple and primarily a Mac format, it's been adopted by others, such as Silicon Graphics (SGI), as well. It is able to reproduce 8- or 16-bit samples (a.k.a., great-quality stuff). These files have an .aiff or .aif filename extension.

- **WAVE:** Developed by Microsoft and IBM and included in Windows 3.1, it's the PC standard for audio. It's similar to AIFF. The extension is .wav.

- **MPEG: Moving Pictures Experts Group:** MPEG audio compression is the most complex and most excellent sound quality on the Net (MPEG files are large). New versions of QuickTime can handle MPEG files without any hardware additions on a Mac. A Windows version may be introduced soon.

- **RealAudio:** Tagged with an .rpm extension, these files are similar to AIFF and WAVE in that they are of good sound quality and not very large.

- **QuickTime:** Cross-platform and flexible, the QuickTime format can be used for audio as well as video tracks on a Web site. For information, jump to http://quicktime.apple.com/.

Building Your Own Sound

The toughest part of adding sound to your Web page is creating the sound file. You can get sound files off the Web (from other sites, with permission, of course), or you can create them yourself.

I like to create sound files by connecting my Macintosh to an external microphone. (You can use the Record function that's been built into every Mac since the mid-1980s.) Windows folks can download or purchase lots of different applications to add to their systems to create sound files, and if your PC is equipped with a sound card, you can input sound.

To include HTML code that will play a MIDI file that is stored on your Web server (MIDI is one of the sound formats you'll find on the Web), follow these steps:

1. **Open your Web page in Claris Home Page.**

2. **Click on the Edit HTML Source icon (the third icon from left on the Claris Home Page menu bar) or choose Edit HTML Source from the Window menu in the menu bar.**

3. **Add HTML code appropriate for the type of sound file you're using.**

   To add code that would play a MIDI file called hiphop.MID, for example, you enter an HTML tag called BGSOUND SRC (for background sound, source).

   Enter this code after the <HTML> tag near the very beginning of your Web page. The raw HTML code you enter should look something like this:

   ```
   <BGSOUND SRC="hiphop.MID"LOOP=INFINITE>
   ```

   This line of code tells the browser that funky background music will play over and over while the reader accesses that page. After you leave the site, or log off, the sounds stop.

   To add sound files accessible through helper applications, such as RealAudio (see the section "Plugging In an Audio Program" earlier in this chapter), the following HTML code is used:

   ```
   <A HREF="/directory/subdirectory/filename.rpm"
   ```

   In this case, filename.rpm refers to a RealAudio-compatible sound file saved on your Web server. Your browser looks at the file and searches the helper applications you have in your Netscape Navigator Helper Applications preferences. (Set them in the Helper Applications preference menu accessible through Netscape's General Preferences menu.) Then the application that plays the sound is automatically launched.

If you're using browsers other than Netscape Navigator, sound files "look" to see if your browser supports sound and then enable the appropriate helper application if it's available on your computer. If not, the sound is ignored, but the visual images and text on the page remain visible and intact.

4. Save your Claris Home Page file by choosing File⇨Save.

5. Test your code by using your browser or the Preview mode (click on the second icon from the left on the Home Page menu bar).

Want some handy hints for including audio on your Web page? Here ya go:

✔ Make sure that you tell your readers what kind of sound format you're using, how large the files are, and approximately how long it may take to download them. A simple message like the following will do the trick:

```
Audio clip: QuickTime, 64K, 20 seconds @ 28.8bps
```
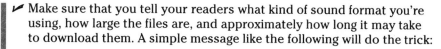

✔ If you're making your own sound files, search the Net to find information about *downsampling,* a technique used to provide a smaller sound file size with acceptable sound quality. (A good place to begin would be to search: http://www.yahoo.com for "sound" and "tools.")

✔ If you must use high-quality sound files, think about including a smaller, lesser-quality version of the file on your site for those who are "bandwidth challenged" and don't have the speed to enjoy your masterpiece.

As a final word to the wise, remember that most of us still have painfully slow connections to the Internet, so sound and video just tie us up. Use audio judiciously and be ruthless in fine-tuning your selection for optimum playback on the Net. Well . . . time to put another quarter in my Internet jukebox. Happy audio!

Chapter 16
Web Cinema

*W*ouldn't it be really cool if you could show a video on your Web page? Maybe some Jimi Hendrix or Sonny and Cher? Well, okay, how about settling for a quick tour of your school or a message from your superintendent?

You're in luck. Video, in the form of digital movies (as shown in Figure 16-1), can be incorporated into your Web page with relative ease. In this chapter, I tell you about one of several ways to add video to your Web page by using a program called QuickTime, developed by Apple Computer.

QuickTime is a multi-platform, multimedia tool that is used to create and deliver synchronized graphics, sound, video, text, and music. QuickTime is the Internet standard for video. QuickTime even offers continuously displayed video (called *streaming video* in Internet-speak).

In addition to QuickTime, other file formats can be used to add video to Web pages, including *VfW* (Video for Windows, identified by the file extension .avi) and *MPEG* (a high-end format that's complex and fairly difficult to use). You can also use *Java,* a relatively new (compared with a traditional programming languages such as C) and powerful programming language that provides cross-platform compatible computing across the Internet. Or you can use a scripting language called *VBScript* (for Visual Basic Script) to add video. (I won't talk about how to use Java or VBScript to add movies to your pages in this chapter — that would require a whole other book!)

To view videos on your page, visitors to your Web site must have a special helper application, called a *plug-in* (a small program that works with your Web browser for additional functionality). By using certain plug-ins, visitors can access sound, video, 3-D models, online presentations, and much more.

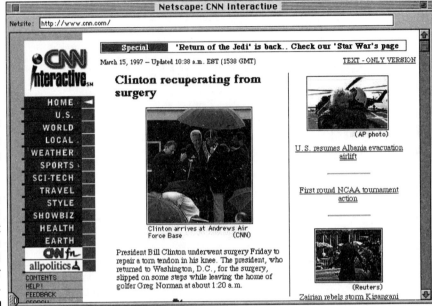

Here's some good news: The QuickTime video plug-in is free, and it works with both the Macintosh OS and with Windows NT, Windows 95, and Windows 3.1. (In the next section, I explain how to download QuickTime from the Web.)

Downloading (transferring) video files to your computer's hard drive and viewing them with an external program (called a *player*) is also possible. When you grab QuickTime from the Internet, the player comes with it. And it's free!

Downloading QuickTime

The QuickTime plug-in comes with the newer versions of Netscape Navigator for Macintosh and Windows, but if you're using an earlier version, you need to download QuickTime. Just follow these steps:

1. **Launch your Web browser and Go to the QuickTime Web site at** http://quicktime.apple.com.

2. **Click on the Download Software link.**

3. **Navigate through the QuickTime site until you find the plug-in that works with your Macintosh, PowerMacintosh, or Windows OS computer.**

4. **Click on the link for your system and then click on Download to download the file.**

   The plug-in automatically downloads to your computer.

5. **Quit or Exit your Web browser.**

6. **Copy the QuickTime plug-in into your browser's Plug-ins folder or subdirectory.**

   You can find the Netscape Navigator Plug-ins folder within the Program subdirectory or folder under the Navigator subdirectory or folder.

   If you're using Internet Explorer, you can find the Plug-ins folder in the IE subdirectory or folder.

7. **Re-launch your Web browser.**

   The QuickTime plug-in automatically loads, and you can then see the QuickTime option under the Claris Home Page Insert menu.

Plenty of tools that increase the functionality of QuickTime are available on the Net. One tool is called MovieStar. It enables you to view QuickTime movies as they download — saving lots of waiting time. Grab this handy plug-in at

```
http://130.91.39.113/moviestar/plugins/
```

Why video for the Web?

Any educator knows that some students are primarily visual learners, some are auditory learners, some are tactile learners, and some learn in a combination of ways. Incorporating video into your Web page offers an educational option to students who have differing learning styles. In addition, some stories really can't be told as effectively in print as they can withpictures. A virtual video visit to a museum in another country or state, for example, is a great alternative to purchasing a costly plane ticket and hassling with permission slips and other travel details.

As data transmission speeds increase, more and more video will be used on the Internet. In the near future, textbook companies will deliver video content over the Web, saving you from fumbling with VCRs and the continual problem of finding out that the tape you want to use has been checked out by the teacher down the hall.

Internet video is just one tool in the bag of teaching and learning tricks at a your disposal. Use this tool wisely, and you and your students will enjoy a terrific learning experience.

Adding QuickTime Video to Your Pages

Including a video in your Web site is as simple as including a standard graphic image. (The tough part can be preparing or obtaining the movie in digitized format.) By using Claris Home Page, you can add *cross-platform* QuickTime movies (optimized for both Macs and PCs) to your Web page.

The process of preparing a movie for publication on your Web page is called *flattening*. You can find a bunch of free tools for flattening movies (for both Macs and PCs) at Apple's QuickTime site at: `http://www.quicktime.apple.com/dev/devsw.html`. Another excellent and easy-to-use tool called the Flattener is available free at

`http://www.ralentz.com/old/mac/qt/flattmoov.sit.hqx`

Claris Home Page enables you to add video to your Web page easily by using the QuickTime Movie item in the Claris Home Page Insert menu. To add a QuickTime movie to your Web page, follow these steps:

1. **Locate or create a flattened QuickTime movie.**

   To create a flattened movie, you need to use a tool like Movie Cleaner Pro (from Terran Interactive at `http://www.terran.com`). Programs such as Movie Cleaner Pro (and there are others — check `http://www.downloads.com`) have an option that enables you, when saving a movie, to flatten the resulting image.

   On many Macs, you can plug a TV, VCR, or camcorder directly into your computer to create QuickTime movies. QuickTime and most of the tools you need to create the movies are built into the operating system. (Upgrades available free at `http://www.quicktime.apple.com`.)

   On a PC, you need to download QuickTime for Windows and drop it in your Plug-ins folder. (See the section "Downloading QuickTime" earlier in this chapter.) To make a QuickTime video (or any digital video) with your PC, you probably need to purchase a video-in card and install it in your computer. Most video cards also come with powerful editing software.

2. **Choose QuickTime Movie from the Home Page Insert menu.**

3. **Select the desired QuickTime movie file from the Open dialog box.**

4. **Click on Open.**

   The QuickTime movie appears on your Web page with the movie's *poster picture* (usually the first frame of the movie) showing.

After the movie has a *placeholder* (a box showing where the movie will display) on the page, you can use the menu bar icons to center-, right-, or left-justify the movie on your page.

Want to change the size of the movie or make it play in a continuous loop? You can change the attributes of the movie file by using the Movie Object Editor. Just follow these steps:

1. **Double-click on the QuickTime movie to open the QuickTime Movie Object Editor (see Figure 16-2).**

2. **Click on the triangle in the lower left corner or click on the Both tab to see all of the settings in the QuickTime Movie Object Editor.**

3. **Change the appropriate settings as desired.**

   Table 16-1 lists the attributes you can assign to QuickTime movies.

4. **Press Tab or click on the Close box of the QuickTime Movie Object Editor.**

Figure 16-2:
Use the QuickTime Movie Object Editor to change the attributes of your movie.

Keep video files as small as possible. Video files can be minimized by reducing the frames per second, reducing the frame size, and limiting the number of colors.

Table 16-1	Attributes for QuickTime Movies
Attribute	*Description*
Width	Changes the width of the movie (in pixels or percentages).
Height	Changes the height of the movie (in pixels or percentages).
Loop	Specifies continuous or one-time play.
Auto-play	Automatically plays the movie as soon as someone enters the page.
Controller	Reveals or hides the QuickTime user control panel (play, pause, forward, and so on).
Plug-in Page	If users don't have the proper QuickTime plug-in to view the movie, they are automatically transferred to whatever Web site you enter in this field (probably `http://quicktime.apple.com`) when they click on the movie link. Readers can then download the plug-in from that site and then, after restarting their browsers, view the movie.
Extra HTML	Adds additional HTML code to further customize the movie. You can, for example, use additional HTML to resize the movie, to add a controller toolbar to the bottom of the movie, or raise and lower the volume of movie playback.

Provide information about the file size and format with all your audio and video links. In some cases, you may include options for different levels of quality and size of files (such as a movie in $1/4$-screen size or $1/2$-screen size) and let the users determine how long they are willing to wait for the movie to transfer.

Viewing Your Movies

In order to see your final masterpiece, you have to preview your Web page in a browser.

Because QuickTime is controlled by a browser plug-in on your Macintosh or Windows computer, you must launch your browser to view the movie. (You can't view your movie from within Claris Home Page or from within many other Web creation tools.)

Ten tips for great Web video

Although you and your student may be experts at shooting video with your school's video cameras, you may not be happy with the results when you transfer those movies into digital (QuickTime) format. When editing for the Web, you've got to consider such factors as download time (which relates to file size) and frame speed. (Your TV displays images at 30 frames per second.)

Here are ten tips that can help ensure that your next Web video efforts result in an eye-popping (and not an eye-fatiguing) addition to your Web page.

✔ **Keep it small (edit ruthlessly!).** Movies smaller than 250K get viewed more often than those that are 1MB or more.

✔ **Use the highest quality camera you can get your hands on.** (S-VHS or Hi-8 is best.)

✔ **Lose the special effects.** They don't compress well. If you must use effects for transitions, stick to cross-fades or quick cuts.

✔ **Step out of the dark ages.** Use lots and lots of light. QuickTime plug-ins tend to darken the image during broadcast.

✔ **Tell the user approximotely how long it'll take to get the entire movie downloaded.** 300K, 45 seconds @ 28.8 or similar messages can help set expectations.

✔ **Offer options.** If a QuickTime movie is essential to your Web page content, offer key frames to hold a still image for those who don't have the plug-in or don't have the patience to wait for your cinematic creation.

✔ **Get rock steady.** Use a tripod or stable flat surface when filming. Jerky shooting looks even more jerky when viewed on the Web.

✔ **Compress the video as much as you can without making it look like an amateur puppet show.** Consider using such tools as Terran Interactive's Movie Cleaner Pro (http://www.terran.com).

✔ **Bright colors and subtle backgrounds make for clearer viewing.**

✔ **Stay away from on-screen subtitles and the like.** If you must use them, make sure that the color of the title text contrasts highly with the background.

Here's how to check your progress:

1. **Click on the Home Page toolbar's Preview In Browser button (it's the one that has the globe in the upper-right corner) in order to launch your browser from within Claris Home Page.**

Your browser launches (and loads the QuickTime plug-in in the process), loads your page, and displays the QuickTime movie as a still image.

2. **Click on the QuickTime movie image to start the movie.**

In some cases (depending on how the original movie was saved), you may see a toolbar (under the movie window) that lets you increase or decrease playback volume or stop and start the movie.

Peeking at QuickTime HTML Code

The HTML code that Claris Home Page generates looks something like the lines of code that follow. The movie shows the *controller* (the movie control button panel), the movie will play only once (no "loop" that replays the movie over and over), and readers are required to click on the poster-screen of the movie to activate it (as opposed to its running automatically when a reader links to the page).

QuickTime VR: Virtual reality in Web page form

QuickTime has an amazing cousin — QuickTime VR — that enables the Web page reader to view still images that are *interactive.* It's the closest thing to virtual reality that you see on the Net (for now).

For example, with QuickTime VR, you can navigate within a 360-degree area of still pictures that are "stitched" together to form a panorama. To get an idea of how QuickTime VR performs, you and your students can travel on a 3-D visit to NASA Space Camp (http://www.spacecamp.com/). (See the figure in this sidebar.) You can experience a real "you are there" feeling by spinning your point of view around in any horizontal direction (and in a limited number of vertical directions) to look at the wonders that NASA brings us. Because this site is digital *and* interactive, you can also zoom in and take a closer look at the interesting images before you.

Running QuickTime VR requires the appropriate plug-in installed in your browser's Plug-ins folder. Visit http://quicktimevr.apple.com for a free copy of the plug-in for your Mac or Windows browser.

The following code is for a movie called *Schooldaze* that is displayed in a 320 x 260 window on the browser screen.

```
<EMBED SRC="schooldaze.mov"
PLUGINSPAGE="http://quicktime.apple.com"
WIDTH=320 HEIGHT=260
CONTROLLER=TRUE
LOOP=FALSE
AUTOPLAY=FALSE>
```

The URL that follows the PLUGINSPAGE code enables Web page readers to download the QuickTime plug-in to their browser automatically if they don't already have it in their Plug-ins folder. (The *Plug-ins folder* is a special folder on a computer's hard drive. This folder holds helper programs that add functionality to your Web browser.)

Chapter 17

Pouring Some Java into Your Pages

· ·

· ·

*N*ext time you grab some quick Java while on a break, you may be surfing the Net rather than sipping cappucino. One of the hottest things to hit the Internet lately is the *Java* programming language created by Sun Microsystems. In this chapter, I tell you a little bit about how Java works and how to use it with Claris Home Page.

Java enables software developers to create programs called *applets,* which live inside Web pages. When a Web browser that is capable of running Java encounters a page that contains an applet, the browser downloads the applet and hands it off to your computer to be run on an as-needed basis to add action to Web pages. By using Java applets, you can instruct objects (such as graphics or text) to jump, rotate, wiggle, and make many other strange movements. Java applets also enable you to embed powerful tools, such as *chat* (live two-way conversation) windows, automatically updating information resources (like stock tickers or banners reporting the latest baseball scores), 3-D movie players, and much more.

JavaScript is a scripting language created by Sun Microsystems and Netscape Communications to enable scripting within the Netscape Navigator browser. *Scripting languages* are relatively easy-to-use programming languages that enable end users to control existing programs. *Scripts* are text files containing English-like commands that browsers follow when they encounter the script. Although Java is very much like the C++ programming language, JavaScript is much more like AppleScript or *HyperTalk* (HyperCard's scripting language). Java-ready Web browsers, such as Netscape Navigator, search for JavaScript code embedded amid the HTML in a Web page and follow the instructions as the Web page is displayed.

More and more Web sites feature Java and JavaScript elements. The de facto "mother of all Java samples" site is `http://www.gamelan.com/`. This site is a great place to search for Java samples and learn more about JavaScript writing. (See Figure 17-1.)

The cool part of this is that the images you see through your browser and on your computer screen can become animated. The not-so-cool part is that the Java language is fairly complex (more job security for Webmasters, I guess). Another disadvantage is that the programming code is large, meaning potentially long downloading times for your readers. (Whether the downloading time for Java programs is brief enough to hold the attention of hormonally challenged middle schoolers remains to be seen.)

Want to see a great educational use of Java? It's an online thematic coloring book. After you've colored your picture, you can e-mail it to a friend. Amazing. Check out `http://www.jayzeebear.com/color/colorbig.html`. Figure 17-2 shows a Java birthday card I made for a friend by using this site.

Another site (one I couldn't resist) gives you an idea of the potential of Java for entertainment and simulation on the Internet. Visit this one at `http://www.cruzio.com/~sabweb/arcade/index.html`.

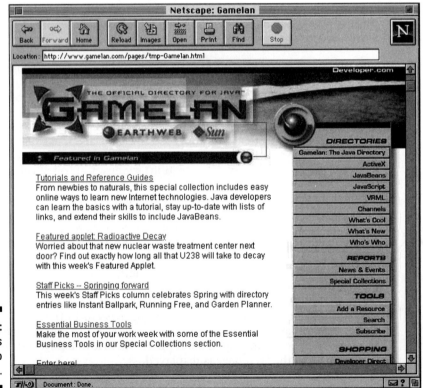

Figure 17-1: Java adds zip to Web pages.

Figure 17-2:
This site
uses the
power of
Java to help
kids create
art on the
Internet.

Want to see how the pros work with Java? When you visit other sites, use
the *View Source* feature in your browser to see how it's done. (The View
Source feature lets you peek at the code that created the page, special
effect, or whatever. Looking to see how other folks create pages can give you
great insight into creating your own.)

(HTML) Tag, You're It!

Claris Home Page inserts the basic structure tags in HTML, but you're on
your own when you begin to write the JavaScript that animates icons,
creates chat windows, and much more.

It turns out that you use plain old HTML code to *embed* (incorporate)
JavaScript and Java applets into your Web pages. Like other HTML tags, such
as <H1> and </H1> (a headline text tag pair), the <APPLET> tag is a *compound
tag,* which means that it requires other information to be complete.

Claris Home Page gives you the ability to build or access basic applets by
using friendly pull-down menus and simple commands. Before I show you
how to do that, however, you need a little background.

Basically, four parts of the <APPLET> tag in the HTML code are at work
behind the scenes:

```
<APPLET attributes>
applet-parameters
alternate-HTML
</APPLET>
```

As with other HTML tags, the attributes and parameters usually just tell your browser how much space to make available on the Web page for your graphic or Java animation. These attributes can also tell the browser what typeface and size to make text on the screen.

Let's say you've got a Java applet called *ticker tape* that plasters a band of electronic stock market information across a computer screen. The display is of current stock prices right from the floor of the New York Stock Exchange. Assuming that you want a band across the screen 25 pixels high and 450 pixels wide, the code would look like this:

```
<APPLET CODE="ticker tape.class" HEIGHT=25 WIDTH=450>
```

Note that the applet name (`ticker tape.class`) is case sensitive (capital letters have to stay as capital letters; lowercase as lowercase, and so on). The `.class` extension is a standard way to let your browser know to expect a Java applet.

Serving Up Some Java

To insert Java code into your home page while you're working in Claris Home Page, follow these steps:

1. Choose Insert⇨Applet.

The Applet object editor dialog box opens. (See Figure 17-3.)

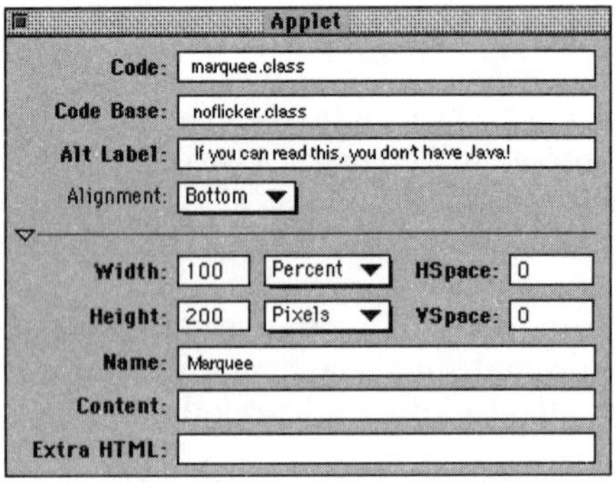

Figure 17-3:
The Applet object editor allows you to enter and edit JavaScript code.

Applet		
Code:	marquee.class	
Code Base:	noflicker.class	
Alt Label:	If you can read this, you don't have Java!	
Alignment:	Bottom ▼	
Width:	100 Percent ▼	HSpace: 0
Height:	200 Pixels ▼	VSpace: 0
Name:	Marquee	
Content:		
Extra HTML:		

2. Fill in the blanks with information about the Java applet you're incorporating.

Table 17-1 helps identify how to fill in the blanks.

3. Click in the close box of the Applet editor window.

The resulting HTML code appears in your Web page; you can use the Edit HTML Source button (the button with two angle brackets) to view the code.

Table 17-1	Information for the Applet Object Editor Dialog Box
Applet attribute	**Function**
Code	Specifies the filename of the applet (watch for .class or .cls extension).
Code Base	Specifies the path to the folder where the applet is located. Leave it blank if the applet is located in the same subdirectory (folder) as the Web page itself.
Alt Label	Sets text that appears when someone who is Java-less visits your page.
Alignment	Determines how the applet is aligned with text around it.
Width	Determines the width of the applet.
Height	Determines the height of the applet.
Hspace	Determines the amount of horizontal space to the right and left of the applet (measured in pixels).
Vspace	Determines the amount of vertical space above and below the applet (measured in pixels).
Name	Assigns a name to the applet so other applets can communicate with it. (Advanced feature.)
Content	Assigns parameter names and values. (Advanced feature.)
Extra HTML	Adds more HTML attributes. (Advanced feature.)

What you enter in the boxes in the Applet editor dialog box depends on what you want the applet to do and how you want the applet to look on the page. This descriptive information, called an *attribute,* can be user-configured in a limited manner with Claris Home Page or by writing your own HTML code. The next section describes attributes and their functions.

The ABCs of Attributes

All `<APPLET>` tags must contain these three attributes: CODE, HEIGHT, and WIDTH. Some optional attributes enable you to align the Java element on the page (left, right, or center) and enable you to hook to other Java applets already published on the Web.

Table 17-1, earlier in this chapter, shows you the required Java attributes and a few of the optional ones. Access the Applet object editor window (double-click on the applet placeholder on your home page to display the object editor) to adjust and enter Java code.

Another major part of the <APPLET> tag is the *applet parameter* by which you can customize an applet. A tag called <PARAM> has two attributes: NAME and VALUE. Because Claris Home Page and certain other Web page creation tools do not directly support these parameters, you may have to enter these manually in Raw HTML mode. (See Chapter 6 for more on using Raw HTML.) Here's what the syntax (code) would look like if it were entered in Raw HTML:

```
<PARAM NAME="parameter name" VALUE="paramater value">
```

Certain types of applets can also run a sound in the background of your page. This is what some sample syntax would like for an applet running sound:

```
<PARAM NAME="sndTrack" VALUE="audio/king/dream.au">
```

In this case, the parameter is `sndTrack`. The value associated with this parameter, `audio/king/dream.au`, is a URL leading to the sound file.

Grabbin' Applets from the Net Tree

If you don't want to take the time to write your own Java applets, it is possible to incorporate applets that are already in use at other sites into your Web page. These ready-made applets from other sites are called *distributed applets*. All you have to know is the name of the site where the applet "lives" and what attributes and parameters (if any) it requires to run as you want it to. Enter the applet information in the Code window of the Applet object editor (refer to Figure 17-3) to access the applet remotely.

Sometimes friendly Webmasters are so proud of their work, they distribute the applets free of charge, and even supply the code. Visit `http://www.homestart.com/support/java/Marquee/` to see an applet that enables you to create text that scrolls across your Web page visitor's browser screen. The code you need (see Figure 17-4) is also on the site. All you and your students have to do to include this Java applet, then, is to cut and paste the code into your Web page!

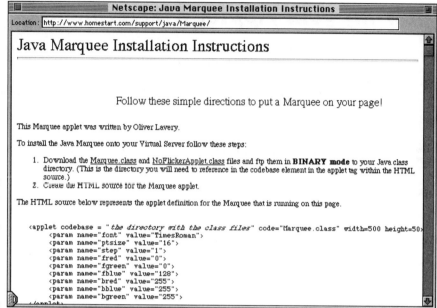

┌───┐
│ **Netscape: Java Marquee Installation Instructions** │
│ Location: http://www.homestart.com/support/java/Marquee/ │
│ │
│ ## Java Marquee Installation Instructions │
│ │
│ Follow these simple directions to put a Marquee on your page! │
│ │
│ This Marquee applet was written by Oliver Lavery. │
│ │
│ To install the Java Marquee onto your Virtual Server follow these steps: │
│ │
│ 1. Download the Marquee.class and NoFlickerApplet.class files and ftp them in **BINARY mode** to your Java class │
│   directory. (This is the directory you will need to reference in the codebase element in the applet tag within the HTML │
│   source.) │
│ 2. Create the HTML source for the Marquee applet. │
│ │
│ The HTML source below represents the applet definition for the Marquee that is running on this page. │
└───┘

```
<applet codebase = "the directory with the class files" code="Marquee.class" width=500 height=50>
    <param name="font" value="TimesRoman">
    <param name="ptsize" value="16">
    <param name="step" value="1">
    <param name="fred" value="0">
    <param name="fgreen" value="0">
    <param name="fblue" value="128">
    <param name="bred" value="255">
    <param name="bblue" value="255">
    <param name="bgreen" value="255">
```

Figure 17-4: Some Java can easily be cut and pasted into your Web page.

Java on — Java off

The good thing about Java applets is that they download automatically to your hard drive, which makes running these Java mini-programs effortless. Unfortunately, seeing exactly what the Java applet is *doing* while it's running is often difficult. Is the applet sending information about what's on your hard drive while running a chat window on your screen?

Because of this potential security hazard, some companies (and some schools) urge their employees to disable their browser's capability to download Java applets. Usually, this step involves a clickable option in your Web browser's Preferences menu. Turning off Java generally won't affect the content of the Web page, but it could substantially affect its appearance.

As with any new technology, there comes responsibility. Hopefully, as programmers, you will encourage your students to conduct themselves properly like 99.9 percent of the folks who develop Web content.

Viewing Your Applet Masterpiece

Although Claris Home Page lets you include applets in your Web page, you have to launch your Web browser to view them in action. Web browsers use *helper programs* (special files that extend a program's capabilities) called *plug-ins* to read Java code. Netscape Navigator Version 2.0 (or higher) and Microsoft Internet Explorer Version 3.0 (or higher) include certain built-in Java plug-ins.

If you use distributed applets, you have to be logged on to the Internet to preview them. If you've created your own code, however, you can view them with your browser without actually signing on to the Internet.

Remember when we wrote six lines of BASIC code just to display a colored box on the screen of our Apple IIs? Now we're doin' the Java waltz! We've come a long way!

Part V

Sharing and Using Your Web Page

The 5th Wave — By Rich Tennant

NOT EVERYONE AT MEDVILLE HIGH SCHOOL EMBRACED WEB PUBLISHING WITH EQUAL PROFICIENCY.

Web publishing is a wonderful combination of creativity, technology, global communications...

...and nightmares.

In this part . . .

As of late 1995, more than 3,000 schools have made the jump to cyberspace and have posted their own Web pages. Since then, far more schools have gained access to the Web through local information providers or online services or through colleges, universities, or libraries with big hearts and even bigger file servers.

This part of the book provides a guide to the process of posting your Web page to the Internet and telling the world about your fabulous creation. I also share tips on using the Internet in the classroom and strategies for sharing the page-updating workload with your students.

Chapter 18

Getting Your Web Page Online

● ●

In This Chapter

▶ Searching for a Web server

▶ Doing it yourself or using a service

▶ Transmitting Web page files

▶ Promoting your Web page

▶ Researching with search engines

▶ Applying tricks of the trade to get noticed

● ●

*H*ere it is: the moment of truth! Now that you and your students have crafted the world's most awesome Web page, it's time to share it with several million other Internet users.

The first goal in your quest to publish your Web page is to find a *Web server*. Web servers are computers on the Internet that run programs that "listen" to the Internet and wait for inquiries to the Web pages they contain. As requests are submitted from Web clients, a Web server locates files and other resources and sends them over the Internet.

Web servers come in all shapes and sizes. A Web server can be anything from a mainframe or mini-computer running *UNIX* (an operating system) to a PC running Windows or Windows NT to a Macintosh. Clients and servers communicate by using a language called *Hypertext Transfer Protocol* (HTTP). This protocol allows computers of all kinds to tap information from your Web server.

Uh-oh . . . I feel the propeller on my beanie spinning. That's a signal that the techno-speak is getting a bit rough. Hang in there, though; this chapter isn't as bad as you may expect. You've already seen most of the hundred-dollar words I'll be handing you.

The Search for Servers and Service Providers

Your search for a file server on which to *post* (send and display) your Web page can be as simple as making a phone call to your school system's district office. Many schools (especially colleges) have Web servers to enable students, teachers, and staff members to create and publish their own Web pages. Those institutions may even offer classes or online assistance in creating Web pages.

The major benefits of publishing on your own Web server are lower cost over time and greater availability of file space. Typically, when you use your own Web server, your school won't be charged by the minute to access the Web — and plenty of space is available for any Web ideas that you and your students can conjure up.

If your school or school system doesn't have its own Internet *node* (a direct connection to the Internet that includes your own www.whatever.edu domain name) with a Web server, you've got a couple of other options. Nowadays, more and more commercial online services are offering users space for Web pages on their huge Net-connected computers. America Online, for example, not only offers its subscribers space, but also has a dandy tool called AOLPress for helping novice users develop their own pages (see Chapter 6 for more on Net tools).

The benefit of using an *online service* (such as America Online or CompuServe) is that it is likely to offer the latest in development tools and lots of online assistance to help you create your pages. Using a service is also a way to get online quickly. Most of the online services provide a walk-through Q & A in which you enter information into an electronic form. Once completed, the data entries are "poured" by the online service into a standard Web page format. It's quick and it's efficient, but it's not a very versatile or flexible way to create a Web page. (For more information on America Online and its Internet services, check out *America Online For Teachers*, also published by IDG Books Worldwide, Inc.)

Another option is to contact an *Internet Service Provider* (ISP). ISPs may be local or nationwide in their service areas. Both local and national providers (such as AT&T WorldNet Service or Mindspring) are another way to connect to the Internet. Some ISPs offer their subscribers a few megabytes of space on which to store their Web pages. For example, MindSpring offers two different types of Web accounts:

✔ The most commonly used one comes "bundled" with an Internet access account at no extra cost. This allows online users, with e-mail and access to the Web, to also have a Web site. Customers are also given five to ten megabytes of Web space for their own site. One thing to keep in mind is that this bundled Web space is just for a basic site. Many of the new and innovative Web technologies can't be used with this type of account.

✔ The second type of Web space that MindSpring offers is the Commercial Web Hosting service for a higher-end Web site. One of the qualifications for Commercial Web Hosting is the customer's URL or Web site address. If, for example, your school wants its URL to be something like `www.ourschoolname.edu`, you will need a Commercial Web Hosting account. This Web hosting option is not a free service like the bundled Web space in the first type of account; however, it offers added features and capabilities you may want.

To find an ISP, I'd suggest asking around your community or checking under Internet Services in the *Yellow Pages*. The backs of computer magazines are also filled with ads for ISPs. The biggest benefit of relying on an ISP for Web page hosting is that the ISP, and not you, is responsible for the maintenance of the Web server, while you retain responsibility for the Web pages on the server. This setup is a little like having a housekeeper come in and clean your classroom windows (who has windows?) and blackboard every night (we can dream, can't we?).

Do you want fries with that? (self-serve Web servers)

If your school has its own Internet node, you may choose to set up your own Web server. To set up a Web server, you need four things:

✔ A fast connection to the Internet (56 Kbps minimum)

✔ A computer running Macintosh OS, Windows NT, or UNIX

✔ A person (or people) who can wear the Webmaster beanie and maintain the Web server

✔ A group of programs that instructs your computer how to act like a Web server

Because the Web was born on a UNIX system, you can use many different ways to set up a Web server on a computer running UNIX. Two of the ways involve freeware programs, CERN HTTPD and NCSA HTTPD. (HTTPD stands for *Hypertext Transfer Protocol Daemon*. See the sidebar "UNIX daemons" in

this chapter for a description of what a daemon is.) These programs are full of great features, but they are a bit hairy to install. Here's where your beanie-wearers come in handy. UNIX is about as friendly as a bus driver on the last day of school. You can find CERN's HTTPD and NCSA HTTPD by jumping to their site from `http://www.netscape.com/`.

Grabbing a Macintosh is one of the easiest ways to create a Web server at your school. A Mac freeware program called WebStar (formerly called MacHTTP) can be up and running inside of 15 minutes. Most anyone can install it, beanie or not. You can find WebSTAR at `http://www.starnine.com/`.

For PC users, some dandy, fast Pentium Internet servers are out there. If your school or district has lots of Windows gurus and you want to give them a challenge, some places on the Web (such as at `http://www.ibm.com/`) show you the way to create a PC Web server. Server software is available to support Windows, Windows 95, and Windows NT solutions. PC servers use shareware Web server programs such as SerWeb (Windows 3.1) and Alibaba (Windows 95 and Windows NT) — grab SerWeb at `ftp://ftp.cica.indiana.edu` and conjure up Alibaba from `http://alibaba.austria.eu.net` — or commercially available software such as Domino from Lotus (Windows NT), that transforms Lotus Notes servers into Internet Web servers. (Check out `http://domino.lotus.com/`.)

UNIX daemons

A *daemon* is a UNIX program that sits and waits for someone to access it. When requests come in to a server, the daemon jumps in and processes each request and then hustles back to the corner to wait for another request. (One of the dictionary definitions of "daemon" is something that has exceptional enthusiasm for work.) Daemons are similar to Windows *TSRs* (Terminate and Stay Resident programs) and Macintosh OS Extensions (those things that hide in the System folder).

Daemons are dandy because they grab processing power only while they're active. Daemons manage traffic on UNIX Web servers. If you've got a UNIX server, you've probably got someone to run it, too. That person can help you exorcise, uhm, *exercise* your daemons!

A quick and easy Web server

In the beginning, Web providers were forced to endure the confusing world of UNIX servers. After all, the Internet started with UNIX as its operating system, and old habits are hard to break. Nowadays, smart folks (like many associated with schools) are flocking to an easier solution — Apple's Internet Workgroup Server bundle. All you need is a PowerMac Workgroup Server (they come in several flavors) and supporting software. Apple's server comes with WebStar (formerly known as MacHTTP), Netscape Navigator (in my opinion the best browser on the planet), BBEdit (for writing Web pages), PageMill (for creating Web pages in a user-friendly, drag-and-drop, point-and-click Mac environment), and lots of other goodies. Best of all you can be up and running within 15 minutes!

The bundle includes the capability to build a secure Web site and construct *firewalls* (software blockades to keep prying eyes away from your server resources). The Mac software has fewer security holes than UNIX does; but just in case, plan to dedicate a server to Web tasks instead of using your LAN's (Local Area Network's) main server.

Apple's solution is about half the price of a UNIX solution and is much easier to administer. The downside? Only high-end PowerMacs currently support multitasking, so some processor-intensive tasks (like a zillion people logging on at the same time) may slow down network access. One solution is to use a number of servers and let the powerful Domain Name Server software balance the load. (For more information, visit http://info.apple.com.) When the load gets too large, each server then passes users along to the next server.

Leave the driving to them: using Internet service providers

If your school or district doesn't have its own Web server, don't worry. Many Internet providers allow subscribers to publish their own Web pages with little or no cost beyond their monthly Internet access fee.

In Atlanta, for example, a company called Mindspring (http://www.mindspring.com/) uses revenue from corporate customers to allow it to give one free dial-up account, with accompanying space for a Web page, to practically every Georgia public or private school that wants one. These folks at Mindspring have the right idea. Call your local Internet provider and wave that in their face!

To find a listing of Internet providers in your area, check out the Internet Access Providers links on the popular Yahoo Internet catalog. You can find it at

```
http://www.yahoo.com/Business/Corporations/
    Internet_Access_Providers/
```

After you've created a list of Internet service providers to explore, ask each of them three questions:

✔ **How much storage do I get for my Web site?**

Ten megabytes (10MB) of storage space is recommended for a start. Most sites will sell you more space in increments of 10MB for just a couple of dollars a month.

✔ **How much bandwidth am I allocated?**

Bandwidth refers to how much data can be moved across the Internet by the server. If your HTML code uses up about 50K and your graphics eat up about 100K, the server will suck up sufficient bandwidth to blast out 150K of data. If ten people access your site, your total bandwidth usage is 1500K. Some providers charge you if your site exceeds certain limits for access. Ask in advance if this is an issue for your school's site.

✔ **What happens if I need help?**

Because not everyone on Planet Earth has a Web server, having some-place to turn to when challenges arise is important. A good ISP offers easy-to-access, 24-hour telephone support. Because your connection is worthless to everyone if it doesn't work, this is an important question to ask!

You can also publish Web pages on commercial online services, although right now access and space (plus your ability to be creative) are limited with commercial service Web-page authoring systems. Most of the commercial online services haven't yet caught up to the high demands that users are making on their systems.

I definitely recommend that at first you work with a service provider. Having your own server is a little like buying that hundred-acre farm that you always wanted — it's great until you have to get up at 5 a.m. and milk the cows. Web servers require expertise and maintenance. May as well let someone else get "udderly" frustrated (ouch!).

FTP and Me: Transmitting Your Web Page Files

FTP (File Transfer Protocol) is a *protocol* (set of rules) for data transfer. It allows files (programs, pictures, sounds, movies, and so on) to be exchanged between different kinds of computers, without regard to how the computers are connected or what operating system they are running. Through FTP, you transfer files from a host computer to your computer.

If you're using a Web server that's located at an Internet Service Provider (as opposed to your own Web server that may be down the hallway from your classroom), you also use FTP to transfer your Web files (HTML pages) and associated graphics and multimedia to the server where your Web page will live. (If you have your own server, you can transfer the files by copying them over the network; you don't need FTP.)

FTP can be used as a noun and as a verb. As a noun, it's used like this: "That file is available via FTP from C|net." You also may hear, "Get that file by FTPing it from Harvard's server." The whole Internet is turning out to be the birthplace of as many new techno-terms as it is new ideas.

After you've established a site for your Web page, the next step is to actually publish your Web page to the Internet Service Provider's Web server. Basically, this process involves four easy steps:

1. **Determine which Web server subdirectory you will use to post your Web page.**

   To determine the subdirectory to use, contact your network administrator or network information provider. Either can give you the directory path that you need in order to post your Web pages to the proper place.

2. **Use FTP to send a *text* version of your HTML script file to the Web subdirectory on your Web server.**

   After your network administrator has given you a directory path to follow, FTP programs such as Fetch and NetPresenz (Macintosh) or WS_FTP (Windows) makes the data transfer pretty effortless (as shown in Figure 18-1).

   To make this task extra easy for you, I've included both these programs on your *Web Publishing For Teachers* CD-ROM!

3. **Use FTP to send all associated GIF (an image file format on the Web), sound, or movie files to the same subdirectory on the Web server.**

4. **Test your Web page (for the umpteenth time — you can't be safe enough) by logging in to the Web server and accessing your Web page.**

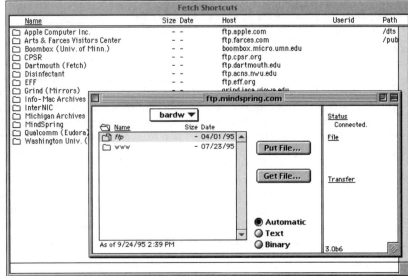

Figure 18-1:
FTP
programs
make it
easy to
transfer
your HTML
code and
graphics to
your Web
server.

When you transmit a file, make sure that it has the letters `html` appended to the filename. That very important appendage tells the browser that you've made an HTML page.

When sending *graphics* (image files), make sure that you've named them exactly the way that you named them in your Web page. (Use the View HTML Source option in Claris Home Page to check it out.) Note that if your Web page is also accessing documents from other sources, you may have to edit your HTML script so that it knows where to look for those resources when it needs them.

Don't forget to try accessing your brand new Web page from several different types of computers using several different Web browsers. You may be surprised (either pleasantly or not) at the differences you see.

Getting the Word Out about Your Web Page

Because nobody administers the entire Internet, there's no district office to which you submit the name of your Web server in order to have your Web page broadcast to the rest of the Internet. You can choose from a few simple ways to publicize your Web site:

✔ Post messages to newsgroups.

✔ Send e-mail to `news@ncsa.uiuc.edu`.

✔ Get your URL posted on the "What's New" page on your Internet Service Provider's home page.

✔ Visit `http://ep.com/faq/webannounce.html`.

✔ Check out CERN at `http://www.cern.ch/`.

✔ Write an article for your local (or national) paper.

✔ Create a business card containing your school's Web address.

✔ Send e-mail to everyone you know and have them pass the word.

The little search engines that could

Whether you're looking for some sample Web sites or you want to find ways to get the word out about your new school site, Web search engines are an effective way to begin your research.

Search engines are essentially directories of Web sites (for example, FTP sites, newsgroups, or even Web sites belonging to individuals). They are updated, for the most part, by digital *spiders* — programs that crawl around the Web and grab new URLs as they find them.

Here's a list of the most popular search engines:

Search Engine Name	Location
Lycos	`http://www.lycos.com/`
AltaVista	`http://altavista.digital.com/`
Web Crawler	`http://webcrawler.com/`
World-Wide Web Worm	`http://www.cs.colorado.edu/home/ mcbryan/wwww.html`
Open Text	`http://www.opentext.com`
All4One	`http://www.all4one.com`
Infoseek	`http://www2.infoseek.com`
Inktomi	`http://inktomi.berkeley.edu`
Yell	`http://www.yell.co.uk` (UK specific)
Yahoo!	`http://www.yahoo.com`

What Does It Cost?

You may be wondering how much it costs to publish a Web page. The best answer to that question is, "How much do you have?" Depending on whether you work with a current Internet service provider, or an online service, or you opt for your own Web server, the cost can range from just pennies to thousands of dollars per month.

The toughest part of cranking up your own server is paying the monthly maintenance fees for ISDN, T-1, T-3, or other high-speed telecommunication lines. Most schools and districts balk at the $60 to $2,000 monthly fee. But wait! Before you fall out of your chair, you should know that ISDN and other similar high-speed telecommunication lines are

- ✔ Becoming more common
- ✔ Becoming less expensive
- ✔ Often discounted for educational institutions
- ✔ Becoming easier to set up
- ✔ Becoming easier to manage

With all this good news, how can you help but jump online?

Tricks for Getting Noticed by the "Big Kahunas"

I've managed to meet lots of people in my surfing sojourns in preparation for writing this book. As I met each Webmaster, or more often, Webmistress, I ask each for their best trick of the trade for getting noticed on the Web. Although some of these folks are admittedly full of techno-speak, after you've surfed around to other Web sites and built your own Web page, you come to understand what they are talking about. Here's the top list of tips to get attention:

- ✔ **Use an effective page title.** Your title is an important factor in getting your page recognized by the big search engines, such as Yahoo! and AltaVista.

  Use the first header HTML style (H1) for the title style and make sure that the title contains your most important keywords. For example, if you think that surfers will seek "Georgia High Schools," a page titled "Georgia High School: Parkview HS" will be among those frequently visited.

✔ Use the <H1>...</H1> HTML tag pair somewhere near the top of your home page to repeat the page's title. Putting an attractive logo at the top of the page is fine, but a logo doesn't mean anything to a search engine. For the best results, consider using both a logo and a text header.

✔ Select your keywords with care. (Keywords appear in the HTML code of your document but aren't displayed by your browser. Use View HTML Source in Claris Home Page 2.0 to see examples of keywords and keyword syntax on your favorite Web pages.) Determine the two or three dozen keywords that seem to be the most essential to your site; then make sure that the most important of these are in your title and mentioned early on in the text in your Web page. Examine sites similar to yours on the Web and see what they've done with their keywords. Where do their keywords show up in a page when the keywords are included in a query?

✔ Don't repeat your keywords too many times; it can work against you. In fact, Infoseek (one of the bigger search engine sites) warns that using a keyword more than seven times in a *meta description* (the first few lines of text on your Web site) causes the description to be ignored.

In the past, Web pages rose to the top of the search engine's list if the pages used certain words repeatedly. Some crafty Webmasters even began to embed *hidden text* (white colored text on a white background) in Web pages to get themselves to the top of the search list. Eventually, the creators of the larger search engines got wise to this trick and placed blocks against this kind of data manipulation (which, incidentally, was dubbed "spamdexing"). (Eek, they took all the fun out of it!) Pages with repeated words are now penalized and no longer appear prominently on the lists of searching results.

✔ Include a descriptive paragraph on your home page. This paragraph will be used in the HTML Head (use View HTML Source in Claris Home Page to see what the program classifies as a Head) and in your introductory blurb. It is what search engines usually display to the user if your page is among the results of the query. If a page lacks descriptive text, then there is little chance this page will rank high in results from a search engine query.

✔ If you want your Web page to be found by people who are using some keywords, be sure to include those words near the beginning of the Web page. A *spider* (a Web-page-seeking program running on search engine servers) makes a determination about relevant words based on the way the words are used on the page. Search engines catalog the text read from the pages they have visited. Some search engines catalog ALT text and text in the comment and meta tags. To be sure, a straight HTML description is recommended. If you really can't put a text description there, use the <META> tag.

✔ Consider offering a text-only version of your site. If your home page has lots of graphics or JavaScript (see Chapter 17 for information on JavaScript), consider creating a text-only Web page that describes your school.

✔ Supply the basic "who/what/when/where" information in your site. A page of this sort is a huge assistance to people seeking specific information, for the visually impaired who use text-to-voice translators, and for people who use text-based browsers, such as Lynx. Put this text-only page in your top-level directory, link it to your home page, and create a prominently placed button that links readers to the information.

An instant e-mailing list with just one form

Wouldn't it be great if visitors to your site could automatically be notified of any changes taking place at your school or district just by visiting your site? Wouldn't it be convenient if teachers and community members were informed when a new class schedule was posted or an event, such as a fundraiser, was coming up?

Guess what? They can if you use some HTML code and create a handy form to include in your Web page. This simple form (you can copy the code that follows in this sidebar) provides you with a list of visitors to your page who would want regular updates on your school. (For more info on using forms on your Web page, see Chapter 19.)

Visitors can enter their e-mail address into the form, and those addresses are automatically mailed to you as requests for updates. All you have to do is create a return message, something like "What's New This Month at XYZ High School" and e-mail it back to your visitors.

Here's an example of code you can enter into Claris Home Page to create such a form:

```
<FORM METHOD="GET" ACTION="http://www.netmind.com/cgi-bin/uncgi/
    url-mind">

Enter your e-mail address to receive e-mail when this page is
    updated.<br>

Your Internet e-mail address:<br>

<INPUT TYPE=TEXT SIZE=40 NAME="required-email"><br>

<INPUT TYPE=HIDDEN VALUE="PUT YOUR URL HERE" NAME="url">

<INPUT TYPE=SUBMIT VALUE=" Click Here to Register ">

</FORM>
```

Enter this code into your Web page, and then sit back and wait for the e-mail to flow in. Try it; you'll love it!

What's the bottom line on getting your page online? After you've made the decision as to whether you'll build your own Web server or trust an ISP or online server to host your site, the rest is just transferring your files from your computer to the server. For most schools, using someone else's Web server may make sense, especially because the average school doesn't exactly have an MIS support staff of 25. If you really get the bug to do your own Web-hosting thing, however, do some careful research before you choose the server and server software you'll use.

Well, there they are — a few tips from the masters of Web media! Enjoy them. May their force be with you and your students!

Chapter 19

Managing Your Web Site

· ·

In This Chapter

▶ Knowing your role and sticking to your plan

▶ Evaluating Net content

▶ Creating an Internet learning center

▶ Working with limited resources

▶ Updating your page

· ·

*I*f you're a science educator, chances are that at some point in your teaching career you've been involved in that wonder-of-wonders project — creating a volcano. As a newbie science teacher back in nineteen-eighty-something, I distinctly remember breezing past building a stream table with my students to simulate water erosion (and a mighty river it was) in order to reach Volcano Day. You know the drill: Get all the materials together, set the stage for the grand event by placing the experiment in the context of your learning goals, and then make the earth tremble with the mighty gush of the volcano.

When those classes began, the students were already bustling with excitement. As I carefully explained the experiment, they were anxious to see the outcome. Ingredients were measured, data tables were drawn, and lab notebooks were poised for the big event. When the final ingredient was added, the baking soda volcanoes dribbled forth a fizzing river of white goo.

That's when it happened. One of my better science students, a front-seater named Christy, raised her hand and said, "Mr. Williams, this is boring. Why didn't it blow up?" (Gulp.) As I was masterfully explaining how some volcanoes dribble and don't go off with a shower of sparks and *ejecta* (that's flying rocks for you non-science folks), I realized that Christy had a point. The little science guy sitting on my shoulder whispered in my ear that properly manufactured volcanoes should show the power of nature by casually blasting molten rock and boulders from here to there.

I'll bet you know where this is going. I tripped back to my lab cabinet and selected various volcano-making chemicals and other goodies (small quantities, of course) and proceeded to build a better volcano. I lit the fuse of the second volcano and proceeded to experience a small, but safe, explosion that (to the delight of the class) had the requisite sparks and flames. Unfortunately, the experiment also created what was described by the questioning science-whiz student as a "cloud of stink" that floated lazily out of the classroom and down the hallway, creating what can only be described as total panic.

Teachers complained. Students complained. The principal visited. The smell was sulfur, of course (not something any self-respecting scientist would crinkle a nose at, but which to most people smells worse than yesterday's tuna). The experiment had been a success, sort of, and had created at least one unexpected outcome that was good (a few extra sparks and flames that fizzled safely away) and one that was not so good (the amazing stinking cloud).

As you begin to coordinate the development of your Web presence, think about the stinking cloud I just described before you turn the process over completely to the students. Chances are that you and your students will experience varying degrees of success with every Internet journey. Developing your own home page is no exception. Think ahead and you'll quickly learn to expect the unexpected and be equally prepared for positive and negative outcomes.

Know Where You're Going and What You're Doing

There are a number of parallels between Volcano Day and your experiences in the classroom with building Web pages with your students. Here's a quick list of things to think about before you and your students begin Net-surfing:

- Make sure that you have a plan (establish a reason for posting information to the Internet).

- Make sure that you've prepared your students with reasons for the project (frame your reason in the context of your instructional goals and objectives).

- Make sure that you've completed a "pre-volcano" (or in this case, a pre-surf) checklist. Consider the pitfalls in the process and plan for them.

- Time is a huge factor in Web page creation — great pages aren't completed overnight.

✔ Make sure that you're prepared for unexpected outcomes — the good and the not-so-good ones.

✔ Lead, follow, or get out of the way (know when to give direction, when to jump on the surfboard with students and teach them more about the Web, and when to step back from your computer and let students create on their own).

The last item I just listed will probably be the most difficult to handle at first, but you'll quickly get the hang of deciding which of the three roles is most appropriate for each learning activity. Getting out of the way empowers students with the freedom to create and experience the same joy that you have found in discovering unknown Internet treasures. You've probably heard a great deal about not-so-appropriate things on the Internet, but there's really little to worry about as long as your surfers stay goal-focused.

Work Your Plan

As you plan for your use of the Web (or the Internet) in general, it's important to learn a lesson from some of our underwater friends. Scuba divers have a saying: Plan your dive and dive your plan. It's obvious that good planning is essential to any classroom activity, and following your plan will lead your students to their projected outcomes as efficiently as possible.

When planning to use the Internet with students, think about using the Net to

✔ Expand and enhance problem-solving skills (throw out a topic and see what resources can be identified).

✔ Build critical-thinking skills through focused, outcome-based activities.

✔ Evaluate what students see, hear, or read based on a predetermined set of parameters.

Reread the last item I just listed. This one's a biggie. It's scary to think about the folks out there who believe everything they read in a newspaper or see on television. It's even scarier to think about students surfing the Internet where there is even less journalistic control and fewer folks who might be guided by truth and other desirable virtues. Later on in this chapter, in the section "Making the Grade: Evaluating Net Content," I talk more about assessing the quality of information on the Internet.

Manage Expectations of Student Learning

What is a successful outcome from an Internet session or Web page development effort? It's important to think about your expectations before you challenge students to use Internet resources or create pages of their own for the Internet. Because of the dynamic nature of the medium, not every online session or attempt at publishing may be successful.

The Net is vast, but it still doesn't have quality, credible information on every topic imaginable. More often than not, sessions need to be supplemented with good old books and other print media to develop a clear picture of the topic. All this presents some interesting challenges when it comes time to evaluate student progress and assess outcomes.

How do you evaluate students on Internet projects (including the development of Web pages)? The answer depends largely on your goals. Think about whether the goal of your lesson is to do one or more of the following:

- ✓ Teach students something about the Internet
- ✓ Teach students how to use the Internet
- ✓ Teach students by using information gained from the Internet
- ✓ Teach students how to create publications for the Internet
- ✓ Teach students how to apply current classroom objectives to an Internet-based Web page project

Regardless of whether you're focusing on the Internet, the process of using the Internet, or the way the resulting information is used, you can use the same techniques of evaluation that you use for other classroom projects. Checklists, rubrics, peer evaluation, pen-and-paper exams — they all work just fine.

Avoid allowing students to aimlessly wander around the Internet as a reward for completing their other assignments. If you do, you're setting yourself up for some disappointing outcomes. Many students can save their random surfing for their at-home Internet connections (*under parental supervision*). If students are browsing just to discover what's out there, at least give them an interesting topic to research (such as "rock and roll on the Internet") or assign an outcome goal (for instance, finding out if there's a skateboard magazine on the Net).

Making the Grade: Evaluating Net Content

Talk with your students early on about taking a careful look at each source of information and at what they're reading. Work to develop a list of essential questions to determine the credibility and truthfulness of each source they stumble upon.

Think about keeping a log of not-to-be-missed Web pages next to your computer. You may even create a form that students or teachers can complete so that others can benefit from their searching. Include questions such as

> ✔ What is the name of the Web page?
>
> ✔ What is its Internet address (URL)?
>
> ✔ What are four positive things about the page?
>
> ✔ How might the content (or design) of the page be improved?
>
> ✔ Which topic or subject area would get the most use out of this page?
>
> ✔ What is the best thing about this Web site?

As a follow-up to compiling a log of favorite Web sites, suggest that a small group of students sort through the information and create a "Top Tips for Creating a Web Site" brochure for your classroom (or even for the whole school to use).

Want to find some great evaluation activities and checklists? Launch your Web browser and go to the Wentworth Communications Web site (http://www.wentworth.com/). There you'll find lots of sample articles, hyperlinks to valuable education sites on the Web, and even some home page links to schools on the Internet. The Wentworth folks publish what I believe to be the best monthly education resource for Net surfers — *Classroom Connect* magazine.

To get on the *Classroom Connect* mailing list, send an e-mail message to crc-request@wentworth.com. In the body of the message, enter the word subscribe. Leave the subject of your message blank. If your e-mail program requires a subject, enter subscribe in the subject box. You also can visit their FTP site for some great educational software and documents. Use FTP to get to ftp://ftp.wentworth.com.

It's also a good idea to have students cite Internet resources when they use the information for classroom assignments, presentations, or other research activities. Check out the nearby sidebar, "How to cite electronic media sources," which shows you what the good folks at the MLA (Modern Language Association) said about citing resources.

Limiting student access to the Internet

Because the Internet offers access to millions of people worldwide, both as consumers and producers of information, its content is as varied as the individuals who use it. As such, you can find things on the Net that will make you chuckle, cry, or cringe. Because not everything on the Internet is appropriate reading and viewing for everyone, several products have recently emerged that make limiting access to the Net easier than ever.

Currently, more than 200 Internet newsgroups contain sexually explicit material. Some Web sites even contain motion pictures and text that depict sexual relations. Until recently, there's been no way to control access to this information — that is, until Surfwatch.

Surfwatch is one of the first, and still one of the best, software products that allow you to block access, either from individual computers or through networks, to sexually explicit sites (or sites with any other kind of potentially objectionable content). A password-protected on/off switch lets you allow access or prevent it. Surfwatch is available for both Macs and PCs running Windows.

Surfwatch comes with a listing of Internet addresses for hundreds of sites containing material that the folks at Surfwatch believe may be offensive or upsetting to your kids.

They also offer a subscription program that updates the list of unwanted sites automatically.

Admittedly, the Surfwatch standards are subjective, but you can request customized lists for your particular situation. Surfwatch controls access to specific World Wide Web, FTP, Gopher, and chat sites, and can restrict access to selected newsgroups. It works with any Macintosh or Power Macintosh with System 7.x or Windows 95 or Windows 3.1 with any modem, ISDN, or high-speed Internet link. Surfwatch is not designed to work with commercial online services. If this program interests you, contact Surfwatch by e-mail at info@surfwatch.com or visit their Web site at http://www.surfwatch.com/.

Other similar programs that limit access to the Internet include CyberPatrol (http://www.microsys.com), NetNanny (800-340-7177), CYBERsitter (http://www.solidoak.com), Purview IM (800-541-5223), and Apple's At Ease (for limiting access to the browser completely) (http://www.education.apple.com). These programs offer varying control options. For the record, I don't generally think that teaching Net responsibility by Net control is the answer — but it's nice to have programs for those who do want to use this method.

Splash the Net on the Wall for All to See

Exploring the Net with your entire class sometimes makes sense. Hook your computer to a good-quality LCD panel and project your Internet session on your classroom walls. This strategy for whole-group instruction makes good sense, especially when you're all just learning to surf for the first time.

TIP

How to cite electronic media sources

After your students find information on the Net they'd like to share with others or include in their Web page, how do they properly give the author of the information credit?

What follows is a list of MLA (Modern Language Association) citation standards that you and your students can use as a guideline:

✔ Electronic mail messages

Include name of author (last name and initials). Year, month, and day message is posted. Subject of message (for example: [e-mail to receiver's name]. [Online]. Available e-mail: the receiver's e-mail address).

Here's an example:

Templeton, P.K. (1995, June 5). Project Deadline [e-mail to `fred.flintstone@ slate.com`], [Online]. Available e-mail: `fred.flintstone@slate.com`.

✔ Articles available via mailing lists

Root, C. (1994). ESL and learning disabilities: A guide for the ESL practitioner. TESL-EJ 1. Available e-mail:`LISTSERV@CMSA. BERKELEY.EDU`. Message: `GET TESLEJ01 A-4 TESLEJ-L F=Mail`.

✔ Online chat rooms

Bard Williams. [Online]. Available IRC: `telnet` (site address), IRC channel name, date of session.

✔ Online images (graphics)

Picture name. [Online Image]. Available `http://address/filename`, date of document or download.

✔ Online sounds

Description or title of sound. [Online Sound]. Available `http://address.filename`, date of document or download.

✔ Online video

Description of title or video clip. [Online Video Clip]. Available `http:// address/filename`, date of document or download. [Quicktime Format]

✔ FTP or telnet

Kehoe, B.P. (1992). Zen and the art of the Internet (2nd. Ed.), [Online]. Available FTP (Telnet) `quake.think.com`, Directory: `pub/etext/1992`. File: `Zen10.text`.

✔ Computer programs

Sandford, J.A. & Browne, R.J. (1985). Captain's log: Cognitive Training System (Version 1.0). [Computer program]. Indianapolis: Psychological Software Services, Inc.

✔ Online databases

The educational directory. (1992). [Online]. Available: Knowledge Index File: The Educational Directory (EDUC6).

✔ World Wide Web

Bard Williams. Net-Ready Educator's Home Page. [Online]. Available `http://www. mindspring.com/~bardw/bard. html`, date of document or download.

These guidelines, and more, are adapted from the MLA Citation Guide at `http:// www.cas.usf.edu/english/walker/ mla.html` and `http://www.pitsco. inter.net/p/cite.html`.

Are Internet programs really free?

Using software programs and including them on your school's Web site is one of the major issues you and your students face in managing your Internet projects. Are the programs you download from the Net really free and usable on your Web site? You'll find that some are and some aren't. By sorting the files on the Internet into three categories (public domain software, freeware, and shareware), you can make sense of the software that's out there.

✔ *Public domain* programs and files carry no copyright restrictions. There are no limits on their redistribution, modification, or sale.

✔ *Freeware* programs and files are free for you to use and give away, but not to sell or modify. The author retains the copyright to these programs.

✔ *Shareware* programs and files allow you to road-test programs for a short evaluation period and then either pay the author a small fee or erase the program from your computer. The author retains all copyrights, and although you can give shareware programs to your friends, all shareware information must accompany the program, and those friends also have to pay the author.

You can set a good example for your students by always paying shareware fees and by discussing the issue of intellectual property rights with them. Most of the programs that come with this book are programs that wouldn't be available if there weren't lots of honest computer users like you out there.

Jot down 10 or 12 random topics related to your subject area (or any other worthwhile subject area) and ask students to pick one of them from a hat. Use these topics as a starting point (and as a goal) for your on-the-wall activity.

I usually model this endeavor by beginning with a search engine (a site on the Internet that allows you to search other sites), such as Excite (http://www.excite.com/), and then showing students how moving from link to link until you find the information you need is, at best, a hit-or-miss exercise.

To keep the entire class involved, question students frequently about what they're seeing and how the surfing expedition is proceeding. Ask them questions such as

✔ Does this Internet site contain information that is credible, truthful, and helpful for our learning goals?

✔ Does this Internet site contain all the information we need? If not, what are the unanswered questions?

✔ Now that we have the information we need, what should we do with it?

Having one or more students keep a log of all sites that you've visited is also helpful. After the activity is complete, create a "road map" that shows where you surfed and how one link led to another. This helps students understand the dynamic nature of the Internet and encourages them to think about the complexity and vastness of the Internet as a classroom resource.

Establish an Internet Learning Center

One strategy for using the Internet more fully in a resource-limited environment is the creation of a learning center. Meet with fellow teachers to develop short, meaningful Internet excursions. Design these excursions to be step-by-step-oriented and focused on a specific learning goal with some sort of written product in the end. With this configuration, you can easily rotate students of just about any age through the learning center with all of them having success.

Carefully written directions and a whole-class discussion of the technical aspects of the activity prevents floundering and frustration on everyone's part. Have students write something about their journey or have them print out data to share with you and the rest of the class as evidence of their success in this learning adventure.

Control the time-on-task factor by using clocks or timers and make sure to give students a starting point (such as an Internet URL) from which to explore. Allow students to work in pairs, if possible, to encourage synergy and reduce the likelihood of floating past unanswered questions.

One more thing: If students don't make good use of their time, restrict their access to the Web. You'll quickly find that this is just as effective as the "no video games until you do your school work" rule at home.

Flying Solo with a Single Computer

If your school's like most, you probably don't have Internet access in every classroom. In fact, chances are that if you have any connection at all it's in your school's media center or tucked away in a computer lab. It's also likely that your school has only one computer directed to the on-ramp to the information superhighway. (Luckily, this barrier to Internet-assisted instruction is rapidly falling!)

One computer connected to the Internet is kind of like having one set of encyclopedias for an entire class. It's not an ideal configuration, but (crafty, innovative teachers that we are) we can usually find a way to make it work.

The nearby sidebar "Working without a Net" presents are a couple of ideas for using the Internet when you're restricted to a single computer or phone line. Think about your goals for the Net activity; then read on. These are, of course, only a few of the possibilities for working with the Internet.

Tending to Your Crops with Regular Web Page Updates

Many Web pages wither away and die from lack of attention. As educators, we have a special duty to keep the information posted under the school's name fresh and interesting. Don't create a "do it once and you're done" site!

Working without a Net

If you don't have access to the Internet via a direct Internet connection, try using an online service, most of which offer Internet connections. If you don't have any access at all to the Internet, try asking a friend who does have access to print out samples of data mined from the Net. Ask your friend to include screen shots and URLs, and share these with your students to give them a taste of what Net-surfing is like.

I've listed a few more activities to heighten awareness of the Net while you await your Internet connection:

- Have students collect newspaper and magazine articles focusing on the Net and create a bulletin board filled with these clippings.

- Test student knowledge of the Internet by challenging them to draw a picture of the Internet (this activity can be lots of fun — who knows what you'll get!)

- Invite a parent or a local businessperson to give a presentation to your class using their Internet connections.

- Invite students to create a classroom dictionary of terms found in books and periodicals relating to the Internet.

- Have students create storyboards containing rough sketches of the design of a proposed Web site.

Meanwhile, put on your best lobbying face and begin to work behind the scenes to make sure that your Internet connection becomes a reality. For statistics to back you up in your quest, check out *The Internet For Teachers*, 2nd Edition (from IDG Books Worldwide, Inc.).

Some do's and don'ts of Web publishing to keep in mind are

- ✔ Do use lots of navigational cues, such as arrows and menus, to keep your readers from getting lost.

- ✔ Do go for content over hype — being cool is one thing; being cool and *useful* is better.

- ✔ Do minimize large graphics or use alternative graphics or text to reduce downloading time for your readers.

- ✔ Do leave an e-mail address or include a "mailto" hypertext link so people can write and give you compliments.

- ✔ Do make sure your school's location and phone number (and the name of a Webmaster or contact person) is on the top-most page.

- ✔ Don't let the page's content get stale.

- ✔ Don't concentrate more on format than content.

- ✔ Don't take on all the content development or formatting yourself. Your students will quickly become very adept at this!

- ✔ Don't do what everyone else has done. (You can do better!)

There you have it. Managing your Web site means setting expectations for the use of your site, helping students evaluate the content you'll display (as well as the content you mine elsewhere on the Internet), and regularly "tending to the crops" on your site so people will want to come back and visit again. It is, of course, appropriate that your students do most of the crop-tending. You have to watch for a few weeds they may stick in the patch now and then, but overall your harvest of information should be very rich!

Part VI
The Part of Tens:
Tens of Ideas,
Tens of Sites

The 5th Wave   By Rich Tennant

"Oh, I'll get us in - I used to teach Web publishing to teenagers."

In this part . . .

Whether you want ideas for cool Web projects for your classroom, samples of cutting-edge Web page designs from schools around the world, or tips for teaching others about the Web, you'll find them in this part of the book! I also take a look into the cyber-crystal ball and give you my predictions about where the Web might be headed in the future. (Future, in the Internet world, means "after today" — things move so quickly!)

Feel free to use the information in this part to enrich your staff development for teachers and enhance "basic training" for your students. Here's a hint: It's better to absorb this stuff in small bites than to cram the whole Internet publishing world into your brain at one time. Take things slow and easy and the end results can be startling.

Chapter 20

Ten Hot Web Projects

1 can think of only three reasons why you wouldn't want to do a project that involves using the Internet:

✔ You don't have easy access to the Internet. (It's a money thing.)

✔ You don't understand the Net. (It's a learning thing.)

✔ You have 120 kids at school, 3 kids at home, and a spouse who thinks that a trip to the hardware store for a Phillips-head screwdriver, or to the mall for a tube of lipstick, is infinitely more important than shopping for an online project. (It's a time thing.)

Folks, let me tell you. This Internet stuff is easier than you think. No matter what the challenge, a way can be found to get around nearly every one of them. Learning more about the Net ensures that you can jump these hurdles like an Olympic athlete rather than a beginning runner. (Of the three reasons I just listed about why you might not be using the Net in the classroom, I must admit the toughest problem is the "time thing." It requires the toughest adjustment: rethinking how you teach and how your students learn, and figuring out how, and if, the Internet fits into what you want to accomplish each day.)

As you scan the projects described later in this chapter (and these projects represent just a fraction of the ideas that are out there for the taking), think about the potential benefits of learning (either your own or your students') and try to determine whether the activity fits with your current learning objectives you're helping your students to achieve.

After each project description, I've provided an Internet address that may serve as a starting point for students. Feel free to make you own selections to begin your search! Make a New Year's resolution (even if it's only September) to try just one of the addresses I've included. I guarantee you'll find that using the Web is addictive.

Talking to the World

The main reason most people use the Internet is to communicate with others. Think of the Internet as a bunch of boxes (or computers) connected by wires (called networks) and driven by lots of people (who are users, all of whom bring their knowledge and wisdom to the Internet community). Online projects that allow you and your students to communicate with your peers (or with experts — or just with other citizens of Planet Earth) can bring big rewards. Using the Web is a *gestalt* of sorts — the whole is a whole lot greater than the sum of its parts.

Animal magnetism (zoo searches)

Wild animals roam throughout the Net. A wealth of information is available about everything from the inhabitants of the London Zoo and national forests to endangered species, or the birth of a rare white Chinese panda.

Ask students to choose a favorite animal and then visit online zoos to collect information about that animal. Also suggest that your students seek out pen pals that live in cities with famous zoos. Your students can then contact these pen pals to conduct interviews with them, exchange pictures (digitally!), or post information about their personal experiences at their own zoos. After your students have located information on the species of their choice, have them create a mobile, a bulletin board, or a brochure about that animal. Be sure to add the project information (and some of the student products) to your school's Web page!

Want a good starting point to learn more about "online zoos"? Check out:

```
http://www.yahoo.com/Science/Zoology/Zoos/
```

Recipe exchange

Close your eyes and think about the best home-cooked meal that you've ever had. Don't you wish you could re-create that magic recipe? The following is a great idea to combine communication, research, and fund-raising in your school.

Challenge your students to poll their families and friends, both on and off the Internet, to get their favorite recipes. Use the best recipes to create a yummy Web page that features a new recipe each week. (Be sure to create a "recipe release" form for your participants to sign!)

If you want to get really creative, try publishing your own cookbook and advertising the book on your new Web page. (One school in Michigan earned more than $2,500 in three weeks with its cookbook!)

Here's a good starting point for creating a recipe Web page:

```
http://www.indi.net/welcome.html.
```

You're moving where?

I recently moved from the sunny South to the snowy North. You wouldn't believe how useful the Net has been in helping me get comfortable. I can sign onto the Net and find subway maps, restaurants, and libraries. I've even discovered Bunker Hill!

Have your students draw slips with the names of large cities from out of a hat. Explain to your students that they are soon moving to the city that they picked and they need to find enough information so that they can decide which neighborhood they would like to live in. Next, they need to get directions on how to get from the airport to that area of the city. (Figure 20-1 shows a great page for getting this kind of information.)

The starting point for this very "moving" exercise is here:

```
http://www.neosoft.com/citylink/ or www.vicinity.com
```

Figure 20-1: MapBlast! provides a starting point for geography and mapping exercises.

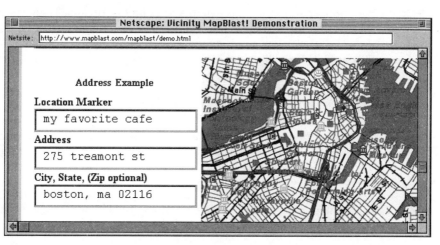

Hitting the Electronic Books

One of the most frustrating things about textbooks is that they're OLD. The second they're printed they go out of date. In today's fast-paced world of cyber-info, gaining access to up-to-the-minute information is becoming more and more important as a way to accomplish next-millennium curriculum objectives. These activities will give you a beginning for some "just-in-time" learning that'll energize your classroom.

News beyond your own backyard

A hot news spot always seems to be popping up somewhere in the world. For example, during the past several years, Bosnia has been a center of attention for the many human dynamics at play there. Staying abreast of international events and other breaking news stories is a great reason to log on to the Net.

Have your students work in groups to use popular search engines, such as Yahoo! (http://www.yahoo.com/) or CNN's Web site for articles and information about Bosnia (or any other global locations of interest). Be sure to have your students search for background material (weather, climate, geography, culture, and such). Then ask your students to write a news story about some aspect of that country. Ask your students to exchange the stories with each other and to edit them until they're worthy of publication. The final newsletter that contains their stories can then be shared with other students around your school.

Starting point for creating a news publication about Bosnia can be found here:

```
http://www.cnn.com/
```

For younger students, find a map and point out Bosnia. Then ask them to search for information such as the type of clothing people wear or what the major cities are like, and then encourage the students to relate that information to their own surroundings.

Researching with ERIC

We educators can't seem to do anything in educational research without our good buddy ERIC. These days, ERIC lives not only in the voluminous binders on library shelves, but also lives in a CD-ROM and on the Net. For those who haven't yet "met" ERIC, it's an acronym for the Educational Resources Information Center— a federally funded project of the U.S. Department of Education, Office of Educational Research and Improvement.

The ERIC database is an internationally accessible collection of practical and research-oriented documents for educational practitioners and researchers at all levels. Don't forget to check with your local college for telnet addresses that you can use for full-text article retrieval.

Here's a starting point for educators on the long road to conducting research with ERIC:

```
http://ericae2.educ.cua.edu/search.htm
```

The market basket (food price comparisons)

How much does a loaf of bread cost in Alaska? Here's a chance to help your students integrate communication skills with higher-order thinking skills while they research and compare prices on ten well-known products.

First, have students visit a supermarket and get the prices on ten "staple" items: bread, Coca-Cola, apples, and such.

Next, arrange to exchange e-mail with a school in another state (or country) and have students practice their graphing and analysis skills as they answer these questions:

- ✔ Which items are more expensive where you live?
- ✔ Which items are less expensive where you live?
- ✔ How much difference is there in the price of each item?
- ✔ Why would the same item cost more or less depending on where you live? (List three reasons.)
- ✔ What kinds of products are grown or produced in your town, city, county, or state? Are these products more or less expensive where you live? Why?
- ✔ How might the information you collect be used to advise a person expecting to move to your area? If your prices are more expensive than those at the comparison sites, how can you justify the extra expense to a prospective resident?

Other projects like this "market basket" exercise are available through mailing lists — or try the keyword **ESH** on America Online.

Try this starting point to fill your market basket:

```
http://pixel.cs.vt.edu/melissa/projects.html
```

Believe it, or not?

Is everything that is published on the Net true? My guess is that most students (and many parents) may think so. Here's a chance for a constructive lesson for students. Have small groups of students choose a topic of interest and collect information about the topic from four different sites on the Net. As they collect the data, have them note which site they visited (by jotting down their URLs). After the information is collected, ask the students in each group to rank the information sources based on their perception of the credibility of each source. Have each group present their analysis of each site to the class and discuss the rankings.

I recommend this starting point to analyzing the truthfulness of information on the Net:

```
http://www.cnn.com/
```

For younger students, discuss some easy tips for determining when information is true or false. This exercise provides a great opportunity for a value lesson on being a good "Internet Citizen" as well!

A taxing situation (searching for IRS forms on the Net)

Imagine that it's 10 p.m. in the United States on the night before tax returns are due to Uncle Sam. You still need one more form to complete your return: the form that lists dependent income. Have your students surf the Web and find the IRS Web page, download the file for this form, and print it. Extend the activity by discussing the context in which the form might be used and some strategies for better tax planning.

A good starting point for "auditing" the forms the IRS supplies is this:

```
http://www.irs.ustreas.gov/prod/cover.html
```

Raising Arizona (the search for the American Indian cultural heritage)

The Web is the perfect medium to foster global thinking, which in turn produces new and creative ideas for how we should be doing business around the world.

Imagine that you and your students have just become ethnographers. First, have your students find out what an ethnographer *is* and what an ethnographer *does*. Next, have your students choose a particular world culture. Finally, have them search the Internet for specific information that might be used to give a clear and honest picture of that culture, or of famous people from that culture.

A recommended starting point for examining world cultures is here:

```
http://www.dreamcatchers.org/
```

WebCo, Ltd.

Have students list their favorite soft-drink company, computer company, fast-food company, book company, or any combination of these. Explain that they have just been hired to create a Web page for that company and that the Web page is to be aimed at their own age group as a target market.

To create the Web page, your students should first search the Web to see if they can locate a page for a company like the one they've chosen. After they've found a similar page, have them note which elements, such as graphics, advertisements, or coupons, the company's Webmaster has chosen to include on the page.

Next, have students consider the demographics of the group of people who will likely purchase your company's product. What age groups might buy the product? Would the product appeal more to males or to females (or to both equally)?

Finally, have your students use a Web publishing tool or their favorite word processor to create a mock-up of a Web page for the business that they have selected. (See Figure 20-2 for a glimpse of how the pros do it.)

The icing on the cake is to have students print out their Web pages and enclose them with a letter to the vendor of the product they're selling that explains the Web page creation process. Who knows? The vendors may write back and offer your students a job!

A starting point for seeing how to design a Web page to sell a product is here at:

```
http://www.airwalk.com/
```

Figure 20-2:
You and your students can learn much from examining professionally produced corporate Web pages!

Breaking New Ground

The following Web activities will engage students in the process of evaluating information and creating new ways to gain knowledge.

I want to take a vacation in . . .

Have students use the Net to collect information about the vacation spot of their choice. Next, have them create a simple brochure explaining the reasons for their choice, describing highlights of the spot or any other facts about it. As an extension to the activity, ask students to search the Net or your online services to find out about the actual travel and lodging costs at each location, or invite students to interview others via e-mail about their travel experiences. Post the final brochures in an "Around the World on the Net" area in your school's media center.

Your students can learn to be their own travel agents at this starting point:

```
http://www.bookport.com/htbin/publishers/thomasfilms/yah/
```

Shopping on the Net

You thought telephone shopping was easy? Wait until you see how easy it is to shop on the Web! Have students search the Web for sites that are selling items such as clothing, music, or food. Ask students to evaluate and analyze each site for content, organization, and "sales appeal." Then ask them to draft a note to the Webmaster explaining their rankings.

Learn how to be an online comparison shopper at this starting point:

```
http://www.shopping2000.com/
```

My own catalog of URLs

Here's a chance to have your fellow teachers compile a list of their favorite URLs. Post a log beside each Net-connected computer in your school. As sudents and teachers enter a URL that they like, ask them to record the URLs in the log to share with others later. Issue an "Internet Teacher of the Month" award for the educator who enters the most URLs.

Here's a handy starting point for collecting your favorite URLs:

```
http://www.yahoo.com/
```

What's next on the Web?

Virtually nothing is changing more quickly than the information on the Internet. With the Internet's explosion of content, plenty of creative people are looking for new ways to search for and display the information. You can now use the Internet as a telephone, movie projector, interactive conference tool, and CD player. Encourage your students to search key sites for ideas on leading edge Web technology — from Java to sound to multimedia.

Challenge your students to write a short paragraph about what they believe the Internet will be like in ten years. Then invite them to search the Web to find initiatives or companies that are working to push the Web to its next level.

Here are a few URLs to get you started:

- ✔ Apple Computer, Inc. at `http://www.info.apple.com/`
- ✔ International Business Machines (IBM) at `http://www.ibm.com/`
- ✔ Netscape Communications, Inc. at `http://www.netscape.com/`
- ✔ Sun Microsystems, Inc. at `http://www.sun.com/`

Web-Surfing Activities for Younger Students

If I were to hand you a lump of clay and ask you to design an activity for high-school students, would you think that lump of clay is a medium just for little kids? After a day or so of pot-throwing, ink-stamping, and Sanskrit-writing, you'd probably decide that the possibilities found within a lump of clay were endless. Think of the Internet as putty in your hands. (Okay, that phrase is a bit hackneyed, but I think that it works!) No matter what age your students are, information that they (or you) can use to enhance, enrich, or remediate is available.

Getting Seussed

Everybody loves Dr. Seuss. There's a great page on the Web that guides you and your students through games, contests, activities, and more — all based on Cats in Hats and Who-people — that your kids can understand and enjoy. It's a must-see! (Figure 20-3 shows you the Seussville home page.)

Find Green Eggs and Ham and the Grinch at this starting point:

`http://www.randomhouse.com/seussville/`

Toys Forever

What if you and your students could design their own toy? What might it look like? What kind of toys are most fun for kids to play with? What kinds of toys did your parents like most? Lots of questions and answers arise from this info-packed Web page designed by two Portuguese children (see Figure 20-4). Use this page as a beginning for activities about invention and innovation. (This site is also available in several languages!)

Figure 20-3: Introduce Dr. Seuss's Seussville to your younger students (and they'll tell you who all the characters are).

COOL WEB SITE

Here's a starting point for information on creating your own toys:

http://www.toysforever.com/english/index.html

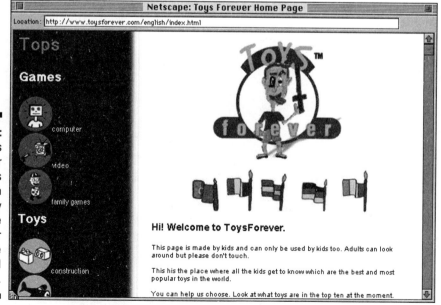

Figure 20-4: Toys Forever offers kids an opportunity to write about their favorite toys and more.

The greatest hurdle to using the Net with younger students is that much of the medium requires reading skills. Nevertheless, a very graphical part of the Net exists that kids of practically any age can understand. Try the activities mentioned earlier, as appropriate, by using parent "coaches" or older student "buddies." You'll be surprised at how successful the young ones can be at Web surfing!

Chapter 21
Ten Winning Webmaster Sites

. . . .

In This Chapter

▶ Web reference bonanza

▶ Diagnosing your Web work

▶ All about Java

▶ Graphics and more

. . . .

*O*ne of the really neat things about the Web is that it's a great place to learn neat things about, well, the World Wide Web. There are literally thousands of Web pages dedicated to helping you and your students build better Web pages of your own. In this chapter, I've supplied a small sampling of the different kinds of pages you might find helpful, from general reference to programming to graphics and even a Web site that looks at the code on your Web site and gives you feedback about what you can do better.

One word of warning — most of these sites are long on useful information, but sometimes fall short on practicing what they preach as far as design style and ease of use goes. Nevertheless, the information inside them is great.

The Ultimate Web Reference?

From Net beginners to Webmasters, `www.webreference.com` is the fastest way to learn about the Web and the art of the Web site. This site is packed with tutorials, tools, graphics, sounds, statistics, and much much more (see Figure 21-1). You can find it at:

```
http://www.webreference.com/
```

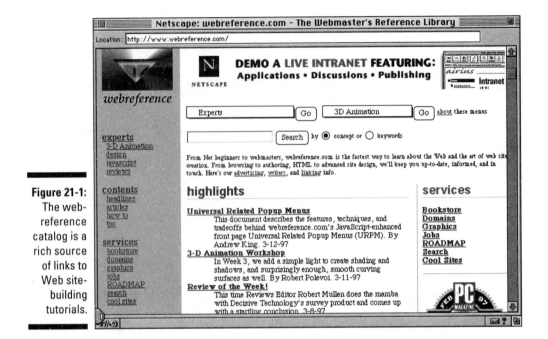

Figure 21-1:
The web-
reference
catalog is a
rich source
of links to
Web site-
building
tutorials.

Reach for the Stars

The WDVL (Web Developer's Virtual Library) is one of the most popular and respected resources for Internet developers and publishers. A gold mine of information with more than 500 pages and thousands of references, it's the only on-line encyclopedia for Webmasters. It's organized with several navigational aids to enable users to quickly and easily find what they are looking for (see Figure 21-2). You can find it at:

```
http://www.stars.com/
```

No Bones about It

The Bare Bones Guide to HTML lists every tag in the official HTML 3.2 specification — plus the Netscape extensions — in a concise and organized format. This is a great place to go when you're ready to move beyond the scope of this book or if you're just curious. You can find the site at:

```
http://werbach.com/barebones/
```

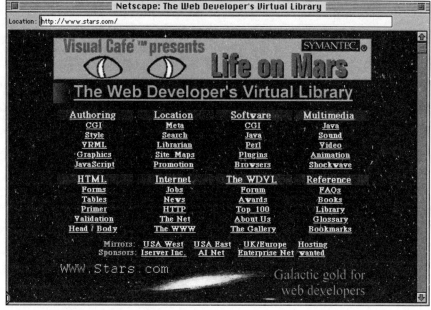

Figure 21-2:
This online
encyclopedia
for
Webmasters
boasts
more than
500 pages!

Diagnosis Perfect!

This is an amazing site (see Figure 21-3) that uses a clever CGI script to
check your HTML programming for "bad code." (Chapter 11 briefly covers
CGI.) It even checks all your links to see if they're still good. This feedback is
as helpful as it is instructive. It's kind of like submitting a paper for your
teacher to grade — those 10 to 15 seconds the CGI script takes to run can
seem like hours. On first trial run of this site, my home page had 22 syntax
errors, but no spelling errors. Oh well, I guess that's good! You can find this
site at:

```
http://www2.imagiware.com/RxHTML/
```

All about Java!

Want to know more about Java language? This is the quintessential source
for links to information about, and examples of, Java and JavaScript.
Whether it's buttons, counters, or dancing ticker tapes you want, this is the
place to begin. You can find this site at:

```
http://www.javasoft.com
```

Figure 21-3:
Is there a
Web doctor
in the
house?

Get Some HotSauce

The inventors describe HotSauce as "a technology demonstration based on MCF (Meta Content Framework). MCF is a new approach to representing meta information about content in any information space." What, huh? In simple terms, it's basically an incredible new way to organize and browse sites on the Web. It simulates being in "meta-space" and you and your students are the pilots. This stand-alone or Netscape Java plug-in application is free and very, very cool. (See Figure 21-4.) You can find this site at:

```
http://hotsauce.apple.com
```

Tools-R-Us

Need a tool to create audio files for your Web site? This site is well-maintained and has Web-creation tools as well as a variety of viewer and helper applications and graphic and multimedia utilities. Visit the NCTWeb Software Tools for the Web site. You can find the site at:

```
http://www.awa.com/nct/software/webtools.html
```

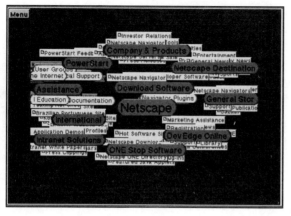

Figure 21-4:
Get some
HotSauce
for your
Mac or PC
for some
cool space
surfing.

Graphics à la Mode

Lynn's most-excellent WebMastery site offers gobs of public domain graphics, sounds, and design elements to snazz up your Web pages. (See Figure 21-5.) A unique "jukebox" even allows you to listen to some digital music while you're browsing the site. You can find the site at:

```
http://fly.hiwaay.net/~nlf/index.html
```

Figure 21-5:
Lynn has
put together
a great
collection
of graphical
elements
you can use
on your
school Web
site.

Go CGI!

Need help writing CGI scripts? (These are programs commonly used to provide a means for online feedback, enable database searches, or provide gateways to Internet services outside the Web.) The CGI Resource Index is packed with samples and libraries of pre-made CGIs. Each script is formatted so it can be easily pasted into your Web page. The site also includes valuable information resources and even job listings. This site is a must-see for budding programmers. You can find it at:

```
http://www.cgi-resources.com
```

Chapter 22

Ten Tips for Teaching Other Teachers about the Web

• •

In This Chapter

▶ Vogue: the staff development way

▶ Doing the right thing the right way for the right reasons

▶ Net by teacher: Internet training tips

• •

*R*emember when computers first began to appear in schools? I remember teaching hundreds of fellow teachers to become "computer literate." Back then, computer literacy meant knowing the difference between RAM and ROM and knowing that, to insert a $5^1/_4$-inch floppy into a disk drive, you "put your thumb on the label." We all sat through courses in BASIC programming, and went to sleep at night with thoughts of

```
20 FOR x=1 to 10
30 FLASH
40 PRINT "I Love <fill in the blank>"
50 NEXT x
60 END
```

We gave "computer licenses" to students and personal floppy disks to teachers. We spent countless hours focusing on the machine itself, but not on what we'd do with it. Not-too-distant memories, right?

As the years rolled on, we discovered that teaching *with* computers was more important and valuable than teaching *about* computers. Courses in applications appeared, and suddenly we were learning about word processors, spreadsheets, and databases. We learned to use these basic tools, both for instruction and for personal productivity. No longer did we have to know, or care to know, about what's under the hood of a computer. Then someone figured out that we still weren't focusing on either educational outcomes or educational objectives.

The winds of developing technology staff have shifted again (this time toward outcome-oriented interdisciplinary instruction), with the computer used as a tool to achieve an educational objective. The technology has become easier to use, more fully integrated into the learning process, and more transparent. Courses in creative writing, for example, now (almost incidentally) include instruction in using a word processor. Now we can get back to the business of focusing on the tasks at hand and not the technology.

We can learn much from these earlier lessons on the introduction of computers. Look around. Do you see "Internet literacy" classes offered? Why not teach a course in "How to Teach Biology 101 — Frog Dissection" and include information about how to access the Web's "virtual frog" page as a part of the course?

The URL for the virtual frog is `http://george.lbl.gov:80/vfrog/`. See, I wasn't kidding.

Everybody's talking about the Internet, and they all want to learn more about it. Here's your chance to light a fire under your peers and really make some exciting things happen!

Many models for sharing knowledge about the Internet with fellow teachers are available. The following are ten tips and ideas that I think might be effective for you. Each of these methods is teacher-tested and can net (pun intended) some really amazing results!

Teachers Teaching Even More Teachers

Think about centering your instruction on teaching teachers how to teach *other* teachers. Focus classroom activities on first developing (or modeling) a scope and sequence for instruction about the Internet. Then focus on producing a variety of activities, written in a lesson-plan format, that you can use to ensure that teachers feel comfortable with a bit of structure and support for their first Net-ventures.

As with any other staff development, think about follow-up activities ("refresher courses") as you plan to make sure that folks can keep up with the dynamic Internet marketplace.

Summer Camp

Try hosting a CyberCamp! Yep — we're talking T-shirts, camp counselors, off-the-computer activities (the wellness people will love this!), and lots of focused Internet- and computer-based activities that are driven by surveys of your camp's participants. Don't be afraid to ask your school's business partner, or the local PTA, to co-sponsor the event. Styled like a summer camp, it could run for a week and would be a great way to develop a Net-surfing wonder-team!

To be sure that the campfire doesn't fizzle, maintain a notebook of activities that participants can carry back to their classrooms. Gather the materials into a three-ring binder and ask participants to add to the package during the year. It goes without saying that these activities should be shared via e-mail or newsgroups with the Internet community as well!

After-School Blitz

Offer a couple of hours a week of open instruction for teachers in your school. Keep the atmosphere light (no one is more tired and stressed out than a teacher after the final bell). Focus the content on real-world activities that are immediately useful in the classroom. In general, a ten-hour course, taught over five consecutive weeks, works well. Don't forget to plan for a "class reunion" later in the year to see how your class time has paid off.

Be sure to take the time to apply for continuing education credit for the participants. Seek out instructors from your local college, university, or regional education agency.

Weekend Cyber-Warriors

Want to have some real fun? Try a casual roundup of teachers on an Internet Saturday. Eight hours of instruction on a weekend can do wonders for getting teachers and administrators fired up about the possibilities of using the Internet for classroom instruction or personal productivity. The Internet, it seems, is one of the few topics that teachers will gladly give up a Saturday to explore. Try it. I guarantee that more participants than you expect will apply!

Keep the curriculum focused and the atmosphere fun, and allow frequent breaks. Begin your day with a short overview of the Internet (puh-leeeese keep the History of the Internet part very short!) and then jump immediately on the Net for a topic-based activity such as planning a trip to an exotic resort, finding a good seafood restaurant in Boston, or searching for information on education reform in the archives of the U.S. Department of Education.

Again, it's imperative that you create a structure for documenting popular activities, useful Internet addresses, and useful tips for teaching. Don't forget to add a bit of time at day's end for general questions and a discussion about classroom management.

Teach Responsibility

Before you take off on teaching your first Internet course for your peers, take a tip from a friend who conducts staff development for vocational education teachers: "Know the tools of the trade before you trade the tools." You'll have greater success if you start out with a good understanding of what the Net is, what it does, and the challenges you may face in using the Net with students.

Setting up rules and discussing Internet ethics with students (no matter what their age) is an important part of your responsibility as a purveyor of Internet wisdom. Even though the Internet is still the "wild, wild West" of cyberspace (itself a virtually lawless and totally free environment), people have been talking about Internet ethics and rules since the Net's inception. Groups such as the Division Advisory Panel of the National Science Foundation's Division of Network Communications Research and Infrastructure (is that a mouthful or what?) have formal guidelines about unethical and unacceptable activities. This panel defines such activities as those that purposely do any of the following:

- ✔ Seek to gain unauthorized access to the resources of the Internet
- ✔ Disrupt the intended use of the Internet
- ✔ Waste resources (people, capacity, computer)
- ✔ Destroy the integrity of computer-based information
- ✔ Compromise the privacy of users

These guidelines can provide a platform for discussion with your peers (and students) about ethics and responsibility and can serve as a starting point for anticipating the questions of parents and administrators. Take the time to incorporate a discussion of ethics and responsibility into every Internet staff-development session. Focus on what responsible Internet citizens should know and how they should behave on the Net. Consider splitting your class into small groups to develop their own Code of Internet Ethics, and then share the results with your district technology coordinator or college dean — you won't be sorry you did.

After you've given your students (whatever their age) a tour of the Net and discussed the list of Internet don'ts mentioned earlier, ask them to work in small groups to develop their own Code of Internet Ethics (such as your peers have done), and post each group's work in your classroom.

Become a Telementor

The Internet learning curve is a bit steep, but you can conquer it easily. The best way is to ask someone who's already an Internet surfer to show you the way. And, guess what? These Net mentors don't even have to be in the same country as you! They can be anywhere in cyberspace. You can use telecommunications such as e-mail, LISTSERVs, and so on, to communicate. Someone recently called this relationship *telementoring.* I think that's a nifty way of saying, "Find a mentor, and have that person teach you about the Net."

Stumbling Stumbleware

I like to think of Internet tools as "stumbleware." You very often stumble onto resources or ideas that you'd never dreamed of finding, which is one of the best things about the Internet. The most efficient way to learn about the Net is to just dive right in and try it. An easy introduction through a commercial online service is also a great way to begin.

During your first visits, focus on one tool or one type of information. As you explore the Net, think about how you can make your next visit more productive. I find lots of sites just stumbling around at random. The site shown in Figure 22-1, for example, prints out navigational directions to drive from one point in the U.S. to practically any other place in the country. (This site is AMAZING!) Visit it at

```
http://www.mapquest.com/
```

Figure 22-1: "Stumble-time" can unearth sites like this one that gives you a map of your neighborhood!

Like any other technology, the more you use it, the better you become at it.

The Display's the Thing!

 As a practical matter, using a good-quality overhead display makes sense for large group instruction. Multiple phone lines also help. Don't be bashful in asking local colleges or universities to let you use their facilities if you don't have access to these important tools.

Focus on *With*, not *About*

Be sure to focus your instruction on teaching *with* the Internet, and not just *about* it. Link your instruction to curriculum-focused activities and think about possible tangible products and the ways in which you may evaluate those products.

Kill the Seagulls!

Well-conducted staff development is a great opportunity to motivate teachers, however veteran they are; and you can quickly see the wheels turning in the minds of even the staunchest techno-phobes.

But the model we typically use in education for staff development is what I call *seagull staff development*. This is a process in which we swoop into a classroom of teachers (usually large groups), deposit out-of-context content, and fly away, never to be seen again.

Seagull staff development simply doesn't work. A one-shot deal may be enough just to motivate, but it's rarely enough to educate. Try breaking your education workshops into several pieces that you deliver a week (or more) apart. Between sessions, assign *homework* (ugh!) and find ways to monitor the learning. We teachers all know this is what makes learning work, but sometimes neglect to practice it because of inconvenience or budget constraints. Make a pact with yourself: No more seagulls (or rather, no more seagull-style education).

Chapter 23

Ten Cool School Sites

As you may imagine, I've spent literally hundreds of hours scouring the Internet to research this book. I know I must've seen more than 2,000 school sites, so narrowing them down to the ten "best" sites was very tough. The ten sites in this chapter represent what I believe are examples of "best practices" in Web design and implementation. As you visit the sites I've listed, think about these elements:

✔ Does the Web site have a compelling theme and purpose?

✔ Does the Web site give you the information you need to establish location, mission, and the feeling of what it's like to be at the school or university?

✔ Does the designer use Web resources, such as multimedia, color, frames, tables, and so on, effectively?

✔ Does the site have links to lots of *quality* interdisciplinary sites?

✔ Would I want to return to the site?

I think all ten of these sites pass these tests with flying colors. (I apologize if I missed your killer Web site.) If you've got nominations for the next edition of this book, please e-mail them to feedback/dummies@idgbooks.com

Loogootee Elementary

Here's an elementary school with a terrific Web page. (I also thought the name was cool — it's in Loogootee, Indiana, of course.) In addition to excellent organization and great use of Web elements such as frames and icons, this site has information for everyone in the community. (See Figure 23-1.) Nice job, Web team!

Figure 23-1: Find out what an innovative bunch of elementary school folks can do with some great ideas and a Web site!

Visit Loogootee Elementary at:

```
http://www.siec.k12.in.us/~west/west.htm
```

O' Canada!

Some incredibly innovative Web page ideas are coming out of Canada. This site celebrates excellence in Web site production across Canadian schools with its "Cool School of the Week" page. It's great PR for their schools and a quality site all rolled into one!

Visit this site at:

```
http://lancer.stvital.winnipeg.mb.ca/~coolsite/
```

Sam Barlow High School

What happens when you mix a high school with a very talented Webmaster team? You have Sam Barlow High School in Gresham, Oregon. (See Figure 23-2.) In addition to its clever design and organization, this site actually makes you want to attend the school. (I miss corn dogs on Thursdays!) There's excellent talent at Barlow — Netscape, are you listening?

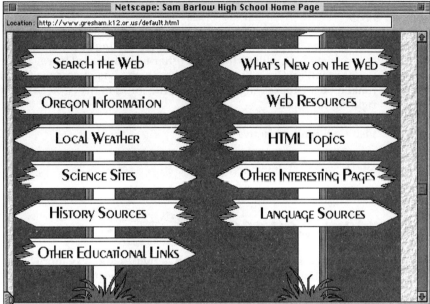

Figure 23-2:
The site developed by Sam Barlow High School in Gresham, Oregon, is a great example of creativity and rich content.

Visit Sam Barlow High School at:

```
http:// www.gresham.k12.or.us/
```

Cal State Does the Web

"It's not beautiful, but it's packed with useful information." That's how one educator described a site created by Dr. Vicki F. Sharp and Dr. Richard M. Sharp, who are Professors of Elementary Education at California State University, Northridge. The Sharps have collected sites and resources from the Internet for teachers to use in their classrooms. There's also a special category for children called "Just for Kids." These sites are entertaining, useful, informative, and fun. They range from lesson plans, creative classroom projects, interactive activities, and visits to museums to trips around the U.S. and other countries.

Visit the Elementary Education site at Cal State Northridge at:

```
http://www.csun.edu/~vceed009/
```

Kidsites

I found this site to have the most complete listing of reviewed sites that are appropriate for children than any other I ran across. The reviewer at Cochran Interactive's Kidsites rates each site based on specific criteria ranked on a 1-to-5 rating scale. From the looks of his choices, I'd say he's right on the mark.

Visit Cochran Interactive's site at:

```
http://www.cochran.com/theodore/noframe/ksites.html
```

Classroom Connect

Wow! Want a site that's packed with activities and way more links than you'll ever have time to visit? That's Classroom Connect. Besides being originators of one of the best newsletters on the planet about using the Net in the classroom, the gurus at Classroom Connect have scored a big one with this content-rich site. Try it once and you'll bookmark it for sure.

Visit Classroom Connect's site at:

```
http://www.classroom.net/
```

Waaaaa-Waaaa-chusett

Wondering how to answer the "We're wired, now what?" question? The folks at Wachusett Regional High School (see Figure 23-3) show what happens when you mix ten or so very talented high-school students and a graphic arts teacher who's got lots of patience and creativity. Besides being a repository for useful information and current events, the WachuNet site illustrates the potential benefits of a school's Internet connection to the community.

Visit Wachusett Regional High School in Massachusetts at:

```
http://199.232.160.4/
```

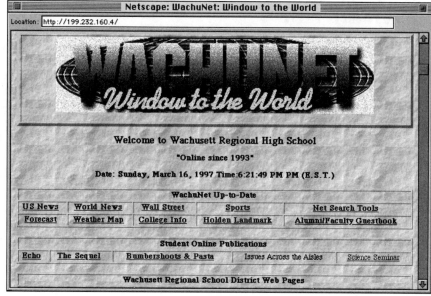

Figure 23-3:
Mix a
computer
club and
an expert
graphic arts
teacher and
here's what
you get!

Ralph Bunche School

From Harlem in New York City comes a terrific site developed by the Ralph Bunche School. Using a "school within a school" concept, Grades 4 through 6 enjoy a high level of access to technology and have created a pretty neat Web site to boot! This site stresses content over design, perhaps reflective of the fact that many of the students maintain, and influence, the content of the site.

Visit Ralph Bunche School at:

```
http://ralphbunche.rbs.edu/
```

Web 66

Be sure to take a trip to the oldest and largest registry of school Web sites on the Net. With some careful TLC from the College of Education at the University of Minnesota, this International Registry of Schools site continues to be the best for surfing from school to school (and a great place for you to prospect for ideas)!

Get to the International Registry of Schools at:

```
http://web66.coled.umn.edu/schools.html
```

It's Nisky Time!

Just one visit to the Niskayuna Central Schools Web site and you realize just how effective a school Web site can be. Besides featuring a dandy use of tables, this site offers easy access to everything you would want to know about the school and its community (see Figure 23-4). It also prominently displays a picture of the school — great for establishing presence and location! Whatta site!

Visit Niskayuna at:

```
http://www.wizvax.net/nisk_hs/
```

There you have it. Ten sites that, while very different, share one goal — providing information that makes for a richer, more diverse teaching and learning environment. Some of the aforementioned sites have more bells and whistles than others, but all show forethought and wisdom in execution.

Your challenge is to work with your students to push the envelope of Web design. Help make the Internet a better place. Design a site everyone will wish to visit and one that represents your school and community well. Who knows, maybe your school will be considered for the next book!

Figure 23-4:
Niskayuna
High
School
uses tables
effectively
to organize
their data.
The site is
deep and
wide in
content!

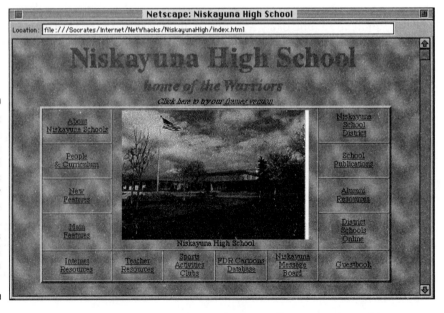

Chapter 24

Ten Webbing Trends to Watch

● ●

● ●

*E*ver taken the time to ponder what life could be like in the classroom of tomorrow? Will you look out at a room full of precious second graders (all wearing multicolored virtual-reality helmets hooked together by infrared signals) and wonder what country/planet/data bank they're exploring today? (They're smiling about something!) The World Wide Web and the Internet could be the vehicle that'll make this possible.

A quick glance at the video game market can tell us what's in store for education. Game manufacturers are creating faster, more user-friendly hardware and more visually stimulating software; and experimentation has already begun with alternative input and output devices. Will the uniform of tomorrow's schools be "Net-ready" clothing — complete with motion sensors, network interfaces, and (of course) the obligatory brand-name logo? Will future students purchase "cyberjeans" made by Apple or Motorola or some other upstart company we haven't even heard from yet?

Kick back and let your imagination wander as you browse through the following pages which explore some of the innovations related to the Net and the Web that are available today. Then go hug a good book.

Total Web Integration

There is already much discussion about whether Internet resources can replace textbooks. Of course, "they" said the same thing about audiotapes, videodiscs, and computers (and even televisions) and it didn't happen — at least not yet. The next generation of textbooks will probably feature Internet addresses inserted in side margins of student and teacher texts. Another visionary idea could involve carefully constructed cyber-journey activities that offer up-to-the-second information, via the Internet, about the curriculum concept or skill being explored.

Content delivery via the Web has already begun. Companies such as the forward-thinking American Cybercasting (`http://www.americast.com/K12`), CNN (`http://www.cnn.com`), and others have already begun to develop specific objective-linked activities that students can explore while online. These activities are designed, for the most part, to complement and supplement, not replace, more traditional classroom activities.

The advantages of curriculum delivery via telecommunications are obvious. Information can be presented in a just-in-time fashion, and Web pages can be easily customized for schools, classrooms, and even individual learners. The major disadvantage is that we are still far from the time when every student has easy access to Internet resources.

Access to computers and the Internet for all school students is the one issue that could really slow the timeline for information exploration in the classroom. New products, such as the eMate (a small, portable, Internet access computer), may just speed things up. (For more information on this technology, check out `http://www.education.apple.com`.)

Web 3-D

Never underestimate the creativity of fellow humans. I'd be willing to wager that at some time in your life you donned a pair of those silly one-red-eye, one-green-eye cardboard 3-D glasses. And let me guess: You were probably viewing some really cheesy sci-fi horror movie (the ghoul reaches out and taps you on the head with a ten-foot sword poking out from the screen), or maybe you were experiencing a multimedia extravaganza at some way cool theme park. Viewing two-dimensional things in three dimensions is neat, but those glasses made folks look silly (and sometimes the effects weren't very stunning at all). You want stunning? Check out *VRML*.

VRML stands for *Virtual Reality Modeling Language,* a standard on the Web that lets Web page developers create an environment that Web users can explore, via the Internet, in three dimensions.

Push Me, Pull You: Two new concepts in Net browsing

Remember Dr. Doolittle's bidirectional creature, the Push-Me-Pull-You, that had two front ends headed in opposite directions? Thanks to some crafty marketeers, two new concepts have been introduced into the world of Web browsing that sound like that two-headed beast: *pull* and *push* technologies.

"Pull" technology works like this: You set up a list of search terms, or questions, for your browser while you're offline. Then, once you sign on, the browser reaches out and grabs specific information from sites based on the directions you've given it. You're *pulling* information from the Net based on your preferences. (There's lots of brainpower now being applied to creating so-called intelligent agents, digital assistants of sort, that can do a lot of the information pulling for you. Now if they could only grade papers . . . .)

In "Push" technology, the contents of the Internet are sent to users' desktops instead of users having to fetch or "pull" information from a Web site. In this model, information based on your preferences that are known by advertisers is *pushed* to your computer's screen 24 hours a day, 7 days a week.

If you've shown interest on in sites on the Internet related to math and education by having visited them, your "push" application dutifully shows you advertisements and news related to those topics as they arrive on the Net or as an advertiser decides to give them to you. Want to find out more about push technology? Push yourself to www.pointcast.com.

Someday, Net surfers will be able to walk down the halls of the Louvre, turning to look at any picture or sculpture they desire, or take a tour of the solar system with planets whizzing past. Because no nerdy bi-color glasses are used, the 3-D effects are limited to the two dimensions of your screen. The overall effect is kind of like peering into a window that looks 3-D (all you Doom or Marathon players out there know exactly what I'm talking about).

VRML was created by Mark Pesce (http://hyperreal.com/~mpesce/), who later partnered with Tony Parisi (a browser whiz) and the "Father of the Web," Tim Berners-Lee. This team of cyber-rangers is currently busy working on ways to make VRML available to greater numbers of computer users.

If you and your students are ready for in-your-face 3-D Web action, try surfing to Silicon Graphics (the developer of the WebSpace 3-D VRML browser) at http://www.sgi.com (see Figure 24-1). A competing product, called WorldView, is under development at ftp://tcc.net.org or http://www.intervista.com/worldview.html. By the time that you read this, both WebSpace and WorldView should be available for Windows, Macintosh, UNIX, and Windows NT machines.

Figure 24-1:
A 3-D Web page tool called WebSpace allows users to explore a new dimension in information access.

Way-Ahead Stuff

Nobody can really predict what'll happen with technology. The creativity of the human mind seems unlimited. (Yes, someday that roustabout in your third-period class may own a $2 billion company!) Government and special interest groups could, with just the stroke of a pen or the touch of a keyboard, alter how technology is implemented and used by the public (and the schools).

This section gives you a little teaser about some Web technology initiatives that are in the works. These initiatives deal with technologies that may have a profound impact on the way that you teach and learn.

Don't wear the harvest gold bathrobe!

Current software and hardware allow you to do much more than just type a letter to your friends. With technology such as CU-SeeMe, you can actually see the person on the other end of the Internet connection *in almost real time.* What's the message here? *Don't wear that harvest gold bathrobe* (you know, the one that's been your friend since 1972) while you're surfing! (I, myself, plan to hide behind a picture of Brad Pitt that I've cut out of the latest movie magazine.)

The hardware for live Internet video conferencing requires:

✔ A camera, such as the really cool-looking "eyeball camera" called QuickCam from Connectix (at www.connectix.com)

✔ A computer

> ✔ Special software (some of which is available on the Net — the most common being CU-SeeMe)
>
> ✔ A high-speed connection (such as an ISDN or T-1 phone line)

Internet video conferencing technology isn't perfect — yet. Unless your connection is a very high-speed line, the images tend to make everyone look like a 1990s Max Headroom. As the technology improves, however, your students should be able to converse live with authors, engineers, politicians, and anyone else who can click a mouse.

Talk shows online

Audio can also be transmitted on the Internet. Plenty of sites currently offer sound files, digitized by their creators, that can be downloaded (copied) to your computer for your listening pleasure. Recent advances in file compression (which reduces the size of files so they're more manageable) make the downloading of those files much less painful than it once was.

Live audio (including *telephony,* in which your computer is used as a telephone) has also arrived on the Net. Enterprising folks have whipped up products, such as Real Video (www.realvideo.com), that can deliver *streaming* (continuous) audio and video at acceptable quality. While Ma Bell and the Baby Bells shouldn't get too nervous, it looks as if real-time audio quality will continue to improve, and people will turn to their computer screens for inexpensive long-distance conversations.

Everybody's on the Net

If the number of people gaining Internet access continues to grow at the current rate, everybody on the planet will be online within ten years. Will you and your students be among some of the first (nudge, nudge)? (In Parts II and III of this book, I take you on a step-by-step journey to create your own World Wide Web page.)

Nowadays, it seems like almost everyone is a personal Web page publisher — and those who aren't want to be! The 10-year-old down the street is just as likely as a Fortune 500 company to have his or her own Web presence. All the major online services (AOL, CompuServe, Microsoft Network, and Prodigy) are making personal Web publishing easier with built-in graphical tools that allow subscribers to create their own simple Web pages.

Elvis lives! (on the Net)

Remember being amazed when wristwatches first stored telephone numbers, and VCRs (through VCR+) could first program themselves? Get ready to be amazed once again. The creative folks at the Voyager Company (`http://www.voyagerco.com`) now have a way for your Internet connection to talk to your computer's CD-ROM drive.

Imagine that your students are surfing the Net, looking for information about pop music, and they stumble upon a Web page from *Spin* magazine. Scrolling down through the lists of clickable Internet links, they spot Elvis. (Now you know where he's really been all these years.) One click and the screen flashes to lots of great information about The King, and a flashing button on the screen reads "Don't Be Cruel" (an admonition perfect for students).

Your students click on the button, and suddenly the room is instantly filled with the sounds of The King himself — in stereo. Amazing, huh?

The King's crooning comes from a CD (one that you've sneaked into the CD-ROM drive of your computer beforehand) that was activated by a Web browser helper application called *CDLink*. The folks at Voyager believe that the possibilities of CDLink are endless.

Web sites can now interact with multimedia CD-ROMs to bring life to the two-dimensional Web. Educators can author Web pages that serve as a front end for myriad multimedia CD-ROM-based data. So now you know: Elvis is alive and well on the Internet.

e-Buck$

I guess it was inevitable that we'd soon be purchasing products and services through the Internet. After some very careful study of the subject, I've finally decided that the *secure sites* (those sites that offer encrypted — that is, protected — transactions, marked by the appearance of an unbroken key icon on the lower left corner of your browser window) are safe enough to use. Since that decision, I've ordered flowers (many times), birthday presents, magazine subscriptions, and even some new income tax software through the Net. The trust is building. So far, so good.

For schools, the advent of "e-commerce" could have wide-ranging impact. Will educators be given a resource budget and then be able to download (and pay) for new content from the Web? Or, for those out there with the entrepreneurial spirit, will you be able to use your skills as an educator to offer training services, via the Internet, and actually get paid for your sideline work? I believe the answer is "yes" to both questions. Start designing a business card now. The worker of tomorrow is likely to be a *knowledge* worker, rather than a production line worker. And guess whose responsibility is it to help that worker get the skills he or she needs? (Perhaps you should also get malpractice insurance. Oh well, we'll take the bad with the good!)

You're on WebTV

We've come full circle in computing. Remember when you used to plug your little old Apple II computer into your TV set via a simple RCA cable? Life was simpler then. Guess what? Now your TV set once again becomes a computer screen with the invention of WebTV.

WebTV offers a relatively low-cost, easy-to-use Web browser projected onto your TV screen. (Now there will be a crop of cyber-potatoes instead of video game spuds.) The catch is that these WebTV devices aren't very smart — they're really for *surfers,* and not *users,* of information.

Few options exist for storing what you've found on the Web, and the resolution on most TV screens isn't too wonderful. But, wait! I'm supposed to be thinking into the future. Coming soon to a living room near you — *Web-ready* TV sets, complete with retractable phone cords, higher-definition TV screens, and wireless keyboards.

Will WebTV replace the computer in your home or classroom? I don't think so. The computer continues to evolve as an increasingly faster, more portable, and more powerful tool for data management. While WebTV is great for the "family that surfs together to stay together," the personal computer is simply more *personal.*

A Web browser screen built into the phone on your desk may make sense too, wouldn't it? Don't you just love this stuff?

Famous Last Words

Will the Internet ever replace the textbook? Probably not in our lifetime. I do believe that telecommunication skills (information management, search and retrieval strategies, and the evaluation of data sources) will become as essential as the three Rs. In view of the latest evolution of Internet-access tools, I'd say that it's a safe bet that you'll see the integration of Internet and other telecommunications methods spread like wildfire (and you'll find that this information access will become less expensive, less time-consuming, less difficult, and more fun!).

Part VII
Appendixes

The 5th Wave — By Rich Tennant

"WE RUN THE COMPANY A LOT LIKE A COLLEGE. WE STAY UP LATE CRAMMING TO FINISH SOFTWARE PRODUCTS, WE ENCOURAGE STUDY GROUPS BY EMPLOYING MULTI-USER NETWORKS, AND ON FRIDAY AFTERNOONS WE ALL GATHER IN THE CAFETERIA, DANCE, DRINK, AND THROW UP ON OUR SHOES."

In this part . . .

Here's a place to go when you're cyber-stumped. You'll find a glossary of terms written in *plain* English and a handy dictionary of HTML tags (for the advanced Web page creator). You'll also find a sample acceptable use policy that you can use as a framework for your own policy for appropriate and intelligent administration of the Web in your school.

Appendix A
Glossary of Terms

address (e-mail, mail server, Web server)

A bunch of letters or numbers that tell the world *who* you are followed by more letters or numbers that tell them *where* you are. Your Internet address will look something like this: `username@domain_name`. The *username* part is your login name or account number. The *domain* part is the name of the computer that connects you to the Internet. The domain name can be a few words strung together with periods. An Internet address usually doesn't have any spaces between words or symbols, but when there are spaces, they are indicated by an *underscore* character as in `fredf@bedrock_slate.com`.

alt

A newsgroup that deals with "alternative" topics. This newsgroup is often thought of as the place where topics are born. When they grow up, they move to other classifications. Beware when you are stomping around in `alt` territory; some things in the bushes shouldn't be in your classroom.

America Online (AOL)

A public online service that has access to the Internet. AOL has the largest U.S. subscription base of any of the commercial online services. Many of its subscribers are educators.

anchor

One end of a link between two files. When you're looking at a Web page, the underlined, colored text that you see is an anchor at one end of a hypertext link. Clicking the text brings up another Web page, which is the anchor at the other end of the link.

anonymous FTP

When you log on to someone else's computer, you may need to provide a login name and password. On some systems, logging in as "anonymous" and using your e-mail address as a password is enough to give you access to public files.

applet

A Java program (or a really small apple).

ASCII

American Standard Code for Information Interchange. Another word for characters (letters and numbers) in a text file.

attribute

In HTML, an attribute is a set of characters after the first set within an HTML tag. It modifies the tag's purpose. Example: In the tag `<IMG SRC="budpic.jpg">`, the attribute is `SRC`.

bandwidth

How much data can be crammed into the data pipeline. Measured in baud or bits per second. Also the amount of information one person can manage at one time, as in "Sorry, I don't have the bandwidth to do bus duty right now."

baud

A unit of transmission speed. The greater the baud rate, the faster data moves from point to point.

BBS

Bulletin board system. A system that lets people post messages, read others' messages, and, sometimes, exchange programs and files. Usenet newsgroups are kinda like the world's largest distributed BBS.

binary file

A file that may contain words, sounds, pictures, even movies, in their *raw* form.

BinHex

A program that converts a binary file, specific to a particular machine, to a text file so that it can be transferred over the Net. The program can then be used to convert the file back to binary for use on your computer.

bookmark list

A list of your favorite Web pages. You can add to your bookmark list while surfing the Net by selecting Add Bookmark from your browser's menu bar.

bounce

When you send e-mail and it comes back marked as undeliverable.

browser

A program used to look at World Wide Web documents. Mosaic was the first popular browser, and Netscape Navigator is currently the market leader, with Microsoft Internet Explorer gaining momentum.

chat

The electronic equivalent of a CB radio. Person-to-person, real-time conferencing.

clickable image map

A graphic that includes areas called "hot spots" that, when clicked, take you to different Web pages or locations within a Web page. Many large Web sites use clickable image maps on their home pages to entice the user to move farther into the site.

Common Gateway Interface script (CGI script)

A program used to transfer data from an HTML form to an application. The CGI script runs on the server that hosts the Web page that has the form.

communications program

A program that enables you to dial through a modem and access another computer. Examples are *Microphone* and *Z-Term* for Macintosh computers and *CrossTalk* and *Procomm Plus* for computers that are running Windows.

CompuServe

The granddaddy of all online communications networks. Focuses mostly on the business user.

Cyberspace

The digital world of computers and the information that passes between them. Comes from the sci-fi novel *Neuromancer* by William Gibson.

dial-up connection

You've got one of these if you access a network or the Internet by dialing a telephone number. The opposite, a *direct* connection, means that the computer is always hooked into the Net.

domain name

A domain name represents a Web site. In the U.S. the domain name can end in .com (for businesses), .edu (for educational institutions), .org (for non-profit organizations), or the prestigious .net (for organizations that are part of the structure of the Web itself). Other countries can use different suffixes. Additionally, a country code such as .uk, for United Kingdom, can be added to represent a country or region. The part before the suffix is either the name of the group that puts up the Web site or something that attracts people to the site. Domain names can start with "www" if desired, but it's not necessary.

dotted quad

The techno-weenie words that describe a numerical Internet address (actually a TCP/IP address) such as this one: 128.33.43.55.

download

To move data from another computer to yours. Compare with *upload*.

downloadable image

An image that's associated with a Web page but not displayed unless the user clicks on a graphic to display it.

edu

An Internet identifier for a college, university, or K–12 school.

electronic mail (e-mail)

A message sent from one computer user over a network to another computer user. The most popular service on the Internet.

Eudora

A great mail program for Macintosh or Windows computers. Both shareware and commercial versions are available.

FAQs

Frequently Asked Questions. Commonly asked questions about a variety of topics, including learning about the Internet. Reading FAQs will save you a great deal of time and embarrassment. You'll find FAQs in public areas of most FTP sites and in the Internet areas of commercial online services.

Fetch

A handy Macintosh FTP program from Dartmouth that enables you to transfer files.

firewall

Software or hardware protection for areas of a Web server computer that protects against unauthorized access.

flame

A sarcastic, critical, or obnoxious message posted to a newsgroup or sent via e-mail. Flames are neither nice nor necessary.

forms

Sections of HTML documents that accept input from users. Forms are used for user feedback, ordering, password protection, and searching.

frame

Rectangular Web page areas that contain separate chunks of text, graphics, and other information. Frames are used to segment Web pages so that some parts change while others stay the same.

FTP

File Transfer Protocol. A method of transferring files across the Internet from one computer to another. Also refers to the name of a program that transfers files.

GIF

Graphics Interchange Format. Can be pronounced "jiff" (most common) or "gif" (with a hard *g*). A format for encoding images, including computer-generated art and photographs, for transfer among machines. GIF is the most popular means for storing images for transfer over the Internet and is supported by all graphical Web browsers.

hexadecimal

A way of counting that uses 16 "digits," 0–9 plus A–F, instead of the 10 digits that common decimal numbering uses. Hexadecimal numbers are often used for describing values stored inside a computer. In hexadecimal numbering, 0–9 have their normal values, but A represents 10, B represents 11, and so on through F, which represents 15. Place values are also different; each successive place represents the next greater power of 16. Example: 2F in hexadecimal translates to 47 in decimal; the 2 represents two 16s, and the F represents fifteen 1s.

hit

One access by someone on your site. Folks in Cyberspace count hits with a counter (a small program you can embed in your Web page).

home page

A Web page that you intend users to come to directly. If a Web site has multiple pages, the home page usually serves as a guide to all the pages.

host

A computer that offers resources that are usable by Internet users. You can access a host computer via telnet, FTP, or the World Wide Web. Technically, in TCP/IP, any machine connected via IP is considered to be a host computer.

HTML

HyperText Markup Language. The language used to create pages for the World Wide Web. The commands enable users to specify different fonts, graphics, hypertext links, and more. You can use a word processor to create a Web page if you know the HTML commands to embed.

HTTP

HyperText Transfer Protocol. The way World Wide Web pages are transferred over the Web. Every Web address begins with `http://`.

hypertext

Text found on Web pages that you can click to go to another location, page, or document or link to sounds, graphics, or movies.

image map

See clickable image map.

information superhighway

This is a goodie. It means lots of things. Most people think that the Internet *is* the information superhighway. They're mostly right. Stuff such as cable TV and phone company networks also qualify, though.

interlaced GIF

A GIF graphic displayed gradually by showing every fourth line, then showing the next one-fourth of the lines, and so on, until the entire image is displayed. This process quickly displays a blurry version of the graphic that sharpens as time passes and the missing lines are filled in. Interlaced GIFs save users time by allowing them to see the initial, blurry version quickly and, if desired, move on before it is entirely displayed.

Internet

The hardware and software that together support the interconnection of most existing computer networks, allowing a computer anywhere in the world to communicate with any other computer that's also connected to the Internet. The Internet supports a variety of services including the World Wide Web.

intranet

An internal network used for distributing information broadly within an organization but not to the general public. Many intranets work just like the Internet and World Wide Web, only on a smaller scale.

IP

Internet Protocol. The networking specification that underlies the Internet. IP's most important feature is its support for routing of the packets — small chunks of information that make up a communication — across multiple connections to their final destination.

ISP

Internet Service Provider. It offers connections to the Internet and support for Internet services, such as the World Wide Web.

Java

A programming language that supports the creation of distributed programs, called "applets," whose functionality can be easily and flexibly split between a client computer and the server that it's connected to. Java provides a way for the Web to support easy sharing of programs as well as data.

JPEG

Joint Photographic Experts Group. A format for storing compressed images. JPEG images were once supported by helper applications but are now directly supported by many browsers. JPEG is the best format for most photographs.

link

A connection between two documents on the Web, usually specified by an anchor in an HTML document.

MacTCP

An extension that allows a Macintosh to connect to the Internet. In newer versions of system software, it's called TCP/IP, and it's found in your control panel folder.

Microsoft Network

A commercial online service run by Microsoft and usable only if you have Windows 95. If your MSN user name is BillGates, your Internet e-mail address is billgates@msn.com.

modem

A marvelous piece of electronics that translates what you type and create on your computer into a signal that can be sent through a phone line and recreated by another modem on the other end of the line.

multimedia

Literally means "many media," and in this sense, a Web page with graphics is multimedia. However, multimedia is usually understood to mean either more than two types of media; or alternatively, to mean time-based media (such as animation, sound, or video) and space-based media (such as 3-D and virtual reality). On the Web, multimedia is also used to mean any extension of the Web beyond the basics of text, hyperlinks, GIF graphics, and JPEG graphics.

network

Basically, a bunch of computers strung together by wire. They can be wired together at one site (local area networks, or LANs) or can be connected via telephone or satellite (wide area networks, or WANs).

newbie

Someone who's new to the Internet. I must still be a newbie, because I discover something new every time I log on.

newsgroup

A bulletin board system on the Internet that's organized by topic.

newsreader

A program that enables you to read and respond easily to newsgroups on the Internet.

node

A computer that's hooked to a network.

NREN

National Research and Education Network. An effort to bring high-speed computing to schools everywhere.

pathname

A description of the location of a file.

PKZIP

A file-compression program for DOS and Windows.

plug-in

A small program that works with a Web browser to allow multimedia files to be displayed in a Web page or that otherwise extends the capabilities of the browser.

PPP

Point-to-Point Protocol. An alternative to SLIP for dial-in access to the Internet. PPP is more reliable (and sometimes faster) than SLIP. For Macintosh users, a control panel called MacPPP is used to connect to the Internet if you have a dial-in connection.

protocol

A set of rules that controls communications on or between networks.

QuickTime

A multi-platform standard from Apple Computer, Inc. for multimedia.

QuickTime VR

A multi-platform standard for image-based virtual reality.

service provider

A company that supplies you with the connection that you need to access the Internet (also ISP, or Internet Service Provider).

shareware

Software that you download and try out for a limited time. If you keep the software, you're honor-bound to send the author a small fee.

SLIP

Serial Line Interface Protocol. A way to connect directly to the Internet so that programs you download come to your local hard drive and not to your Internet Service Provider's hard drive. If you have a SLIP account, your computer is actually *on* the Internet and is not just a dumb terminal. If you're SLIP- (or direct-, or PPP-) connected, others can telnet to *your* computer, too — if you have the software to allow this. A control panel called MacSLIP (or InterSLIP) is used to connect to the Internet if you have a dial-in connection.

spam

Posting commercial messages to lots of unsuspecting users. A huge no-no on the Internet (also a mysterious luncheon meat and the topic of a Monty Python skit).

StuffIt

A Macintosh file-compression program.

syntax

A syntax is the ordering of the elements in a language or protocol.

tag

An HTML element that contains information besides the actual document content, such as formatting information or an anchor. Example: the `<B>` tag starts bolding of the characters that follow it, and the `</B>` tag ends bolding. So to make a word or phrase bold, surround it with the `<B>` and `</B>` tags.

TCP/IP

Transmission Control Protocol/Internet Protocol. The system or language used between computers (hosts) on the Internet to make and maintain a connection.

telephony

The process of converting sound into electrical signals, transmitting the signals through wires or cables, and then converting them back into sound on the receiving end.

telnet

A way to log in to someone else's computer and use their computing resources.

terminal

A stupid, brainless front-end machine that relies on the computing power of a host computer. You can run programs on your computer that will make it act like a stupid, brainless terminal to enable you to dial in to some host computers.

tool

In computing, a tool is similar to a program but more narrowly focused on a single task or set of tasks. It's capable of being used more flexibly with other tools, and it's more likely to be provided from an online source or even used directly online, rather than run on the user's computer.

transparent GIF

A file stored in Graphics Interchange Format and modified so that the area around the objects of interest is assigned the color "transparent." This capability makes the rectangular frame around the objects seem to disappear so that the graphic appears to "float" over the page on which it is displayed.

UNIX

A computer operating system. Get *UNIX For Dummies,* 2nd Edition, by John R. Levine and Margaret Levine Young (IDG Books Worldwide, Inc.) to become an instant expert.

upload

To move data from your computer to a host computer. Compare with *download.*

URL

Uniform Resource Locator. Basically, the address of any Gopher, FTP, telnet, or WWW site. URLs for Web pages look like this: `http://www.domain.top-domain`. For a Gopher site, a URL may be `gopher://domain.top-domain`.

Usenet

A collection of thousands of newsgroups.

uuencode/uudecode

Programs that encode and decode newsgroup (and some other) files for sending over the Internet.

VRML

Virtual Reality Modeling Language. A set of standards for displaying 3-D data on the Web.

Web authoring

Creating documents for use on the World Wide Web, including text documents with HTML tags, suitable graphics, and, in many cases, multimedia files.

Web page

A text document with HTML tags to specify formatting and links from the document to other documents and to graphics and multimedia files.

Web server

A computer that connects to the World Wide Web and hosts HTML-tagged text documents, graphics, and multimedia files to be downloaded by Web clients.

Web site

One or more linked Web pages accessed through a home page. The URL of the home page is made available to users on the Web (and often through other advertising and marketing means as well).

WinSock

A program that conforms to a set of standards called the Windows Socket API. *WinSock* programs control the link between Windows software and a TCP/IP program. You'll need this API (software driver) if you're using a computer running Windows to connect to the Internet.

World Wide Web (also known as the Web or W3)

An Internet service that provides files linked by HyperText Transfer Protocol. The Web specification allows formatted text and graphics to be viewed directly by a Web browser and allows other kinds of files to be opened separately by helper applications specified in the Web browser's setup. The Web is the most popular Internet service, partly because it can also be used to access other Internet services, such as newsgroups and FTP.

Appendix B

HTML Code Dictionary

*T*he most commonly used HTML tags are presented here as a quick and handy reference. Plenty more tags exist out there (in fact, you may want to regularly check the Web at http://www.netscape.com for updates), but the following tags are the ones you'll use most often.

Here are a few things to keep in mind about HTML tags:

- ✔ Claris Home Page allows you to use all of the following coding tags, but has shortcuts (automatic tag formatting) for only some of them.
- ✔ Enter the tags in Raw HTML mode (Window⇨Edit HTML Source).
- ✔ HTML tags are not case-sensitive — so whether you have caps on or caps off, they work the same way.

If you're looking for more information on working with HTML, check out *HTML For Dummies,* Second Edition, by Ed Tittel and Steve James (IDG Books Worldwide, Inc.).

Structural Tags

Use these HTML tags to indicate document endings, beginnings, and comments:

`<HTML>...</HTML>`	Beginning and end of an HTML document
`<HEAD>...</HEAD>`	Beginning and end of a document header
`<TITLE>...</TITLE>`	Beginning and end of page (document window) title
`<BODY>...</BODY>`	Beginning and end of body of document
`<!- ... ->`	Comment (does not show up when viewed by browser)

Formatting Tags

Use these formatting HTML tags to format text, including adding ruler lines and inserting breaks:

`<p>`	Begins a new paragraph
`<H1>...</H1>`	Sets the size of text (the lower the number, the larger the text size; range is from H1 to H6)
`<PRE>...</PRE>`	Sets preformatted (WYSIWYG) text
`<HR>`	Inserts horizontal line
` `	Forces a line break

Browser-Independent Tags

These tags display the same way, no matter what kind of browser you're using:

`<B>...</B>`	Boldface
`<I>...</I>`	Italics
`<TT>...</TT>`	Monospace (such as a typewriter font)
`<U>...</U>`	Underline (not supported by all browsers — yet)

Browser-Specific Tags

These tags may display differently depending on the browser your readers are using:

`<EM>...</EM>`	Used for emphasis. (Each browser treats this text differently; some browsers display it as italics; some as underlined text.)
`<STRONG>...</STRONG>`	Used for strong emphasis. (Some browsers display as boldface; others as underlined text.)
`<CODE>...</CODE>`	A code sample or Internet address. Appears in most browsers as Courier or other monospace font.

`<SAMP>...</SAMP>`	Used for illustrative text or examples. Appears similar to `<CODE>` text.
`<KBD>...</KBD>`	Used to indicate something to be typed by the user. Appears in monospace (Courier) font on graphical browsers.
`<ADDRESS>...</ADDRESS>`	Displays address information, usually in italics.
`<VAR>...</VAR>`	Used to name a variable. Some browsers show this text as italics or underlined text.
`<CITE>...</CITE>`	Citations for bibliographics. Usually shows text as italics.
`<DFN>...</DFN>`	Word or phrase to be defined. Usually shows the word as boldface.
`<BLOCKQUOTE>...`	Indents text to separate it from the `</BLOCKQUOTE>` surrounding text. Used for quotations or other extracted material.

Tags Specific to Netscape Navigator and Internet Explorer

These HTML tags are useful for Web pages that are best read by Netscape Navigator 2.0 and higher versions and Internet Explorer 3.0 and higher versions.

`<BASEFONT SIZE=n>`	Sets base font size for document. (n=1 point through 7 points)
`<BIG>...</BIG>`	Uses a larger font than the default size
`<BLINK>...</BLINK>`	Makes the selected text flash; not recommended.
`<FONT SIZE=n>...</FONT>`	Sets font size for a section (n=1 point through 7 points; you can use a plus sign (+) before the *n* to specify relative size)
`<SMALL>...</SMALL>`	Opposite of `<BIG>`
`<SUB>...</SUB>`	Subscript
`<SUP>...<SUP>`	Superscript

`ALIGN=n` (replace n with `TOP`, `BOTTOM`, or `MIDDLE`)	Used to align images

Hypertext Links

Use these tags to set up hypertext links to other sites:

`<A HREF=" destination URL">link description </A>`	Links to another Web page or a different server
`<A HREF="#target name">destination description </A>` or `<A NAME="target name"> destination </A>`	Links to another place, same Web page
`<APPLET CODE= "filename" HEIGHT=number WIDTH=number></APPLET>`	Accesses a Java applet

Lists

Use these tags to create different kinds of formatted text lists:

`<UL>…</UL>`	Bulleted list
`<OL>…</OL>`	Numbered list
`<MENU>…</MENU>`	Menu list
`<DIR>…</DIR>`	Directory (horizontal) list
`<DL>…</DL>`	Glossary list (for first lines of entries in glossaries)
`<DT>`	Definition text (for glossary list text)
`<DD>`	Definition description (for glossary list text)
`<LI>`	List item

Images and Sound

Use these tags to insert special effects or link to special effects in another file:

`<IMG SRC=" filename.gif">`	Inserts image (graphic)
`<IMG SRC="filename. gif" ALIGN=TOP>`	Inserts image (graphic) and aligns top of accompanying text with top of image (`MIDDLE` and `BOTTOM` work, too)
`<IMG SRC="filename. gif" ALT="alternate text">`	Inserts image (graphic) and alternative text for non-GUI browsers
`<A HREF="file:// filename.mov"> click for movie </A>`	Links to sound, movie, or other external file

Special Characters

Some characters, such as an ampersand (&) or a quotation mark ("), require special formatting to be seen by most browsers. I've provided some of the most common symbol characters in the table below. You can find the rest at `http://www.w3.org`.

Key sequence	Displays
`&lt`	<
`&gt`	>
`&amp`	&
`&quot`	"
`&#169`	©

Appendix C
Acceptable Use Policies

- -

In This Chapter

▶ Why define an Acceptable Use Policy?

▶ Whose policy is it?

▶ How flexible should the policy be?

▶ Who should you share the policy with?

- -

*1*t's halfway through your third-period class when a tall, lanky student enters the room. The student quietly shuffles up the middle aisle and a hush falls over the room. He hands you a note and turns to walk away, but not before flashing an all-knowing little grin.

You open the note and it says, "Call Mr. Jones about the Internet ASAP. Then see me. Signed, The Principal." (Gulp!)

It's inevitable, folks. Sooner or later, someone in your school (maybe even you) will be called upon to defend the use of the Internet in the classroom, just as many before you have had to defend the use of certain textbooks, movies, audiovisual aids, computers, and even the quill pen (back in the earlier years of progressive education). How you feel at the moment you're handed "the note" will be directly affected by one simple question: What is your school or district policy on Internet use? If your answer is "We don't have one" or "I don't know," you're in for a hefty case of indigestion, far worse than the feeling you had when you ate the green hot dog by mistake in the school cafeteria thinking it was part of a St. Patrick's Day menu.

You Need an AUP!

Let's face it: Most people get most of their knowledge of the Internet from television, newspapers, and radio reports. The news media seem to work hard to flush out every little negative thing about the Internet that they can. You can't turn on a television these days without seeing a news story about some kid in East Smallville downloading a picture of a naked something-or-other.

Few people really understand what the Net actually is and how it works. That's why it's important for you and your school to help educate your community about the positive aspects of the Internet. An *Acceptable Use Policy* (AUP) is a great way to help both your peers and your community understand how and why you use the Internet in the classroom.

Although some highly publicized cases of abuse or criminal activity involving computers and online services (or the Internet) have made the news, these reported cases happen pretty infrequently. The fact that some crimes are being committed online is not a reason to avoid using online services, any more than the fact that shoplifting occurs should keep you away from the local mall. A better strategy is to help kids become "street smart" about what they can do to safeguard themselves against possible problems.

Who's the Boss?

One issue you should think about right off the bat is who should be assigned to lead the effort to develop the AUP. Should the policy be developed by your school's media and technology committee? (You do have a media and technology committee, don't you?) Should parents and other community members be involved in the creation of the policy? Or should the policy be created at the district level and approved by your local Board of Education?

This is a big issue. It could be a bigger issue than school libraries circulating *Catcher in the Rye* was. (When did you first check out that book?) In general, most educators would prefer a district-wide policy. (In many school systems, an Internet "rider" is added to the same policies and procedures that govern textbook adoption and curriculum material review.) One difficulty in the implementation of a district-wide policy is that in order to encompass all uses of the Net in your school system, the policy has to be very broad. Some schools, however, need to make a more specific policy, either because of their communities or their school cultures.

So, what are the benefits of district-wide policies? They tend to promote consistency among schools in your district, are usually more broad in their scope, and if things go wrong, you don't take the blame (hmm . . . definitely something to think about!). Discuss this issue with all parties involved before deciding who should take ownership of the policy, if there is a policy at all.

The Keyword Is: Flexible

A flexible policy contains general guidelines about who can use the online service, under what circumstances they can use the service, and what (if any) restrictions are placed upon that use. But be advised (for you overachievers out there) that flexible does not mean that you should generate a 40-page document to cover all the exceptions to the rules. A brief, well-constructed, collaboratively developed but also flexible and dynamic document is the best bet.

Before you develop a policy, put together a group of parents, teachers, students, and other community members. Don't forget to invite a representative from your local public library (the library's support could be critical if the policy is challenged).

Spend some time educating the committee about the positives of the Internet, partly to counteract the nasties in the media, partly just to make sure that everyone's on the same (home) page. Next, shoot for a policy that can fit on one sheet. (Don't allow the wordy people to use puny nine-point type either!)

Another Key Word Is: Comprehensive

Based on the issues raised earlier in this chapter and a few from newsgroups on the Net, what follows is a handy little checklist of things you may include in your policy.

An effective AUP may cover several topics, including statements that:

- ✔ Address adherence to state, local, and federal laws
- ✔ Outline the limits (if any) of access
- ✔ Provide a definition of authorized use and authorized access
- ✔ Explain the responsibility of the student, parent, and teacher or administrator
- ✔ Set forth a penalty for not abiding by the rules
- ✔ Declare who can grant or revoke privileges of Net access
- ✔ Caution against revealing personal information or establishing face-to-face meetings with other people who are online

Don't forget signature lines for parent, student, and school representative approval or authorization!

I'm a big fan of *not* reinventing the wheel. To that end, I suggest zipping around the Web and searching for sites that have already created and posted their AUPs. As a starting point, visit http://www.altavista.digital.com and enter the search terms **acceptable use plan.**

Rules for online safety (for kids)

As part of a project supported by all the major online services, the National Center for Missing and Exploited Children (1-800-THE-LOST) and the Interactive Services Association developed a great pamphlet entitled *Child Safety on the Information Highway* (1994).

The pamphlet contains, among other things, a list of items called "My Rules for Online Safety." These rules are excellent for use as part of, or as an addendum to, an acceptable use policy. They are written in terms that both parents and children can understand. The rules recommended by the NCMEC include the following:

- I will not give out personal information such as my address, telephone number, parents' work number or address, or the name and location of my school without my parents' permission.

- I will tell my parents right away if I come across any information that makes me feel uncomfortable.

- I will never agree to get together with someone I "meet" online without first checking with my parents. If my parents agree to the meeting, I will be sure that it is in a public place and bring my mother or father along.

- I will never send a person my picture or anything else without first checking with my parents.

- I will not respond to any messages that are mean or in any way make me feel uncomfortable. It is not my fault if I get a message like that. If I do, I will tell my parents right away so that they can contact the online service.

- I will talk with my parents so that we can set up rules for going online. We will decide on the time of day I can be online, the length of time I can be online, and the appropriate areas for me to visit. I will not access other areas or break the rules without their permission.

Sharing Your Policy

Don't let the protocol monster bite you in the node. Before you even think of sharing your policy with external audiences, make sure that your district media or technology coordinators get the chance to have their say on the subject. Their input can be critical in defending the policy later on.

When you're ready to publish the AUP, remember that the reason you created a policy in the first place was to be proactive. Introducing the policy to external audiences before something happens might save you stress, time, and (in some cases) your job. Whether the policy is created at the district or local level, there are several ways to spread the word, and if you're really shrewd, you can end up with some much-needed "fundage" to help you with your school's technology needs.

Take some advice from some schools around the nation for spreading the word about your AUP and appropriate use of the Internet:

- ✔ Educate your community about how the Net is used (hold open houses or seminars, or offer training for parents).

- ✔ Make sure that teachers and administrators know and understand the policy (another item to add to the faculty meeting agenda).

- ✔ Make the policy readily accessible to all teachers and students (plaster it everywhere).

There's one last thing you need to do. Be sure to share your policy with the Internet education community. Who knows? Your AUP could end up in a book like this one someday! Share you ideas via online services (check out the EdConnection library in the Electronic Schoolhouse [Keyword: **ESH**] on America Online) or post it to an education newsgroup.

C'mon and give it a try. Creating an AUP is a lot of work, but it promotes constructive dialogue besides educating many of your peers and members of the community on how to intelligently use the Internet. An AUP is a great way to help others create and manage their own Internet use policies. I'd call that a lasting contribution to education as we know it!

Appendix D
About the CD

*N*ow that you're all excited about creating Web pages, you'll be looking for some tools to help you and your students do the job. Of course, most of you probably fall into the "I never read the instructions" category, so you can just pop in your *Web Publishing For Teachers* CD and wing it. Others, however, may want to know just what's in store for them and will want to know if their computers have the brainpower (in other words, the RAM) to run the software I've included. (For that, just read the section "System Requirements" that follows.)

There are some terrific tools on the CD. The disc includes programs for your Macintosh as well as for a computer running Windows 3.1 or Windows 95. Here's a handy table so you can see all the goodies in one place. (Following the table, I give you more information about each program.)

Tool Type	Tool Name	Macintosh	Windows 3.1	Windows 95
Compression tools				
	DropStuff	X	-	-
	StuffIt Expander	X	-	-
	StuffIt Lite	X	-	-
	WinZip 6.2	-	X	X
Internet tools				
	Adobe Acrobat Reader	X	X	X
	AT&T WorldNet® Service	X	X	X
	Claris Emailer 1.1	X	-	-
	NetPresenz	X	-	-
	SiteMarker	X	-	-
	SurfBoard Demo	X	-	-
	WS_FTP LE	-	X	X
Webmastering tools				
	Adobe PageMill 2.0 Trial	X	-	-
	Allaire HomeSite	-	-	X
	Claris Home Page 2.0 Trial	X	-	X
	HTML Web Weaver Lite	X	-	-
	WebWhacker	X	X	X

(continued)

Tool Type	Tool Name	Macintosh	Windows 3.1	Windows 95
Graphics tools				
	GraphicConverter 2.7	X	-	-
	Paint Shop Pro	-	X	X
	VuePrint	-	X	X
Sound tools				
	Convert Machine	X	-	-
	Cool Edit	-	X	X
	Sound Machine	X	-	-

System Requirements

Check under the hood of your Mac or PC to see if it meets the requirement for accessing the programs on this CD. Here's what's recommended:

- ✔ Any Macintosh or Mac-compatible with a 68030, 68040, or PowerPC processor, or any PC with a 486 or faster processor running Windows 3.*x* (that is, 3.1 or 3.11) or Windows 95.

- ✔ *At least* 8MB of total RAM (16MB of RAM is recommended for best performance with Power Macintosh computers and PCs with Windows 95).

- ✔ At least 37MB of hard drive space available to install all the software from this CD (you'll need less space if you don't install every program).

- ✔ A CD-ROM drive (double-speed [2x] or faster recommended).

- ✔ A sound card with speakers, if you want to add sound to your Web pages (PCs only, Macs have built-in sound support).

- ✔ A monitor capable of displaying at least 256 colors or grayscale.

- ✔ A modem with a speed of at least 14,400 bps (you don't need a modem to create the Web pages, of course, but you do need one to publish your pages and view them after they're on the Internet).

If you need more information on Macintosh, PCs, or Windows basics, check out *Macs For Teachers,* 2nd Edition, by my friend Michelle Robinette; *PCs For Dummies,* 4th Edition, by Dan Gookin; *Windows 95 For Teachers* (another Michelle Robinette original); or *Windows 3.11 For Dummies,* 3rd Edition, by Andy Rathbone (all published by IDG Books Worldwide, Inc.).

What Do I Do First with the CD?

You'll find installation of all (or some) of the programs on the CD is easy and relatively painless, whether you're using a PC with Windows 3.1 or Windows 95, or a Macintosh.

For Windows users, I've included the "CD Assistant." It's a master program on the CD that lets you install or run any software on the CD just by clicking on selections from the CD Assistant's window.

Mac users can skip all that stuff and go right to "Getting started with a Macintosh." Windows 95 users can begin with "Getting started with Windows 95 with AutoPlay CD-ROMs." Windows 3.1 users can jump right into "Getting started with Windows 3.1 and non-AutoPlay CD-ROMs."

Getting started with Windows 95 with AutoPlay CD-ROMs

If you're running Windows 95, just insert the CD in your computer's CD-ROM drive and wait a few moments to let Windows 95 start the CD Assistant automatically.

When the license agreement appears, click on the Accept button. Now a window that shows a stack of books and a brick wall appears. Congratulations! That's the CD Assistant. You can move on to the section, "What's on the CD?"

If nothing happens after a minute or so, you've probably got a CD-ROM drive that can't run the CD Assistant without some help from you. Move on to the section "Getting started with Windows 3.1 and non-AutoPlay CD-ROMs."

Getting started with Windows 3.1 and non-AutoPlay CD-ROMs

All Windows 3.1 users (and some Windows 95 users) need to install an icon to their Program Manager (or the Windows 95 Start menu) to run the CD Assistant. To install the icon, follow these steps:

1. **Insert the CD into your computer's CD-ROM drive.**

2. **For Windows 3.1: In Program Manager, choose File⇨Run.**

   For Windows 95: Click on the Start button and then click on Run.

3. **In the Run dialog box, enter the following:** D:\SETICON.EXE

Substitute your actual CD-ROM drive letter if it's something other than D.

4. **Click on OK.**

An icon for the CD Assistant is installed in a program group named For Teachers.

To start the CD Assistant, open the For Teachers program group. (Windows 95 users can find an item named For Teachers on their Start⇨Programs menu.) Double-click on the icon in Windows 3.1 (in Windows 95, select the icon from the Start menu) to run the CD Assistant.

Getting started with a Macintosh

The CD takes advantage of the Mac's easy-to-use desktop. Just pop the CD into your CD-ROM drive and double-click on the Web Publishing FT CD icon after it appears on your desktop. A window appears that shows folders named after each category of software on the CD. Installing the programs on your Mac is easy. Just double-click on each program's installer program icon (if there is one) or just drag the program's folder to your hard drive to copy the folder. You can find out more about the categories of software in the section "What's on the CD?"

Restarting the CD Assistant in Windows

If you're using Windows 95 and were able to start the CD Assistant just by popping the CD into your CD-ROM drive, restart the CD by double-clicking on the My Computer icon and then double-clicking on the CD-ROM icon. This method works only if your CD-ROM drive automatically started the CD Assistant when you first popped the CD in your CD-ROM drive.

If you had to follow the steps in "Getting started with Windows 3.1 and non-AutoPlay CD-ROMs," you can restart the CD Assistant by opening the For Teachers program group (Windows 95 users can find it on their Start⇨ Programs menu) and double-clicking on the CD Assistant icon named after this book.

Remember that you have to keep the CD in the CD-ROM drive to use the CD Assistant.

What's on the CD?

If you're a Mac user, just open a category folder to find more folders or icons for the software. Some of the software may require you to install the software on your Mac by double-clicking on the program's installer icon. For other programs, installing may be as simple as dragging the program's folder from the CD's window to your hard drive. The easiest way to tell if a program requires installation and not drag-and-drop is to look for the words "Installer" or ".sea" in the icon's name, or an arrow(s) within the icon. These items should be double-clicked on to install a program.

If you're using Windows, follow these steps to use the CD Assistant.

1. **Start the CD Assistant. (See the section "What Do I Do First with the CD?" earlier in this appendix if you haven't a clue as to what I'm talking about.)**

2. **Choose a software category you'd like to explore by clicking on the category title.**

   When you click on the title, the window changes to show you a list of software for that category.

3. **Click on the name of the software you're interested in.**

4. **The window changes again to show you a brief description of the program. If you would like to install or run the program, just click on the Continue button at the top of the window.**

5. **If you don't want to install the program, just click on Cancel to backtrack.**

6. **To exit, just click on the Exit button at the bottom right in the categories on any program window.**

First, what's shareware?

Shareware is not a type of software, per se, but a way of selling software to you. Many of the programs on this CD are given to you through the shareware process in which a program's author distributes the program freely through the Internet or online service. You download it and play with the software for a while and, if you like it and plan to use it, send money (a small fee — typically between $5 and $35 for most programs) to the program's author.

The "Software Cops" aren't going to break your door down if you fail to pay for the software, but you should feel like a heel for not paying for the program. Also, if no one pays for the program, the author might feel that no one needs the program and stop developing it further. Support the little guy in the software industry and pay your shareware fees, okay?

Here's a summary of the software that you can find on this CD.

Sound tools

Cool Edit: From Syntrillium Software, `http://www.syntrillium.com` on the World Wide Web. For Windows. Shareware.

Cool Edit is a digital sound editor for Windows. With this software, a sound card, and microphone, you can record and edit any sound. You can even add special effects to spice up your sounds.

Sound Machine and **Convert Machine:** By Rod Kennedy, `http://www.kagi.com` on the World Wide Web. For Macintosh. Shareware.

SoundMachine is a sound player for Macintosh. It can play many of the common sound formats available for computers, from AIFF to ulaw, Windows WAV formats, and more.

ConvertMachine is a drag-and-drop sound converter. For example, assume you have a QuickTime movie file with a soundtrack. After you've chosen the ConvertMachine program's preferences, just drag the movie icon over to the ConvertMachine icon to create (instantly!) a sound file based on the movie icon's sound in the format you specified in ConvertMachine.

Graphics tools

GraphicConverter: From Lemke Software, `http://members.aol.com/lemkesoft` on the World Wide Web. For Macintosh. Shareware.

GraphicConverter is a very popular graphics editing, viewing, and conversion program for Macintosh. GraphicConverter can convert images from dozens of graphic formats for Windows and other systems.

Paint Shop Pro: From JASC Inc., `http://www.jasc.com` on the World Wide Web. For Windows. Shareware.

Paint Shop Pro is a popular graphic image processor for Windows.

VuePrint: From Hamrick Software, `http://www.hamrick.com` on the World Wide Web. For Windows. Shareware.

VuePrint is a widely used Windows image viewer. You can view and print graphics made in the most commonly used formats.

Compression tools

StuffIt Lite, StuffIt Expander, and **DropStuff with Expander Enhancer:** From Aladdin Systems, `http://www.aladdinsys.com` on the World Wide Web. For Macintosh. StuffIt Lite and DropStuff are shareware. StuffIt Expander is freeware.

One problem with a Mac is that, after a while, you have lots of folders, files, and programs. What you won't have left, as a result, is sufficient hard drive space to keep more stuff. Here's where the StuffIt line of products enters to help you out. StuffIt Lite is a program that allows you to create StuffIt *archives,* which are files that contain items you have compressed to save disk space. You can't do anything with the contents of a StuffIt archive until you unStuff (decompress) the archive.

StuffIt Expander is a free program that lets you drag any StuffIt archive (and a few other archive formats like BinHex-encoded files from the Internet) and instantly decode (unStuff) the items. DropStuff does just the reverse; it creates a StuffIt archive for any items you drag to it. DropStuff also adds additional abilities to StuffIt Expander, such as decompressing the PC's version of StuffIt archives, the ZIP archive.

WinZip 6.2: From Nico Mak Computing., `http://www.winzip.com` on the World Wide Web.

Sooner or later, you're going to run low on space on your computer's hard drive. WinZip is a program that can take programs and documents and squish them (or *compress* them, for you technonuts) into files, or archives, that take up less room on your hard drive. You can't use the files while saved in the archive, but you can always unsquish, or *unzip,* them later.

WinZip is shareware (and *great* shareware, if I do say so). If you like it and want to keep using it, please pay for the program. It's cheaper than buying and installing a new hard drive.

Webmastering tools

Claris Home Page 2.0 Trial: From Claris Corporation, `http://www.claris.com` on the World Wide Web. For Windows 95. Trialware; program stops working after 30 days.

If you want to make a Web page but don't want to learn much or any of the HTML programming language that Web pages use, Claris Home Page 2.0 is a great way to start. Claris Home Page is a fully featured Web page processor that lets you design a page as if you were cutting and pasting pictures and text for a newsletter. (Be sure to check out the super educator-only coupon in the back of this book for the full version of Home Page!)

Allaire HomeSite: From Allaire Corporation, `http://www.allaire.com` on the World Wide Web. For Windows 95. Shareware.

HomeSite, originally created by author Nick Bradbury, is an excellent program that enables you to create and edit HTML, the markup language for making Web pages. If you're feeling brave about editing HTML yourself, this program makes it much easier to get started.

HTML Web Weaver Lite: From Miracle Software, `http://www.miracleinc.com` on the World Wide Web. For Macintosh. Shareware.

HTML Web Weaver Lite is the shareware version of Miracle Software's commercially available World Wide Web Weaver. Though it doesn't have many of the stronger features of its commercial sibling, HTML Web Weaver Lite is easy to use and takes up only a bit of your hard drive space and memory, making it a perfect editor for older Macs.

WebWhacker: From The ForeFront Group, `http://www.ffg.com/whacker.html` on the World Wide Web. For Windows. Trialware; allows you to download only four sites.

WebWhacker is a handy tool that downloads entire Web sites, including their text and images, to your hard drive so you can look at them offline. When you view a copy of a Web site that's been "whacked" to your hard disk, the page appears on your screen blazingly fast. This is the _perfect_ tool for building an intranet in your school.

PageMill 2.0 (trial version): From Adobe (`http://www.adobe.com`). For Macintosh.

This graphical Web page processor enables you to create Web pages with drag-and-drop simplicity. To build your page, simply type in your text or drop in content and images from your favorite office and graphics programs. Creating hyperlinks is just as easy! At every step, the intuitive PageMill interface shows you what visitors to your Web site will see. You don't have to know a thing about HTML! And if you do, the integrated source-code editor lets you add and format HTML directly. This version is fully enabled _except you won't be able to save files._

Internet

AT&T WorldNet® Service: From AT&T, http://www.att.com/worldnet on the World Wide Web. For Windows and Macintosh.

For those who don't have an Internet connection, the CD provides sign-on software for AT&T WorldNet Service®, an Internet service provider. Depending on the sign-on software version available for your computer, AT&T WorldNet® Service offers a customized version of either the Netscape Navigator Web browser or the Microsoft Internet Explorer Web browser.

AT&T WorldNet® Service requires you to pay to use their service, so have your credit card ready while you're installing the software.

If you're an AT&T long-distance residential customer, please use this registration code when prompted by the account registration program: **L5SQIM631**

If you use another long-distance phone company, please use this registration code when prompted: **L5SQIM632**

If you already have an Internet service provider, please note that AT&T WorldNet® Service software makes changes to your computer's current Internet configuration and may replace your current provider's settings.

Adobe Acrobat Reader: From Adobe Systems, http://www.adobe.com on the World Wide Web. For Windows and Macintosh. Freeware.

Adobe Acrobat Reader is a free program that lets you view documents (often displayed on Web pages as .pdf files) created with the commercially available Adobe Acrobat 3.0, which creates documents that save the graphics and formatting of the original document it copied.

WS_FTP LE: From Ipswitch Corporation, http://www.ipswitch.com on the World Wide Web. For Windows. Freeware for students, educators, government agencies, and non-commercial home users.

WS_FTP Limited Edition is a program that allows you to send and receive programs and files by the Internet's *file transfer protocol,* or FTP. You'll need this program when sending your completed Web pages and related materials to the FTP server that others call up to see your Web page. For hefty FTP features, you may drop by the Ipswitch Web site for more information on WS_FTP Pro, the commercial sibling of this program.

Claris Emailer 1.1: From Claris Corporation, `http://www.claris.com` on the World Wide Web. For Macintosh. Commercial software-turned-freeware.

Claris Emailer is a powerful Internet e-mail program, perfect for managing more than one e-mail account at a time. Because Claris Emailer Version 2.0 was recently released, we convinced the Claris gurus to give you Version 1.1 for free (a great tease for the new software!).

NetPresenz: From Stairways Software, `http://www.stairways.com` on the World Wide Web. For Macintosh. Shareware.

NetPresenz is an FTP server program for Macintosh. With this program, you can turn your Mac into an FTP server, where others on the Internet can send and receive software.

Surfboard Demo: From Abbott Systems, `http://www.abbottsys.com` on the World Wide Web. For Macintosh. Trialware; cannot save new Web sites that you add.

Surfboard is a cool "remote control" of sorts that lets you save Web sites in an organized floating "TV-tuner-like" panel on your desktop. You'll love this simple-to-use tool.

SiteMarker: From Rhythmic Sphere, Inc., `http://www.rsphere.com` on the World Wide Web. For Macintosh. Shareware; disables itself after 20 uses.

This powerful tool does more than just manage URLs; it's also a powerful, integrated environment for finding, organizing, and sharing Web information. Not only can Web users store and fluidly access an unlimited number of URLs, they can also easily share them with each other.

If You've Got Problems (Of the CD Kind)

Sometimes you just have a bad day. Your car won't start, your grade book blew across the playground, and your computer just won't cooperate. Although I've tried my best to compile programs that work with the most commonly encountered system requirements, sometimes things may not go the way that you'd hoped.

The two likeliest problems are that you don't have enough memory (RAM) for the programs you want to use, or you have other programs running that are affecting the installation or running of the program. If you get error messages like `Not enough memory` or `Setup cannot continue`, try one or more of these methods and then try using the software again:

✔ Turn off any anti-virus software that you have on your computer. Installers sometimes mimic virus activity and may make your computer incorrectly believe that it is being infected by a virus.

✔ Close all running programs. The more programs you're running, the less memory is available to other programs. Installers also typically update files and programs. So if you keep other programs running, installation may not work properly.

✔ Some of the software on this CD may require special utility programs, such as QuickTime. Try reading any "Read Me" notes included in the software's folder on the CD or with the installed software on your hard drive for more information.

✔ Have your local computer store add more *RAM* to your computer. RAM (*random access memory*) consists of strips of computer chips that can let your computer run more programs at the same time and may help speed up your computer as well. Windows 95-equipped PCs work at their best with at least 16MB of RAM. If you have only 8MB of RAM, you can probably get your computer upgraded with more memory for about the price of a cheap VCR or a bicycle. Consider adding more RAM if your computer tells you that not enough memory is available, or if you can't open more than two programs without your computer slowing down dramatically, crashing, or freezing often.

✔ If you're having trouble installing a program, please make sure that you are using the version appropriate for your operating system.

If you happen to encounter any trouble with installing the items from the *Web Publishing For Teachers* CD, please call the IDG Books Worldwide Customer Service phone number: 800-762-2974 (outside the U.S.: 317-596-5261).

Index

● ●

Claris Home Page

Build Dynamic Web Pages In Minutes

The World Wide Web is an exciting tool for students, teachers, and administrators alike. Now, with Claris Home Page software, anyone can develop powerful, customized Web pages in minutes—without having to learn HTML.

With its intuitive interface and extensive toolset, Claris Home Page is the ideal solution for teaching students how to design Web pages and understand the Internet as a means for mass communication. Students, teachers, and administrators can develop interactive Web sites for classroom projects, class information, school

> "Makes Web site creation as easy as word processing"

announcements, and more. Because it's available for both Mac OS and Windows 95/NT systems, Claris Home Page is ideal for schools that have a cross-platform computer environment.

Users new to Web authoring will find Claris Home Page easy to learn and use. If you've used ClarisWorks software or a word processor, you can create Web pages. That's because Claris Home Page has a simple, intuitive interface that uses familiar word processing tools with which you're already familiar. Knowledge of HTML is not required.

Claris Home Page–the best way for every member of your school to build dynamic Web pages.

AT&T WorldNet℠ Service

A World of Possibilities…

Thank you for selecting AT&T WorldNet Service — it's the Internet as only AT&T can bring it to you. With AT&T WorldNet Service, a world of infinite possibilities is now within your reach. Research virtually any subject. Stay abreast of current events. Participate in online newsgroups. Purchase merchandise from leading retailers. Send and receive electronic mail.

AT&T WorldNet Service is rapidly becoming the preferred way of accessing the Internet. It was recently awarded one of the most highly coveted awards in the computer industry, *PC Computing*'s 1996 MVP Award for Best Internet Service Provider. Now, more than ever, it's the best way to stay in touch with the people, ideas, and information that are important to you.

You need a computer with a mouse, a modem, a phone line, and the enclosed software. That's all. We've taken care of the rest.

If You Can Point and Click, You're There

With AT&T WorldNet Service, finding the information you want on the Internet is easier than you ever imagined it could be. You can surf the Net within minutes. And find almost anything you want to know — from the weather in Paris, Texas — to the cost of a ticket to Paris, France. You're just a point and click away. It's that easy.

AT&T WorldNet Service features specially customized industry-leading browsers integrated with advanced Internet directories and search engines. The result is an Internet service that sets a new standard for ease of use — virtually everywhere you want to go is a point and click away, making it a snap to navigate the Internet.

When you go online with AT&T WorldNet Service, you'll benefit from being connected to the Internet by the world leader in networking. We offer you fast access of up to 28.8 Kbps in more than 215 cities throughout the U.S. that will make going online as easy as picking up your phone.

Online Help and Advice
24 Hours a Day, 7 Days a Week

Before you begin exploring the Internet, you may want to take a moment to check two useful sources of information.

If you're new to the Internet, from the AT&T WorldNet Service home page at www.worldnet.att.net, click on the Net Tutorial hyperlink for a quick explanation of unfamiliar terms and useful advice about exploring the Internet.

Another useful source of information is the HELP icon. The area contains pertinent, time saving information-intensive reference tips, and topics such as Accounts & Billing, Trouble Reporting, Downloads & Upgrades, Security Tips, Network Hot Spots, Newsgroups, Special Announcements, etc.

Whether online or off-line, 24 hours a day, seven days a week, we will provide World Class technical expertise and fast, reliable responses to your questions. To reach AT&T WorldNet Customer Care, call **1-800-400-1447**.

Nothing is more important to us than making sure that your Internet experience is a truly enriching and satisfying one.

Safeguard Your Online Purchases

AT&T WorldNet Service is committed to making the Internet a safe and convenient way to transact business. By registering and continuing to charge your AT&T WorldNet Service to your AT&T Universal Card, you'll enjoy peace of mind whenever you shop the Internet. Should your account number be compromised on the Net, you won't be liable for any online transactions charged to your AT&T Universal Card by a person who is not an authorized user.*

*Today, cardmembers may be liable for the first $50 of charges made by a person who is not an authorized user, which will not be imposed under this program as long as the cardmember notifies AT&T Universal Card of the loss within 24 hours and otherwise complies with the Cardmember Agreement. Refer to the Cardmember Agreement for definition of authorized user.

Minimum System Requirements

IBM-Compatible Personal Computer Users:
- IBM-compatible personal computer with 486SX or higher processor
- 8MB of RAM (or more for better performance)
- 15–36MB of available hard disk space to install software, depending on platform
  (14–21MB to use service after installation, depending on platform)
- Graphics system capable of displaying 256 colors
- 14,400 bps modem connected to an outside phone line and not a LAN or ISDN line
- Microsoft Windows 3.1x or Windows 95

Macintosh Users:
- Macintosh 68030 or higher (including 68LC0X0 models and all Power Macintosh models)
- System 7.5.3 Revision 2 or higher for PCI Power Macintosh models: System 7.1 or higher for all 680X0 and non-PCI Power Macintosh models
- Mac TCP 2.0.6 or Open Transport 1.1 or higher

- 8MB of RAM (minimum) with Virtual Memory turned on or RAM Doubler; 16MB recommended for Power Macintosh users
- 12MB of available hard disk space (15MB recommended)
- 14,400 bps modem connected to an outside phone line and not a LAN or ISDN line
- Color or 256 gray-scale monitor
- Apple Guide 1.2 or higher (if you want to view online help)
  If you are uncertain of the configuration of your Macintosh computer, consult your Macintosh User's guide or call Apple at 1-800-767-2775.

Installation Tips and Instructions

- If you have other Web browsers or online software, please consider uninstalling them according to the vendor's instructions.
- If you are installing AT&T WorldNet Service on a computer with Local Area Networking, please contact your LAN administrator for setup instructions.
- At the end of installation, you may be asked to restart your computer. Don't attempt the registration process until you have done so.

IBM-compatible PC users:
- Insert the CD-ROM into the CD-ROM drive on your computer.
- Select *File/Run* (for Windows 3.1*x*) or *Start/Run* (for Windows 95 if setup did not start automatically).
- Type *D:\setup.exe* (or change the "D" if your CD-ROM is another drive).
- Click *OK*.
- Follow the onscreen instructions to install and register.

Macintosh users:
- Disable all extensions except Apple CD-ROM and Foreign Files Access extensions.
- Restart Computer.
- Insert the CD-ROM into the CD-ROM drive on your computer.
- Double-click the *Install AT&T WorldNet Service* icon.
- Follow the onscreen instructions to install. (Upon restarting your Macintosh, AT&T WorldNet Service Account Setup automatically starts.)
- Follow the onscreen instructions to register.

Registering with AT&T WorldNet Service

After you have connected with AT&T WorldNet online registration service, you will be presented with a series of screens that confirm billing information and prompt you for additional account set-up data.

The following is a list of registration tips and comments that will help you during the registration process.

I. Use one of the following registration codes, which can also be found in Appendix D of *Web Publishing For Teachers*. Use L5SQIM631 if you are an AT&T long-distance residential customer or L5SQIM632 if you use another long-distance phone company.
II. During registration, you will need to supply your name, address, and valid credit card number, and choose an account information security word, e-mail name, and e-mail password. You will also be requested to select your preferred price plan at this time. (We advise that you use all lowercase letters when assigning an e-mail ID and security code, since they are easier to remember.)
III. If you make a mistake and exit or get disconnected during the registration process prematurely, simply click on "Create New Account." Do not click on "Edit Existing Account."
IV. When choosing your local access telephone number, you will be given several options. Please choose the one nearest to you. Please note that calling a number within your area does not guarantee that the call is free.

Connecting to AT&T WorldNet Service

When you have finished installing and registering with AT&T WorldNet Service, you are ready to access the Internet. Make sure your modem and phone line are available before attempting to connect to the service.

For Windows 95 users:
- Double-click on the *Connect to AT&T WorldNet Service* icon on your desktop.
  OR
- Select *Start, Programs, AT&T WorldNet Software, Connect to AT&T WorldNet Service.*

For Windows 3.*x* users:
- Double-click on the *Connect to AT&T WorldNet Service* icon located in the AT&T WorldNet Service group.

For Macintosh users:
- Double-click on the *AT&T WorldNet Service* icon in the AT&T WorldNet Service folder.

Choose the Plan That's Right for You

The Internet is for everyone, whether at home or at work. In addition to making the time you spend online productive and fun, we're also committed to making it affordable. Choose one of two price plans: unlimited usage access or hourly usage access. The latest pricing information can be obtained during online registration. No matter which plan you use, we're confident that after you take advantage of everything AT&T WorldNet Service has to offer, you'll wonder how you got along without it.

AT&T

Explore our AT&T WorldNet Service site at http://www.att.com/worldnet

IDG Books Worldwide, Inc., End-User License Agreement

READ THIS. You should carefully read these terms and conditions before opening the software packet(s) included with this book ("Book"). This is a license agreement ("Agreement") between you and IDG Books Worldwide, Inc. ("IDGB"). By opening the accompanying software packet(s), you acknowledge that you have read and accept the following terms and conditions. If you do not agree and do not want to be bound by such terms and conditions, promptly return the Book and the unopened software packet(s) to the place you obtained them for a full refund.

1. **License Grant.** IDGB grants to you (either an individual or entity) a nonexclusive license to use one copy of the enclosed software program(s) (collectively, the "Software") solely for your own personal or business purposes on a single computer (whether a standard computer or a workstation component of a multiuser network). The Software is in use on a computer when it is loaded into temporary memory (RAM) or installed into permanent memory (hard disk, CD-ROM, or other storage device). IDGB reserves all rights not expressly granted herein.

2. **Ownership.** IDGB is the owner of all right, title, and interest, including copyright, in and to the compilation of the Software recorded on the disk(s) or CD-ROM ("Software Media"). Copyright to the individual programs recorded on the Software Media is owned by the author or other authorized copyright owner of each program. Ownership of the Software and all proprietary rights relating thereto remain with IDGB and its licensers.

3. **Restrictions on Use and Transfer.**

   (a) You may only (i) make one copy of the Software for backup or archival purposes, or (ii) transfer the Software to a single hard disk, provided that you keep the original for backup or archival purposes. You may not (i) rent or lease the Software, (ii) copy or reproduce the Software through a LAN or other network system or through any computer subscriber system or bulletin-board system, or (iii) modify, adapt, or create derivative works based on the Software.

   (b) You may not reverse engineer, decompile, or disassemble the Software. You may transfer the Software and user documentation on a permanent basis, provided that the transferee agrees to accept the terms and conditions of this Agreement and you retain no copies. If the Software is an update or has been updated, any transfer must include the most recent update and all prior versions.

4. **Restrictions on Use of Individual Programs.** You must follow the individual requirements and restrictions detailed for each individual program in the "About the CD" appendix of this Book. These limitations are also contained in the individual license agreements recorded on the Software Media. These limitations may include a requirement that after using the program for a specified period of time, the user must pay a registration fee or discontinue use. By opening the Software packet(s), you will be agreeing to abide by the licenses and restrictions for these individual programs that are detailed in the "About the CD" appendix and on the Software Media. None of the material on this Software Media or listed in this Book may ever be redistributed, in original or modified form, for commercial purposes.

5. **Limited Warranty.**

   (a) IDGB warrants that the Software and Software Media are free from defects in materials and workmanship under normal use for a period of sixty (60) days from the date of purchase of this Book. If IDGB receives notification within the warranty period of defects in materials or workmanship, IDGB will replace the defective Software Media.

   (b) IDGB AND THE AUTHORS OF THE BOOK DISCLAIM ALL OTHER WARRAN-TIES, EXPRESS OR IMPLIED, INCLUDING WITHOUT LIMITATION IMPLIED WARRANTIES OF MERCHANTABILITY AND FITNESS FOR A PARTICULAR PURPOSE, WITH RESPECT TO THE SOFTWARE, THE PROGRAMS, THE SOURCE CODE CONTAINED THEREIN, AND/OR THE TECHNIQUES DE-SCRIBED IN THIS BOOK. IDGB DOES NOT WARRANT THAT THE FUNCTIONS CONTAINED IN THE SOFTWARE WILL MEET YOUR REQUIREMENTS OR THAT THE OPERATION OF THE SOFTWARE WILL BE ERROR FREE.

   (c) This limited warranty gives you specific legal rights, and you may have other rights that vary from jurisdiction to jurisdiction.

6. **Remedies.**

   (a) IDGB's entire liability and your exclusive remedy for defects in materials and workmanship shall be limited to replacement of the Software Media, which may be returned to IDGB with a copy of your receipt at the following address: Software Media Fulfillment Department, Attn.: *Web Publishing For Teachers*, IDG Books Worldwide, Inc., 7260 Shadeland Station, Ste. 100, Indianapolis, IN 46256, or call 800-762-2974. Please allow three to four weeks for delivery. This Limited Warranty is void if failure of the Software Media has resulted from accident, abuse, or misapplication. Any replacement Software Media will be warranted for the remainder of the original warranty period or thirty (30) days, whichever is longer.

   (b) In no event shall IDGB or the authors be liable for any damages whatsoever (including without limitation damages for loss of business profits, business interruption, loss of business information, or any other pecuniary loss) arising from the use of or inability to use the Book or the Software, even if IDGB has been advised of the possibility of such damages.

   (c) Because some jurisdictions do not allow the exclusion or limitation of liability for consequential or incidental damages, the above limitation or exclusion may not apply to you.

7. **U.S. Government Restricted Rights.** Use, duplication, or disclosure of the Software by the U.S. Government is subject to restrictions stated in paragraph (c)(1)(ii) of the Rights in Technical Data and Computer Software clause of DFARS 252.227-7013, and in subparagraphs (a) through (d) of the Commercial Computer–Restricted Rights clause at FAR 52.227-19, and in similar clauses in the NASA FAR supplement, when applicable.

8. **General.** This Agreement constitutes the entire understanding of the parties and revokes and supersedes all prior agreements, oral or written, between them and may not be modified or amended except in a writing signed by both parties hereto that specifically refers to this Agreement. This Agreement shall take precedence over any other documents that may be in conflict herewith. If any one or more provisions contained in this Agreement are held by any court or tribunal to be invalid, illegal, or otherwise unenforceable, each and every other provision shall remain in full force and effect.

Installation Instructions

● ●

*F*or Windows users, the "CD Assistant" is included. It's a master program on the CD that lets you install or run any software on the CD just by clicking selections from the CD Assistant's window.

Windows 95 users can begin with "Getting Started with Windows 95 with AutoPlay CD-ROMs." Windows 3.1 users can jump right into "Getting Started with Windows 3.1 and Non-AutoPlay CD-ROMs."

Mac users can skip the CD Assistant and go straight to "Getting Started with a Macintosh."

Getting Started with Windows 95 with AutoPlay CD-ROMs

If you're running Windows 95, just insert the CD in your computer's CD-ROM drive. Wait a bit to let Windows 95 start the CD Assistant automatically.

When the license agreement appears, click on the Accept button. Now a window that shows a stack of books and a brick wall appears. Congratulations! That's the CD Assistant.

If nothing happens after a minute or so, you've probably got a CD-ROM drive that can't run the CD Assistant without some help from you. Move on to the section "Getting Started with Windows 3.1 and Non-AutoPlay CD-ROMs."

Getting Started with Windows 3.1 and Non-AutoPlay CD-ROMs

All Windows 3.1 users (and some Windows 95 users) need to install an icon to their Program Manager (or the Windows 95 Start menu) to run the CD Assistant. To install the icon, follow these steps:

1. **Insert the CD into your computer's CD-ROM drive.**
2. **For Windows 3.1: In Program Manager, choose File⇨Run.**

3. In the Run dialog box, type the following: D:\SETICON.EXE

Substitute your actual CD-ROM drive letter if it's something other than D.

4. Click OK.

An icon for the CD Assistant is installed in a program group named For Teachers.

To start the CD Assistant, open the For Teachers program group. (Windows 95 users can find an item named For Teachers on their Start⇨Programs menu.) Double-click the icon in Windows 3.1 (in Windows 95, select the icon from the Start menu) to run the CD Assistant.

Getting Started with a Macintosh

The CD takes advantage of the Mac's easy-to-use desktop. Just pop the CD into your CD-ROM drive and double-click the Web Publishing FT CD icon after it appears on your desktop. A window appears showing folders named after each category of software on the CD. Installing the programs on your Mac is easy. Just double-click each program's installer program icon (if there is one) or drag the program's folder to your hard drive to copy the folder.

Restarting the CD Assistant in Windows

If you're using Windows 95 and were able to start the CD Assistant just by popping the CD into your CD-ROM drive, restart the CD by double-clicking the My Computer icon and then double-clicking the CD-ROM icon. This method works only if your CD-ROM drive automatically started the CD Assistant when you first popped the CD in your CD-ROM drive.

If you had to follow the steps in "Getting started with Windows 3.1 and Non-AutoPlay CD-ROMs," you can restart the CD Assistant by opening the For Teachers program group (Windows 95 users can find it on their Start⇨Programs menu) and double-clicking the CD Assistant icon named after this book.

Remember that you have to keep the CD in the CD-ROM drive to use the CD Assistant.

If you happen to encounter any trouble with installing the items from the *Web Publishing For Teachers* CD, please call the IDG Books Worldwide Customer Service phone number: 800-762-2974 (outside the U.S.: 317-596-5261).

IDG BOOKS WORLDWIDE REGISTRATION CARD

RETURN THIS REGISTRATION CARD FOR FREE CATALOG

Title of this book: **Web Publishing For Teachers™**

My overall rating of this book: ❑ Very good [1] ❑ Good [2] ❑ Satisfactory [3] ❑ Fair [4] ❑ Poor [5]

How I first heard about this book:

❑ Found in bookstore; name: [6]

❑ Advertisement: [8]

❑ Word of mouth; heard about book from friend, co-worker, etc.: [10]

❑ Book review: [7]

❑ Catalog: [9]

❑ Other: [11]

What I liked most about this book:

What I would change, add, delete, etc., in future editions of this book:

Other comments:

Number of computer books I purchase in a year: ❑ 1 [12] ❑ 2-5 [13] ❑ 6-10 [14] ❑ More than 10 [15]

I would characterize my computer skills as: ❑ Beginner [16] ❑ Intermediate [17] ❑ Advanced [18] ❑ Professional [19]

I use ❑ DOS [20] ❑ Windows [21] ❑ OS/2 [22] ❑ Unix [23] ❑ Macintosh [24] ❑ Other: [25]_____
(please specify)

I would be interested in new books on the following subjects:
(please check all that apply, and use the spaces provided to identify specific software)

❑ Word processing: [26]

❑ Data bases: [28]

❑ File Utilities: [30]

❑ Networking: [32]

❑ Other: [34]

❑ Spreadsheets: [27]

❑ Desktop publishing: [29]

❑ Money management: [31]

❑ Programming languages: [33]

I use a PC at (please check all that apply): ❑ home [35] ❑ work [36] ❑ school [37] ❑ other: [38] _____

The disks I prefer to use are ❑ 5.25 [39] ❑ 3.5 [40] ❑ other: [41]_____

I have a CD ROM: ❑ yes [42] ❑ no [43]

I plan to buy or upgrade computer hardware this year: ❑ yes [44] ❑ no [45]

I plan to buy or upgrade computer software this year: ❑ yes [46] ❑ no [47]

Name: _____ Business title: [48] _____ Type of Business: [49] _____

Address (❑ home [50] ❑ work [51]/Company name: _____)

Street/Suite#

City [52]/State [53]/Zipcode [54]: _____ Country [55] _____

❑ **I liked this book!** You may quote me by name in future
IDG Books Worldwide promotional materials.

My daytime phone number is _____

IDG BOOKS

THE WORLD OF
COMPUTER
KNOWLEDGE

❏ YES!
Please keep me informed about IDG's World of Computer Knowledge.
Send me the latest IDG Books catalog.